W9-AOL-396

T:25   S.∅
H:25
—————
25/
  4

go with the odds

A guide to successful gambling

go

A CHANCELLOR HALL *Book*

A GUIDE TO

with the odds

SUCCESSFUL

GAMBLING

THE MACMILLAN COMPANY
COLLIER-MACMILLAN LTD., LONDON

Designed and produced by Chancellor Hall, Ltd., New York

COPYRIGHT © 1969 *by* Charles H. Goren

All rights reserved. No part of this book may be reproduced or transmitted in any form or by any means, electronic or mechanical, including photo-copying, recording or by any information storage and retrieval system, without permission in writing from the Publisher.

Library of Congress Catalog Card Number: 78–85784

First Printing

The Macmillan Company
Collier-Macmillan Canada Ltd., Toronto, Ontario

Printed in the United States of America

878

發行人：周	政
住址：台北市中山北路二段一八〇號	
發行所：鍾山書局有限公司	
地址：台北市中山北路二段一八〇號	
電話：五 五 九 四 一 〇 號	
郵政撥滙：台 北 三 二 五 八 號	
印刷所：盛昌印製廠有限公司	
地址：三重市正義北路二十八號	
中 華 民 國 五十九年 　 月 　 日	
登記證內版台業字第一四一五號	

introduction

IT IS scarcely necessary to introduce Charles H. Goren to anyone who has ever seen a deck of cards or heard of the game of bridge. Modestly, Goren disclaims authorship of a bridge system. Yet if you go anywhere in the world, meet a new partner and say, "Let's play Goren," the chances are that this is the method your partner uses anyway. If not, he will know what you mean and be able to establish a workable partnership without further discussion of anything except a few points that Goren himself has said may be played either way.

I met Charley in 1933, and we have been good friends ever since. He was broke then as were most other people. Today he is a self-made millionaire. He didn't make a fortune because somebody brought in a wildcat oil well; he never doubled his money by calling "Banco" at baccarat in Monte Carlo; he never bet more than $10 on a horse race — and that was a sentimental wager because the nag he backed was named after him by some bridge-playing admirer who chanced to own a racing stable. True, the biggest winning he ever made was in Las Vegas. The amount was $1,500 — first prize for an Individual Bridge Championship in which he defeated some of the world's greatest players. But Goren contributed the entire purse to the Damon Runyon Cancer Fund.

The reason Charles Goren doesn't gamble is that he knows the odds. In the course of his travels, he has spent many hours in the world's most famous gambling centers: in addition to Monte Carlo and Las Vegas, the Casino at St. Vincent

introduction

in the Valle d'Aosta of Italy, the dozen or more Casinos in the Caribbean and the Mediterranean where thousands of bridge fans have accompanied him on cruises.

Charley has played bridge for nominal stakes and has made very small friendly bets from time to time. He is so conservative that once, when he bet one dollar on a question of fact, I offered ten to one out of confidence in Charley. He advises his friends not to bet. He warns his readers against playing the games that are stacked against them. And then, knowing that they'll probably bet anyway, he tells them in his book how, if bet they must, to *Go with the Odds*.

For your best chance to win the most — or at any rate to lose the least and have the most fun, knowing you are nobody's sucker, go with Charles Goren.

Oswald Jacoby

contents

contents

Two old favorites

Bridge

Glossary

The idea for *Go with the Odds* is the product of the fertile brain of my great friend and associate, Harold Ogust; the mathematical calculations are largely the work of Jeff Rubens whose genius with figures has made many contributions to the science of play in contract bridge. I am deeply grateful to both or them.

Charles Goren

odds and strategy

a word on odds

To the reader:

My best advice on betting is, "Don't!"

Follow it and you can save yourself the price of this book; already you will have shown a profit.

But it simply is not possible never to bet at all. You can bet on anything from the result of a lottery to the chances that we'll have a war. *In fact, you do!*

YOU don't? I used to say that myself. It is true that I do not go to the casino and play roulette; I do not buy lottery tickets; in fact, I do not even play bridge for high stakes.

Nevertheless, I "bet" every day of my life. I buy a raffle ticket (foolish, except as charity); I buy insurance (wise, if the policy is tailored to my needs); I try to invest my capital as a hedge against all possible events — including war. And since all of us must bet, you should know how to go with the odds. You'll lose less, and if you're lucky, you might even be a big winner.

In this book, I have tried to take into account more than just the mathematical odds, even though the odds are the determining factor in most cases. However . . .

All sorts of fallacies are rife. For example, everybody knows that the odds are even on a coin toss. In the long run, you'll toss heads or tails an equal number of times. So, if a coin has fallen tails up ten times in a row, the odds on the next toss are . . . *exactly even that it will come up tails again!* The long run is very long indeed. The practical gambler, knowing this, will probably bet on another tail, figuring that the previous run of results may mean the coin is loaded.

Of course, you could have gotten astronomical odds against eleven straight tails, so doesn't this prove that the chances are NOT even in each throw? You'll find the answer — and the odds — in this book. But maybe a different example will set you thinking the right way.

Suppose you decide to have three children? What are the practical odds that all will be of the same sex? Start with a certainty: at least two *must be* of the same sex. Apparently then, it will all come down to a bet on the third child — an even money proposition if you ignore the minute statistically greater number of girls. But the even money bet reflects the true odds only *after* the first two children are known to be of the same sex. The chances really are:

first	second	third	first	second	third
B	B	B	G	G	G
B	B	G	G	G	B
B	G	G	G	B	B
B	G	B	G	B	G

In other words, your chances are only two of eight possible combinations so the odds are actually 3 to 1 against.

Planning a larger family? — say, four kids? Obviously, you might think, the odds are even that you will have two of each. But, if you take an even money bet on it, again you are not going with the odds. Here's why: Count out all the possible combinations that may result from each single birth. List them, B, B, B, B; G, B, B, B; G, B, G, B, etc. When you've finished listing all sixteen possibilities you will see that in six examples there are two of each kind, against eight splits of 3-1 and two splits of 4-0. In other words, the odds are 5 to 3 against a four-child family including two of each sex.

These are the abstract odds, but they are not immutable. The geneticists are working on methods of pre-determining the sex of a child so that future parents may be able to get exactly what they want, boy or girl. Even a partial success will materially affect the odds; total success will make it no longer a betting proposition.

How to figure the odds

Many people have asked me how to go about figuring out the odds for different games. Unfortunately, this question cannot be answered in a general way, because different games involve different procedures, and the odds governing the ingredients of each game may be based on a completely different set of premises. It is fairly obvious that you cannot use the same basic figures to compute the odds in a game involving the throw of dice as you do in a game involving the use of a deck of cards, for the dice and cards themselves have their own different odds. Furthermore, no two games use their mechanical ingredients in exactly the same way. When someone says "dice" you may think immediately of craps — but this is just one of a vast array of games which involve dice, and which, therefore, require not just a knowledge of how dice are likely to come up when thrown, and how many times each combination of numbers on the dice will arise, but, most important, how these different numbers will affect the particular game being played.

Here I will explain the general theory of computing the odds. That is, I will explain the method of computing odds without reference to any particular game or games. The interested reader, confronting some game not covered in detail in this book, or even a game of his own creation, may be able to apply these principles for himself and formulate the odds on other games, or other events in some of the more popular games.

Odds are based on a mathematical subject called probability. Probability measures how often things occur, and the probabilities, or chances, of different events are expressed as fractions (or decimals), which are always between zero and one. The smallest possible probability is zero. An event has probability zero if it *cannot possibly happen.* The probability that you will throw a seven if you throw a die labeled one through six is zero, because you can't possibly throw a seven whatever you do. In contrast, the probability that the New York Mets baseball team will win all its games next season is very small — but it is not zero, because this event, however unlikely, is theoretically possible.

The highest probability is one. An event has probability one if it *must* happen. The probability of throwing a number from 1 to 6 on a die labeled from 1 to 6 is 1, because — assuming the die lands properly — this event is a certainty. Thus, the probability the sun will rise tomorrow is very high — but it is not 1 because it is *possible* that it won't. (Let's hope it does.)

In order to determine the probability of an event occurring, you divide the number of ways the event *can* occur by the total number of ways all possible events, including the one you are interested in, can occur. For example, suppose you are asked to find the probability of throwing a 5 when you toss a die labeled 1 to 6. The die has six faces, so there are six possible results altogether. Only one of these results is the number 5, so the chances of throwing a 5, or, expressing it as before, the probability of throwing a 5 is equal to

$$\frac{\text{number of ways to throw a 5} = 1}{\text{number of ways the die may fall} = 6} \text{ or } \frac{1}{6}$$

To use this division formula, it must be true that the ways listed in both the top and bottom parts of the formula represent things that are all *equally likely.* You cannot say: "Tomorrow it will either rain or not rain," therefore, there are two possibilities. Since one of them is that it will rain, the probability of rain is ½. This conclusion breaks down because you do not know that the two possibilities you are considering are equally likely.

Notice that the probabilities of 0 and 1 are consistent with this formula. If something *cannot* happen, the number on the top of the fraction will be zero, so the value of the fraction will be zero. If something *must* happen, the number on the top of the fraction will be the same as the number on the bottom of the fraction, so the value of the fraction will be 1.

Once you know the probability of certain events, it is easy to obtain the probabilities of other events by applying some probability formulas. For example:

1. THE CHANCE OF FAILURE

If you know the chance of some event happening is X, the chance it will not happen is 1 minus X.

This is because everything either happens or it doesn't, so the sum of the two possibilities must add up to 1 (the chance of a certainty).

EXAMPLE: If the chance of throwing a head on a coin is $\frac{1}{3}$ (i.e., it is not a fair coin), then the chance of throwing a tail on the same coin must be $\frac{2}{3}$.

2. THE CHANCE OF AT LEAST ONE EVENT

If you have two events, and these events have respective probabilities of occurrence of X and Y then the chance that at least one of the two events will happen is X + Y, minus the probability that both events will occur.

EXAMPLE: You throw a red die and a green die. What is the chance at least one of the dice will turn up 5?

The chance of a 5 on the red is $\frac{1}{6}$; the chance of a 5 on the green is $\frac{1}{6}$.

Then why, if you throw two dice, have you not doubled your chance of throwing a 5, making the probability $\frac{2}{6}$ and the odds against throwing at least one five 2 to 1? The reason is that when you throw both dice together you are dealing not with six possible throws but with 36. Of these possible combinations, one is double-5 and, since you are not betting on the number of 5s that turn up but on the number of times at least one five appears your chances are not 12 in 36 but 11 in 36. See for yourself:

green	red		red	green
5	6		5	6
5	5		5	5
5	4		5	4
5	3		5	3
5	2		5	2
5	1		5	1

The total is 12 chances, but one throw, 5 − 5, has already been counted in the first column and cannot be counted again in the second. Hence, $6 + 6 - 1 = 11$.

So, to express it mathematically, the chance of getting at least one 5 with a throw of the two dice is $\frac{1}{6} + \frac{1}{6} - \frac{1}{36} = \frac{11}{36}$.

3. THE CHANCE OF TWO EVENTS TOGETHER

If two events are not related to each other (that is, if they do not affect one another) then the chance they will both happen at once is the *product* of the respective chances of each.

EXAMPLE: You throw a die and a coin. What is the chance you will get a head on the coin and a six on the die? Since these events do not affect one another, the chance of both is the product of the individual chances. The chance of a head on the coin is $\frac{1}{2}$ (we assume a fair coin here); the chance of a six on the die is $\frac{1}{6}$. Therefore, the chance of both these things happening is $\frac{1}{2} \times \frac{1}{6} = \frac{1}{12}$.

By combining these three rules, it is possible to determine the chance of a complicated event occurring if you know the probabilities of the component events that go into its makeup. This is the general method of computing the probabilities for games involving decks of cards, dice, or similar gaming equipment.

From probability to odds

Once you know the probability of an event, it is easy to find the odds against it. First, express the probability as a fraction, say $^A/_B$. Then find the difference between the top and bottom numbers (the bottom will always be at least as large, so take the bottom minus the top).

Then, the odds against an event occurring is the ratio of the difference to the number on top.

EXAMPLE: The *chance* of throwing a 5 on a die is ⅙. What are the *odds* against throwing a 5?

The numbers are 1 on top and 6 on the bottom; the difference is 5. So the odds against throwing a 5 on a die are 5 to 1.

Odds and probability are both estimations of likelihood. They express exactly the same mathematical quantity in slightly different ways. Odds are often used to express the results of games because by giving the result in terms of odds you are at the same time giving an expression of what the money odds should be in order to make the game a fair one.

Breaking the bank at Monte Carlo

Much as it may shatter your illusions, I must report that nobody ever really "broke the bank" at Monte Carlo. The stories you've heard are probably based on a couple of protective features that a Casino builds into its rules of play. The house sets a limit at every table, beyond which it will not accept a bet. And the house also sets a limit on the total amount of money it will allow itself to lose at any table — except in special cases where a high-rolling sucker on a lucky streak will be accommodated until his streak ends. When the limit has been lost, the table is closed down. The Casino isn't out of money and the patrons can still get action at another table. But the house is both superstitious and suspicious. They want a chance to check on a possibly defective roulette wheel or a dealer who may possibly have defected.

Nevertheless, in the bridge circles which I frequent, there are two noteworthy stories about big wins — one of which actually did "close" a bank, if only temporarily. However, it wasn't the Casino's bank that shut up shop.

Ely Culbertson's autobiographical *Strange Lives of One Man* tells of the time when he left a gambling salon to go outside and settle an argument in the customary fashion. Quite a while later, he returned to the roulette table to find that a bet he had placed on red was still winning!

I cannot vouch for the veracity of that tale. In fact, I am inclined to be skeptical because Ely was not a man given to indulging in fisticuffs, or to forgetting that he had made a bet — or even to making bets at roulette or other games in which the odds were against him. (In bridge, however, he held to the principle that it didn't matter what odds you gave — as long as you won.) Anyway, I have heard the same casino tale elsewhere.

But the second case I can verify because I was there. During the 1960 World Bridge Team Olympiad at Turin, the players were invited to a banquet at the beautiful Casino in St. Vincent, some fifty miles into the foothills of the Alps in the enclave of Aosta. John Crawford was there, along with his lovely wife Leslie and one daughter. He happened to have brought only $200 with him — having left his traveler's checks at the hotel. He walked past a baccarat table and called "Banco," doubling his money. He put it all into one bet on red at the roulette table, won, and then began to invest his capital of $800. After playing 26 unsuccessfully for a couple of spins, his bridge partner, Tobias Stone, suggested that he switch to 23, Stone's daughter's birthday. Crawford bet the limit on 23, the limit on red and the limit on over 18. The little white ball fell into 23. Johnny repeated the same bet and 23 repeated!

Johnny's family left the Casino with something more than fifteen million lire wrapped up in newspaper bundles and Johnny had the rather pleasant headache of figuring a way to turn this money into dollars or pounds. During the Olympiad, the Bank of Italy had, as a courtesy to the numerous players from other lands, opened a money exchange right in the Fine Arts Palace where the championship was played. But in order to dispose of his lire, Crawford offered $105 worth for $100. As a result, until Johnny ran out of banknotes the bank stayed closed.

To some, Crawford's betting tactics would be impossible to emulate. The usual player with a $200 stake plans his play so as to make his money last a long while. The man who goes with the odds knows that the longer he plays in a casino, where the odds are against him, the more certain it is that he will lose. He plays to win big and quit before the odds catch up with him.

Nothing is as immutable as those odds in favor of the house; still, occasionally, the house is glad to alter them (in a way) in order to cater to certain customers. For example, any time the high-roller feels like a trip to Las Vegas, his hosts at the casino will invest free plane fare and free de luxe accommodations — reducing the odds if you consider the fare and room as part of the original stake.

Since the house makes no such offer to the chap who has $200 to lose and plays to make it last as long as possible, does this mean that perhaps he — and not the plunger — has the right idea? I can only answer that it all depends on whether you are out for a long evening's entertainment at lowest cost or a chance, however slim, of walking out as Crawford did, with $28,000 of the Casino's money on that one night when you're lucky.

Whenever you gamble, two considerations must be paramount because they will override all others.

First: What is your objective: having fun, or winning even if it's hard work?

Second: How much, i.e. how badly, do you *need* to win? How much can you afford to lose?

Keep these in mind when you gamble. They are even more important than going with the odds.

systems, limits, and money management

THERE ARE MORE systems for beating the house in gambling games than there are for bidding hands at bridge. Some of these systems, being based on Astrology, Theosophy, and Dream-analysis, are beyond the scope of this book. Others, being based on the detection of defective roulette wheels, dice, and slot machines, are merely anachronistic in a precision-oriented place such as Las Vegas. Others, based on marked cards and loaded dice, are illegal and dangerous.

That leaves us with systems based on "mathematics." Why the quotation marks? Because these systems aren't really based on mathematics, but on incomplete mathematical reasoning.

Take the case, for example, of the Martingale. This is a system based on a geometric progression. You double your bet each time you lose. Eventually you will win and recoup all your losses, plus a profit of one dollar. The progression in dollars is this:

1, 2, 4, 8, 16, 32, 64, 128, 256, 512 . . .

Suppose you are using the Martingale to bet "red" on the roulette wheel. All right, you lose nine times in a row. (Black will come up nine times in a row $\frac{1}{1024}$th of the time, which is not an "impossible" occurrence.) Your tenth bet calls for $512. That's too bad. The house limit is $500. Bye-bye system. Bye-bye bankroll.

Even if the house had allowed you to make your $512 bet and you had won, you would have come out only a $1 winner for the series.

If you had lost that tenth bet (and the odds are even that

you will) you would be a $1024 loser and in serious trouble. It is absurd to risk such sums of money to win such a trifling amount.

All systems have this very undesirable feature in common: they limit the wins to a pittance without limiting the losses. As long as you manage to avoid the house limit, which you can do by starting with a very low amount, you can probably avoid getting cleaned out, but you can never go home a big winner. And eventually, no matter how low your initial bet is, you will come into conflict with the limit because the inexorable house edge will cause you to lose more bets than you win.

Some systems are cleverer than others, and the Martingale is a particularly crude one. If you find a system you fancy, and play it with a low enough initial bet, it may enable you to stay at the roulette table for a long time before you run out of money. If that is your objective, then I recommend the Labouchère, which goes something like this:

Write down a series of numbers on a piece of paper:

1, 2, 3, 4

Always bet the sum of the numbers at the ends of the line. When you lose, put the amount you lost at the right hand end of the line. When you win, cross off the two end numbers and bet the sum of the visible numbers. Eventually, all the numbers will be crossed off and the series will be closed. At that time you will have won the amount of your *first bet*. Meanwhile, of course, you could hit the standard $500 limit, or simply go broke trying to close the series. But if you play the Labouchère for dimes you could stay at the table a long time.

All system mechanics is, however, completely contrary to the principles of sound money management. If your object in going to a casino is to win money, your strategy should be built around three principles:

1] *Make as few bets as possible.*
The fewer bets you make, the less chance the house edge has to grind you down. If you make 500 $1 bets on the pass line you are overwhelmingly likely to emerge a $7.50 loser. If you make one $500 bet you have only slightly less

than an even chance to emerge a $500 winner. You have a slightly greater than even chance, of course, of winding up a $500 loser. But that is gambling. If your intention is to make money, you must risk money.

2] *Make your bets as large as possible.*
The reason is the same as and related to the above argument.

3] *Bet heavily when playing with the house money, lightly when playing with your own.*

This is the advice which is completely contrary to that of the system-mongers. Your general strategy of money management should be to bet a relatively modest amount until and if you are winning, then escalate your bets as you start to play with the money you have won, and continue escalating to the limit until you have lost a couple of large bets. Then QUIT. If you start out a loser, set a limit in advance on how much you are willing to lose, *and stick to it*. This advice will allow you to win huge amounts of money on the (rare) occasions when your luck is really in, while preventing you from losing your home and car when your luck is out.

Here is an example of how one professional gambler would manage a stake of $100 on the pass line at the dice table:

the amount of his bet would be	until he had won
$ 5	$ 30
10	80
20	160
40	400
60	640
100	1100
150	2000
200	3000

This gambler would jump backward a couple of levels if he lost a bet or two, but if he continued to win would escalate right up to the house limit. He would continue playing until he was either wiped out initially, or went over $1000 ahead and dropped back to $500.

This gambler's approach is bold and hazardous. But in my opinion it is an eminently sound approach to money management in Las Vegas. When he is out of luck he loses $100; when he is hot there is no limit to what he will try to win. This man is, as much as possible, going with the odds.

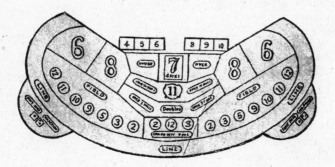

casino games

craps

THE GREATEST volume of action, by far, in any major American casino will be found at the craps (dice) table. More people mill around here, and more money is won and lost, than anywhere else on the floor. The reasons are varied. The action is extremely fast. The complexity of the game can vary, according to the player's inclinations, from very simple to very complicated. And, not least important, the dice table offers, with one exception, *the best odds for the player in a casino.*

The dice table is also a place where one can squander his money by making some of the silliest bets in a casino. The fact that these foolish bets are available to the player is evidence that people make them. If you avoid these, and concentrate instead on the sound bets that are available, you can give yourself one of the best breaks the world of gambling offers. In fact, if everybody who visited a casino made nothing but the best bets available at the craps table, and played no other games, the casino business would become a marginal one.

To get down to the facts: the best pattern of betting at a casino dice table will reduce the odds against you to 0.85%. The worst bets are 16.7% in the casino's favor. That is quite a difference.

What I will say here may seem a bit unpleasant and pessimistic, but it is as surely true as the laws of mathematics: if you play long enough, the casino *must* beat you no matter how you play. If you make the best bets at the dice table you figure to lose 85¢ on every $100 you bet. If you bet foolishly, you figure to lose $16.70 per $100. The best you can ever do is reduce your expectation of loss.

Why bet at all if you are bound to lose in the long run? That is a good question, and I have never really been able to figure out a convincing reply. A fair practical answer, however, is that you are not going to play over the long run, and in the short run you may do very well indeed.

The mechanics of craps

A player, called the shooter, picks up the dice and rolls them onto a surface. His first roll is called the "come-out." If he rolls 7 or 11 on the come-out the dice "pass." 7 or 11 on the come-out is called a "natural." If the come-out is 2, 3, or 12, the dice "don't pass." These initial rolls are called "crap-outs." If the come-out is 4, 5, 6, 8, 9, or 10, the result is not yet settled. The come-out number becomes the shooter's "point." The shooter now continues to roll the dice over and over until either his point or a 7 comes up. If his point comes up before a 7, the dice pass; if the 7 comes up first, the dice don't pass.

Note that I did not say that the shooter wins or loses. At a craps table it is possible for anybody, including the shooter, to bet either that the dice will pass or that they won't. The object of the game, from the bettor's point of view, is simply to predict whether the dice will pass or not. However, it is quite uncommon, for psychological reasons, for the shooter to bet that the dice won't pass.

Let's find out who has the edge in a dice game, and explore some of the odds that you, as a casino visitor, should know.

Since there are two dice and each die has six faces, the dice can come up in 36 different combinations. Here is a table showing each number, the combinations that can produce it,

TABLE 1

number	how produced	no. of comb.	probability
2	1 - 1	1	1 in 36
3	1 - 2, 2 - 1	2	2 in 36 or 1 in 18
4	1 - 3, 3 - 1, 2 - 2	3	3 in 36 or 1 in 12
5	1 - 4, 2 - 3, 3 - 2, 4 - 1	4	4 in 36 or 1 in 9
6	1 - 5, 2 - 4, 3 - 3, 4 - 2, 5 - 1	5	5 in 36
7	1 - 6, 2 - 5, 3 - 4, 4 - 3, 5 - 2, 6 - 1	6	6 in 36 or 1 in 6
8	2 - 6, 3 - 5, 4 - 4, 5 - 3, 6 - 2	5	5 in 36
9	3 - 6, 4 - 5, 5 - 4, 6 - 3	4	4 in 36 or 1 in 9
10	4 - 6, 5 - 5, 6 - 4	3	3 in 36 or 1 in 12
11	5 - 5, 6 - 5	2	2 in 36 or 1 in 18
12	6 - 6	1	1 in 36

the number of combinations that can produce it and the probability of its occurrence in a single roll. The probability is equal to the number of combinations that can produce the result divided by 36, which is the total number of possible combinations.

Notice the considerable difference in the probabilities of various numbers. That difference is the key to the game. Knowledge of these probabilities will help you make goods bets and avoid foolish ones.

As an exercise, let us calculate the odds of the dice's passing. A pass, remember, occurs when the come-out is 7 or 11, or when the come-out is a point and the shooter subsequently rolls his point before a seven shows. A don't pass occurs when the come-out is a 2, 3, or 12, or the come-out is a point and the shooter rolls a 7 before rolling his point-number again.

For the moment let us just consider the come-out.

COME-OUT

Shooter "wins":
$7 = \frac{1}{6}$ chance; $11 = \frac{1}{18}$ chance. Total chance $= \frac{2}{9}$.

Shooter "loses":
$2 = \frac{1}{36}$ chance; $3 = \frac{1}{18}$ chance; $12 = \frac{1}{36}$ chance. Total $= \frac{1}{9}$.

Shooter rolls a "point":
All other numbers combined $= \frac{2}{3}$ chance.

We see that after the come-out the dice have passed $\frac{2}{9}$ of the time and lost $\frac{1}{9}$ of the time. The remaining $\frac{2}{3}$ of the time the issue is yet to be decided. To figure out what will happen from here on, we have to calculate the odds against the shooter's "making" a particular point, and combine that figure with the odds against a particular number *being* his point.

TABLE 2   *Odds against making a point*

point	odds against	probability
4	2 to 1	1 in 3
5	3 to 2	2 in 5
6	6 to 5	5 in 11
8	6 to 5	5 in 11
9	3 to 2	2 in 5
10	2 to 1	1 in 3

The "odds against" is figured as follows: a point can be made with a certain number of combinations (see TABLE 1). A seven can be made with six combinations. The odds against making a point are the number of seven-combinations to the number of point-combinations, or 6 to (the number of point-combinations). For example, if the point is four, it can be made with three combinations. Seven can be made with six combinations. Since the point is "made" only if it is rolled before a seven appears, the odds against making a point of 4 are 6 to 3 (or 2 to 1). The *probability* of making a point of four is 3 in 9, or 1 in 3. This is figured by adding together the number of combinations which will produce the point and the number of combinations which will produce seven and dividing that sum into the number of combinations which will produce the point. In this case the formula is

$$3/(3+6) = \frac{1}{3}.$$

Next, we must combine the probability of making a particular point with the probability of coming out on that point. In other words, suppose you want to make a bet in advance that you will make a pass specifically by coming out on a five and then making your point. What are the odds?

Since you will come out on a "5" $\frac{1}{9}$ of the time (see TABLE 1) and will make your point $\frac{2}{5}$ of the time (see TABLE 2), the probability that you will win this particular bet is

$$\frac{1}{9} \times \frac{2}{5} = \frac{2}{45}.$$

Now suppose you wanted to make a bet that you would make the dice pass by coming out on *any* point and then making your point. The probability that you would win your bet is equal to the sum of the probabilities of your winning via any one point. In other words, the shooter will make the dice pass via a point roll $\frac{97}{360}$ of the time, or about once in four throws.

Now we go back and recall that the dice passed outright on the come-out roll (by showing 7 or 11) $\frac{2}{9}$ of the time. By adding $\frac{2}{9}$ (= $\frac{80}{360}$) to $\frac{97}{360}$ we get $\frac{177}{360}$, which is the total probability that the dice will pass. The dice, therefore, won't pass $\frac{183}{360}$ of the time. The approximate odds against a pass are therefore 183 to 177, or a little less than even.

When you bet at a casino that the dice will pass, the house

TABLE 3 *Probabilities of winning by coming out on and making a particular point*

point	probability of rolling number on come-out	probability of making point	combined probability	
4	1 in 12	1 in 3	1 in 36	
5	1 in 9	2 in 5	2 in 45	
6	5 in 36	5 in 11	1 in 16	(approx.)
8	5 in 36	5 in 11	1 in 16	(approx.)
9	1 in 9	2 in 5	2 in 45	
10	1 in 12	1 in 3	1 in 36	
	Grand total combined probability		97 in 360	(approx.)

will give you *even money.* They have the best of it by $\frac{6}{360}$, or 1.67%. And that is not too bad in any form of gambling against the "banker."

There is a very important concept to be grasped here. *The house does not bet against the shooter. The house only wagers that bettors cannot predict whether the dice will pass or not.* In other words, it is not true that the house wishes the dice wouldn't pass. Because you, as a bettor, can bet that the dice *don't pass,* and the house will give you even money on that, too.

Well, why don't we all rush out to Las Vegas and bet that the dice don't pass? Too bad, the house has studied these odds too. They will give you even money when you bet "don't pass," but there is a hitch: when you bet that way, a come-out of 12 is not a win for you; it is a stand-off. And that reservation is enough to restore the house's edge back to about 1.5%. (Some casinos make a come-out of two a stand-off. This is equivalent to "barring" twelve. If a casino "bars" anything else, avoid the "don't pass" bet.)

Should you bet "pass" or "don't pass?" Really, it is a matter of choice. Nick the Greek, the famous professional gambler, always bets "don't pass." Most players, however, bet pass out of sympathy for the shooter. There is another good reason to bet pass rather than don't pass, and that will be explained later.

Come and don't come

These bets are very similar to pass and don't pass, and feature identical odds. They are designed for the player who wants even faster action than the pass and don't pass lines can provide. By betting the come/don't come lines, a player can get down a bet on every roll of the dice. The mechanics are simple. When you bet "come," you are making an identical bet to "pass" except that for the purpose of the come bet, the *next roll of the dice will be the comeout.* "Come" and "don't come" are perfectly sound bets. My only reservation against them is that if you are not experienced you are likely to become a bit confused about what you are betting on. (But even if you are a babe in the woods, a reputable Las Vegas casino will see to it that you get what belongs to you.)

Another factor to consider is that if you are betting on every roll of the dice and losing, your evening of gambling won't last very long. If you enjoy spending more than a little time at the tables, avoid the "come" bets. If you are running hot, however, by all means get your money down on as many rolls as possible. See the chapter on Systems and Money Management for further advice in this area.

Taking the odds on a point

As reasonable as the odds against you are when you bet the pass or don't pass line, they can be reduced even further by making the most intelligent bet possible in a casino. If you bet pass and the shooter comes out on a point, the casino will allow you to make a further bet, up to the size of your pass bet, that the shooter will make his point. What is so good about this is that on this bet, called "taking the odds," *the casino will give you the true money odds that the particular point justifies.* The casino's edge on this particular bet is *zero!* Any time you have an opportunity to make a bet in a casino where the house has no edge, you should seize it. Better opportunities you will not find.

For example, suppose you put down $2 on the pass line

and the shooter comes out with a five. The casino will allow you to bet an additional two dollars that he will make his point. The odds against making a point of five are 3 to 2, and in fact, if the shooter makes his point, the house will pay you $3 on your additional bet.

If you make this zero-percentage bet every time the shooter comes out on a point you will be reducing the house percentage against you to 0.85%. (If you do *not* make it, the house advantage will be 1.70%.)

If you bet the come line you can take the odds on your new come-out just as if you had bet the pass line. And if you are a "wrong-way" bettor (don't pass, don't come) you can *lay* the odds on the shooter's point once he comes out. In other words, if you are betting "don't" and the shooter comes out on a five, you can bet $3 to win $2 that he will *fail* to make his point. Again, this is a recommended bet.

But there is a word of caution required. Bets on the Las Vegas strip can be made only in multiples of $1, and the house will not pay off fractions of $1. Thus, if you have bet $1 on the pass line and the shooter comes out on a five, it would be foolish to take the odds with another $1 bet, because the house should pay you $1.50 if you win it, but they won't give you the odd fifty cents. If you intend to take the odds on your bets you should ideally bet multiples of $20 on the pass line. Some casinos, however, will allow you to increase your pass line bet in order to take advantage of the odds. If you have to increase your pass line bet as well as betting the larger amount on the point itself after the comeout, don't do it. Once the shooter is out on a point, the pass line bettors are fighting uphill. Even the ability to get the odds-free additional bet won't compensate for the disadvantage you will incur by increasing your bet on the line itself after the comeout.

My advice, then, is to accept the casino's offer if they allow you to take the odds with the next higher amount which will allow them to pay off without increasing your pass-line bet; but otherwise to eschew the offer.

I mentioned earlier that there is an additional reason why players prefer to bet the pass line rather than the don't pass line. That reason has to do with taking the odds. The aggressive theory of gambling is to be on the short end of every bet. In other words, if an event has odds of 3-1 against its occurrence, and you want to bet on the event, it is better to bet that it will happen and put up $1 to win $3, rather than to bet that it will not happen and put up $3 to win $1. The point is that in the long run the house odds will grind you down, so in a given short period of time you should play to win as large an *amount* of money as possible. In other words, you should play the long shot for the higher payoff when you win.

When you bet pass, you are *taking* the odds in your "second bet," when you bet don't pass you are *giving* the odds later. To get the higher payoff on your back-up bet *go with the shooter*. It's riskier, more aggressive gambling, but it's more satisfactory.

Buying and placing numbers

On a Las Vegas craps layout, you will notice a block of spaces labeled "4, 5, SIX, 8, NINE, 10. These are the "place numbers." When you *place* a number you are betting that that number will appear before a seven does. You may make a place bet on any number at any time.

Las Vegas strip casinos provide two ways to bet the place numbers. One is called "*placing* the number," and the other is called "*buying* the number." The difference is this: when you *place* a number the house gives you somewhat less than the true odds against winning, as follows:

number	odds against winning	payoff
4 or 10	2 to 1	9 to 5
5 or 9	3 to 2	7 to 5
6 or 8	6 to 5	7 to 6

When you *buy* a number, the house pays off at the true odds, but you pay a flat 5% fee for the privilege of making the bet. Note that to buy or place a number you do *not* have to make a "line" bet first. That is why these bets carry a percentage for the house, whereas "taking the odds" or "laying the odds" do not.

Should you place numbers or should you buy them? As usual, an examination of the relative odds will yield the answer. Consider the case of the six. If you place the six the house will pay you 7 to 6 on a 6 to 5 proposition. That means that the house edge is 1.52%. If you buy the six you are giving the house an edge of 5%. Obviously it is right to place the six rather than buy it. Consider, however, the case of the ten.

If you place the ten, the house edge is 6.7%. If you buy it, the house has only 5% the best of it. Therefore, if you want to bet the ten, buy it.

In short, *buy* the 4 and 10; *place* the others.

My advice, however, is that *only the placing of 6 and 8 are reasonable bets;* aside from these the house edge is too great for these bets to be worthy of an intelligent gambler.

Bets to avoid at the craps table

1] *Big Six and Big Eight.* These are even money bets that the number specified will appear before a seven does. In reality, the odds against the bettor are 6 to 5. The house, therefore, has one clear win for every eleven plays, an edge of about 9%, which is too large. If sixes and eights are lucky numbers to you, place them. (See previous discussion.)

2] *Field bets.* This is a bet on the next roll of the dice only. The "field" is comprised of the numbers 2, 3, 4, 9, 10, 11, and 12. If the next roll of the dice is a 3, 4, 9, 10, or 11, the house pays even money. If it is a 2 or 12, the house pays at 2 to 1. If it is a 5, 6, 7, or 8 the house wins. Let's figure the odds.

Suppose you bet the Field 36 times and the odds hold absolutely true: over that period of time each combination of the dice appears once. Each Field bet you make is for $1.

You will lose outright 20 times (5, 6, 7, and 8 between them can be made 20 ways; see TABLE 1). You will win at even money 14 times, and you will win at 2 to 1 twice. Thus, you will lose $20 and win $18 over the course of the 36 rolls. The house edge is $2 in 36 rolls, or about 5.5%.

3] *One-roll bets.* The house edge on these bets is as high as any on the table. Seven-in-one-roll, for example, pays 4 to 1 when the true odds are 5 to 1. The house take is an outrageous 16.7%. On a one-roll bet the bettor wins if his number comes up on the next roll and loses otherwise. The *lowest* odds you can get on any of these bets gives the house an edge of 11%. Stay away from them!

4] *Hard-way bets.* These are bets made after the come-out. The bettor wagers that the shooter will not only make his point, but will do it the hard way, that is with a "double." These bets are only possible when the shooter's point is an even number. If the shooter's point is eight, for example, if you bet "the hard way" you are wagering that the shooter will roll specifically 4-4 before he rolls any 7 or any other combination adding up to eight. The house pays 9 to 1 on a hard-way eight. Let's figure the true odds.

You win on one combination: 4-4. You lose on 2-6, 3-5, 5-3, 6-2, and the six combinations that come up seven. In all, you lose ten ways. The true odds are therefore 10 to 1, and the house advantage is 9%. The house edge on the hard six is the same. The hard-way 4 or 10 gives the house an edge of 11%.

Summary of craps

Some of the odds calculations I have shown you may seem a bit complex, but they can all be summarized into a simple method of playing the dice intelligently, which will reduce the house odds against you to a liveable 0.85% or thereabouts — a reasonable tariff to pay for the plush surroundings:

1) BET THE PASS AND DON'T PASS, COME AND DON'T COME LINES ONLY.

2) AFTER THE SHOOTER IS OUT ON A POINT, TAKE THE ODDS.

3) WITH THE EXCEPTION OF PLACING THE SIX OR EIGHT, STAY AWAY FROM THE OTHER BETS.

roulette

and other casino games

ROULETTE is the great game of the European casinos, or used to be before the advent of Baccarat [Chemin-de-Fer]. In the United States it is the great ladies' game. Probably the reason for the relative unpopularity of roulette in Las Vegas is that the house percentage on the game is higher than it is in Europe, where the wheel includes only one zero whereas in the U.S. the casino enjoys two. Roulette, however, can be a pleasant way to pass time with a minimum of thought. I advise that the time be passed with a minimum of expenditure as well, because, at roulette, the house take of 5.26% on all bets — *except one* — (more than double the odds you buck in Europe) is substantially higher than the edge in blackjack and craps. If it is your intention to make some money in a casino, I advise you to try something other than roulette. If, on the other hand, it is your intention to soak up some sun and Las Vegas amusement, and only incidentally to try your hand at some casual gambling, then roulette is for you.

Roulette has the compensating advantages that its pace of play is relatively slow and you may play, even on the Las Vegas strip, for considerably lower stakes than are possible at other games. If you want to make a small outlay last for a long time, roulette is the game to play.

It also is the ideal testing ground for the system you have just devised to break the bank, because you can have a long series of even-money bets, with no complicating side factors. But before you try your new system, read what I have to say in the chapter on systems and money management.

As to the odds in roulette, they are about as easy to

figure as anything in the casino. The wheel consists of 38 numbers (no Virginia, not 36): 36 of them are colored either red or black (18 of each). The numbers 0 and 00 are colored green and are called, with good reason, the house numbers.

You may bet on any number individually, at odds of 35 to 1. You may bet on all the red numbers, all the black numbers, all the even numbers, all the odd numbers, the high 18 numbers, or the low 18 numbers at even money. You may bet on the first 12 numbers, the middle 12, and the high 12 at 2 to 1. If the house numbers come up, all the even-money and 2-1 bets lose. The only bets that win when the ball lands in 0 or 00 are bets on those numbers or combinations which include those numbers.

Some people like to bet the house numbers in the belief that if they win for the casino they will win for them too. This, of course, is nonsense. In an honest game (and games on the Las Vegas strip are as honest as you can find anywhere) 0 and 00 come up exactly as often as any other number, that is, one time in 38. These numbers win for the house because when they appear the house collects all the low-odds bets. You, of course, do not. You get the same 35 to 1 that you get by betting any other number.

The true odds against any number are 37 to 1. The house, therefore, collects two bets out of every 38, for a percentage of 5.26%. This percentage holds true whether you are betting single numbers, parlays, red-black, or anything else, with one exception. The exception is not a friendly one, either. If you bet the "5-number" parlay you will get worse odds.

The "5 number" parlay (also called a "line bet" because the player places his chips on the line separating the numbers 1, 2 and 3 from 0 and 00) pays off at 6 to 1. But since the correct odds are 6.8 to 1, the house percentage goes up to almost 7.9% against you.

In short, there are other games in the casino which offer better odds, but there are none which are played with more relaxation and gentility.

Where you get the worst of the odds

Three games played in every casino attract a large following for reasons that I can never understand. If anybody plays these games for any motivation other than philanthropy toward a hungry casino owner, he has certainly wasted his time and money with this book.

THE SLOT MACHINES

I advise you to throw away 50¢ on one of these machines just to see how the mechanical marvels work. Do not, repeat *not,* insert a second half-dollar. The odds against you are almost unbelievable.

A typical slot machine accepts 50¢ pieces. It has inside it three wheels which can spin freely until stopped by a retarder. Each of the wheels is covered with a printed strip on which are shown twenty squares, each containing a picture of a bell, cherry, etc. Depending on what pictures show in the windows when the wheels stop, the machine pays off according to a schedule. Most of the time, of course, it just sits there hungrily waiting for another coin. A typical jackpot payoff would be $100, and this would occur if three bells appeared in the three windows.

What are the odds? Typically, the middle strip contains 9 bells. About half the time, therefore, a bell will show up just to tease you. The outer two strips, however, have only one bell apiece among their twenty designs. The probability of hitting the jackpot, therefore, is $\frac{1}{20} \times \frac{1}{20} \times \frac{9}{20} = 0.001125$, or slightly better than $\frac{1}{1000}$. The payoff is a munificent 200 to 1. The house edge, therefore, is a mere 80%.

All right, it's not quite that bad. There are winning combinations other than the jackpot. Altogether, though, the percentage against the player is over 65%! A far cry from the 0.85% of the crap table.

THE OTHER CULPRITS

The wheel of fortune and keno are two other games where you will get nothing but sheared. The same is true of bingo, birdcage, and all its variants. In no case does the house take less than a 50% edge. But let us be tolerant. Something has to pay for all that luxuriant splendor, those golf courses, the marvelous entertainment, etc. If you confine yourself to the craps and blackjack tables, however, *you* won't be the one supporting the others!

There is more on Bingo and Keno in the "Lottery" section.

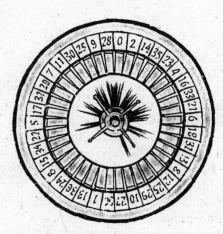

birdcage

BIRDCAGE IS an amusing swindle. It is amusing because one can only wonder what great achievements its inventor might have accomplished had he put his cleverness to work in other ways. It is a swindle because the game gives every appearance of being a fair bet, yet is not.

The basic game of Birdcage (there are minor variations, but they all operate on the same principle) is that a birdcage containing three dice is spun around and the dice are allowed to settle. A player can back any one of the six possible numbers (1 through 6) that appear on the faces of the dice. If the selected number appears on the faces of any of the three dice in the birdcage, the player wins and is paid at even money. If all three dice show other numbers, the player loses.

Unless you think deeply about this game, it seems to be quite fair. There are six possible numbers, one of which is yours. Thus, on each die you have a 1 to 6 chance of getting your number. And there are three dice — so you have three 1 to 6 chances, total 3 to 6 or 1 to 2. So your chances of winning are fifty-fifty and the bet is even money. What could possibly be unfair about that?

Answer: Everything. Actually, of the 216 possible ways the three dice can come up, only 91 of these ways include any one specific number. (If you don't believe it, write down all 216 possibilities and start counting!)

Why is this so? Essentially, it is because the house pays off only once no matter how often the number appears on the dice. Thus, if your number is 6, and the dice come up 3-6-6, if the game were fair you should be paid twice over. Otherwise, you are "wasting" one of your precious sixes. But because the house pays only the standard even money rate, no matter how often a number comes up, it gains whenever a repeated number occurs in the dice (which is surprisingly often!).

To take an example, suppose you back all six numbers and bet six dollars. If any three different numbers come up, you break even — everything is as it should be. But suppose a repeated number comes up, such as the 3-6-6 we discussed above. Now you win on two bets and lose on four: result — minus 2 dollars! (And if all three dice come up the same number, you lose even more!)

As a final argument, let's explode the fallacy that you have half a chance to have your number come up if three dice are thrown. We will extend the argument to the case in which *six* dice are thrown. By the previously given (fallacious) argument, you have six chances at $\frac{1}{6}$ per chance, total 1 — in other words, a *certainty* of getting your number. This is patently false, and it is obvious that the method of computation is faulty. The error lies in the fact that the argument does not take repeated numbers into account.

twenty-one (blackjack)

BLACKJACK IS one of the two casino games (craps is the other) where the player can reduce the odds against himself to nearly the even point.* Like craps and other casino games, blackjack can be played more or less mechanically by a player who is familiar with the odds. Unlike craps and certain other games, however, the calculation of the odds is complex. It is a field which has been the subject of computerized research. So, unlike the presentation in the chapter on dice, I shall not attempt to take you through the actual calculation of any but the simplest of odds. Instead, let me summarize the results and advise you how to take best advantage of the odds.

The mechanics of Las Vegas blackjack

1] The object of the game is to total two or more cards to the highest possible sum that is less than or equal to 21. Cards whose total exceeds 21 are worthless. Two or more cards that add up to 21 constitute a hand that cannot lose.

2] Each card has a value equal to its rank. Picture cards (jack, queen, king) all count ten. Ace counts one or eleven, at the option of the player. (A combination that includes an ace which is being counted as 11 is called a "soft" combination. Other combinations are called "hard"

---

* If you wish to extend yourself (by counting the cards), you can actually show a profit at Twenty-One. However, the mental effort required is considerable.

combinations.) A hard combination that exceeds 21 in value is called a "bust."

3] The player wins if he produces a combination that is higher than the dealer's combination. If the dealer goes bust, the player wins, regardless of his hand (unless he went bust first).

4] The dealer plays last. Any player who goes bust automatically loses, regardless of what the dealer subsequently does. This rule accounts for the entire amount of the house edge at blackjack. (The dealer is always a house man.)

5] Ties between the dealer and a player are standoffs, with neither winning or losing, except as provided in rule 7.

6] Each player places a bet, usually ranging from $1 to $500, before receiving any cards.

7] Each player is dealt two cards face down. The dealer receives one card face up and one card face down. If the dealer's up-card is a ten or face-card, he must examine his down-card. If it is an ace, he turns his down-card up and announces a "natural." If any player has been dealt 21 in two cards he then turns his hand up and the result between that player and the dealer is a standoff. The other players lose their bets and the next hand is dealt.

If the dealer has an ace face up, he must invite the players to purchase *insurance*. Players may look at their two cards before deciding whether to buy the insurance. Any player wishing insurance then places down an additional bet equal to half his original bet. If the dealer has a natural he then pays off at 2 to 1 on the insurance bets, but *collects* the original bets from all players who do not have naturals themselves. If the dealer does not have a natural, he collects the insurance bets and play proceeds.

8] If a player is dealt a natural and the dealer does not have a natural, the dealer pays the player at the rate of

3 to 2. The purchase of insurance by the player does not affect this transaction.

9] After this preliminary business is attended to, play commences. The player to dealer's left has the option of playing his hand as it is, or requesting that another card be dealt to him. If he requests the extra card, he may then elect to stand on his three cards, or receive in order a fourth, fifth, and sixth card. *If at any time, however, the player's hand forms a "hard" combination in excess of 21, he must immediately turn his cards face up on the table and surrender his bet.* (He has been busted.) After the first player has been satisfied or busted, the dealer turns his attention to the second player, and so on around the table.

10] *Finally, after all the players have played, it is the dealer's* turn. If all the players have busted the dealer collects all bets and deals another hand. If one or more players are still alive, however, the dealer turns his cards face up on the table and plays according to a fixed rule:
DEALER MUST "HIT" ON SIXTEEN AND STAND ON SEVENTEEN. That is, dealer can never stand pat with a combination of sixteen or less. He must either achieve 17-21 or go busted trying. If the dealer has a "soft" hand in the 17-21 range some casinos require him to stand pat, while others permit him to continue at his option.

If the dealer busts, all remaining active players are paid off on their bets at even money. A new hand is then dealt.

11] If a player's first two cards are the same value (a pair), he may at his option "split" them by turning each face up and placing an additional bet equal in size to his first one. He then receives an additional card face down on top of each card of his pair and play continues as if the player were managing two separate hands, except that a natural acquired after a split does not receive the 3-to-2 payoff.

12] A player may, at his option, turn his first two cards face up and double his bet; he then receives *only one more card,* face down, and play then passes to the next player. The specifics of this rule vary somewhat from one casino to the next. This procedure is known as "doubling down."

The strategy of blackjack

The commonest misapprehension under which blackjack players labor is that, since the house usually wins, the dealers must be doing something right. The players therefore attempt to emulate the dealer by standing pat on 17 and hitting 16.

The dealers are doing something right, but this isn't it. What they are doing right is playing *after* the other players and allowing the others to bust before they must play. This represents no high skill on the part of the dealers; the advantage derives from the rules of the game. A semi-sophisticated robot could deal a competent game of blackjack, provided he were protected against cheaters.

The fact of the matter is that the players' strategy should be fundamentally different from the dealer's. The player has only one objective in mind: he should beat the dealer. This can be done in two ways:

1) THE PLAYER CAN GET A HIGHER TOTAL THAN THE DEALER;

2) THE PLAYER CAN SIT TIGHT WHILE THE DEALER BUSTS.

The computer studies of the game have provided a fairly simple series of guidelines which will enable the player to play an intelligent game of blackjack. If these guidelines are followed, the house edge in a blackjack game should be no more than 3%.

YOU HAVE: *17-21. Stand.*

Even if the dealer shows a high card you should not draw. The odds are at worst 2-1 that you will win. There is one exception, and it is aggressive, not defensive: IF YOU HOLD A-6 or A-7 and the dealer shows a 4,5, or 6, you should DOUBLE DOWN.

YOU HAVE: *13-16.*

The dealer shows 7 or more. *You should hit.*

It is true that if you draw to a 16 you will bust 3 times in

5. But if you don't draw you will lose 7 times in 20 anyway. By hitting you increase your winning chances by 10%.

The dealer shows 3-6. *Stand.*

The mathematics of this aren't too complicated. If the dealer shows, for instance, a 6, his chances of making his required 17 or better are worse than even. If you draw to 13, your chances of making 17-21 are 3-2 against. If you stand you will win more than half the time as the dealer busts. If you hit you will not do that well.

YOU HAVE: *12.*

The dealer shows 4,5, or 6. *Stand.*

This is not easy advice to take but is mathematically sound. You will have to take my word for it, however, unless you are a mathematician, because the calculations are fairly complex.

The dealer shows anything other than 4,5, or 6. *Draw.*

YOU HOLD: *9.*

Dealer shows 2-6. *You should double down.*

Dealer shows 7-A. *You should take a normal hit* and then reconsider.

YOU HOLD: *10.*

Dealer shows 9 through Ace. *Draw* (obviously).

Dealer shows 2-8: *double down.*

YOU HOLD: *11.*

Dealer shows 10 through Ace. *Draw.*

Dealer shows 2-9: *double down.*

YOU HOLD: *A natural.*

Dealer shows an Ace. *Take out insurance! This is a slick bet.* You cannot lose. Let us see why. Suppose your initial bet was $2. You get a natural and dealer shows an ace. You place a $1 insurance bet. Suppose:

    1) Dealer has the natural. You win your insurance bet and your original bet is a standoff. Net result: +$2 for you.

    2) Dealer does not have the natural: you lose your insurance bet and collect 3 to 2 on your original bet. Net result: +$2 for you.

Either way you win two dollars. *That* is my kind of bet. Now suppose in similar circumstances you do *not* purchase the insurance. If dealer has the natural your bet is a standoff. If dealer does not have the natural you win $3. What is your average expectancy? The odds are about 5 to 2 that declarer does not have the natural. If you repeat this situation seven times you will win $3 five times and nothing twice. Total win: $15. If you took out the insurance each time you would win $14.

You certainly have a right to ask: why advise the insurance when the average expectancy is higher without the insurance? The answer is that the 5 to 2 figure I used as the basis for my calculations is subject to considerable variation. On balance, you will come out about the same whether you purchase the insurance or not. I recommend it on the simple ground that there are precious few "sure things" in gambling, and you should seize one when it presents itself. But maybe you are more of a tiger than I am. (In that case, you won't want insurance.)

There are still a few hand-types to consider:

YOU HOLD: A-2, A-3, A-4, or A-5. Dealer shows 5 or 6: *double down.*

YOU HOLD: *A pair.*
You should always split it if it is Aces, Eights, or Nines.
You should split Sevens if dealer shows Two-Six.
You should never, never split Tens, picture cards, or anything else not mentioned above. Splitting tens is greedy to the point of foolhardiness. Twenty is a powerful hand and should not be given up on speculation. To split two's, three's, four's, five's, or six's is simply throwing good money after bad. You have a bad hand now. If you split you will simply have two worse hands and twice as much money invested in them.

"CASEDOWN" PLAYERS

If you are a casedown player you should not be bothering with this chapter. A casedown player is one who can keep track of the cards as they are played in blackjack and scale his bets and strategy according to what remains in the deck. For example, he may escalate his bets as the end of the deck gets near, because he has much more knowledge of what cards are likely to come up. In addition, his strategy of hitting and standing, doubling down, splitting, and buying insurance is governed by his special insight.

A good casedown player, and their number is few, has a tremendous edge over the house in blackjack. He could almost clean the house out at will. As a result, casinos protect themselves against casedown players in three ways: they bar them from the blackjack tables; they shuffle the cards very frequently; or they use more than one deck at a time. A casedown player has no special advantage on the "early" hands dealt from a deck. Thus, when a casino shuffles several decks together for use in blackjack, it makes the casedown player's life unbearably complicated.

If you wish to take a fling at counting the deck, try ticking off the tens and picture cards. There are sixteen of them in the deck. Just start at sixteen and count backwards. If you are near the end of the deck and very few ten-values are left, you will draw with impunity to a twelve. You can use your knowledge in other ways as well. But I must warn you that it is not as easy as it sounds, and the experienced professionals who deal the blackjack games will likely get wise to you rather quickly and shuffle the deck to thwart you, or perhaps ask you if you don't really prefer roulette.

But *if* you can get away with counting at blackjack you can make a fortune in Las Vegas. A large "if"!

Blackjack at home

The odds for blackjack at home (in which the only rule changes are that the banker pays double for blackjack and wins ties) are very much the same as for the casino game. Requiring the banker to pay double (instead of 3-to-2) approximately cancels the edge he gains from winning ties. The main advantage of the banker is that the player must take the risk of busting before the banker decides whether or not to take additional cards.

Some home games increase the advantage of the banker even further by allowing him to win ties but requiring him to pay only 3 to 2 for blackjack. Here the banker has an additional edge, but there is little that can be done to overcome this in a change in strategy on the part of the other players; they simply lose a little more.

In some games, the right to be banker may be bought and sold. Here you may be faced with a decision as to whether or not to bid for the bank, and if so, how much. The amount you should pay for the bank depends on the amount of the maximum permissible bet. The more money that can be bet, the greater the value of the bank (in terms of expected gains). As a rule of thumb, it is generally a "good buy" to get the right to be banker for three times the amount of the maximum bet. I suggest starting your bidding at that level, on the understanding that if pushed you will bid as high as four times the amount of the maximum bet.

baccarat and
chemin de fer

TRADITIONALLY, baccarat and chemin de fer (the two are essentially the same) are the most exciting of all casino games — but only because so often in fiction, and quite often in fact, somebody swaggers up to a table, calls "Banco," (betting all the money the banker holds) and wins — or loses — a huge sum of money. I wish I could sneer at this practice and let you in on the secret of how to better your chances of winning by betting more scientifically. But the fact of the matter is that the rules that govern play in most casinos have been formulated to give the best winning chances to both banker and punter (the player who bets against the banker). The house doesn't care which side wins or loses since it cuts — usually by 5% — the winnings in each coup.

The longer you play, the more inexorable it is that the bank's cut will wipe you out, so risking in one coup as much as you are prepared to lose turns out to be the best betting strategy. Besides, since there is little freedom of action on the part of the player, you are able to play with more variety at the roulette table and you can get quicker action if you just bet the limit on red or black.

The game is played between banker and punter, using at least three and as many as six decks, shuffled together and dealt from a "shoe" — a device that enables the dealer to slip one card at a time off the top of the deck.

Baccarat

In Baccarat, the game played only in the Old World Casinos, there are two hands dealt against the bank and the punters may bet that either the left or the right hand will win, or that both will beat the bank — a bet *à cheval*. (A bet *à cheval* is withdrawn with no gain or loss if the bank beats one hand and loses to the other.)

The banker announces the amount of his bank; this amount is increased by his winnings, if any. He may not draw down or reduce the amount of his bank, but he may withdraw the entire bank, or the remainder of it, after completion of any deal.

As many as ten places are provided at the baccarat table for punters against the bank. Others in the room may bet as well. But the banker is never obliged to cover more bets than the amount of the bank. If one player calls "Banco" all other bets are withdrawn.

The play is simple. Each player is dealt a hand of two cards. Tens and face cards count zero; other cards count at their pip value. Object of the game is to make 9, or come closer to it than the opposing hand. A count of 8 or 9 in two cards is a *natural* and is shown at once. A natural wins unless tied by another natural or beaten, 9 vs 8. A total of more than 10 counts the amount by which it exceeds 10: 8 and $6 = 14$, counts 4. Barring a natural, each hand may draw one more card but the totals to which the punter must (may) draw are fixed by the rules of play. He must draw to 4 or less, must stand with 6 or 7, may use his own judgment only with 5. (The experienced player usually stands.)

In baccarat, the banker may use his own judgment whatever his count and, since he is playing against two hands, he may pass up a sure win against the smaller bet for a chance to win the larger. The banker has the small advantage of deciding his play with some knowledge of the opponent's cards. The player betting with the smaller pool may have a slight advantage if the banker concentrates on winning the larger wager.

Chemin de fer

In chemin de fer, the banker plays against only one opposing hand. The rules are much the same, but the bank's play is also rigidly dictated: Stand on 6 or 7, draw on 5 or less if the punter stands. There is also a further set of "musts" if the punter draws, depending on the rank of the card drawn.

As played in Las Vegas, the rules differ from those in Europe, where chemmy is now at least as popular as baccarat. The house always deals; the bank's limit is set (at $2,000) regardless of previous wins or losses; the players may back either the punter or the banker.

The rules that govern the play in gambling houses are in accordance with the best chances for punter and for banker alike. About the only way to "Go with the odds" is to buy the Casino.

lotteries
and sports

mathematical
"expectation"

THUS FAR our discussion of the odds has dealt with payoffs of moderate size in proportion to the amount risked. For example, in a card game or other gambling venture of skill, the amount a player stands to win is usually approximately what he stands to lose. In some of the casino games we have discussed (such as craps), this is also true. We have also seen that in some of the casino games there are bets which can be placed with relatively high payoffs, such as the bet on an individual number at roulette, which offers the attractive odds of 35-to-1.

The analysis of betting in cases in which the odds offered may be very high, as well as some instances with moderate payoffs, can best be understood in terms of what is called mathematical expectation. I offer a short discussion of this concept here so that the reader may better understand the chapters (on sporting events and lotteries) which follow.

The mathematical expectation of an event is the *average* expected result if the event were attempted many times. For example, suppose you are engaged in the following highly profitable game. You throw a fair coin and collect $2 if it lands heads or $1 if it lands tails. *On the average,* you collect $1.50 each time you throw the coin. Note that this result is not one which can be obtained with a single toss of the coin. It is, rather, the "fair" price of the game: *the average result which will obtain.* Usually, but not always, such expectations are expressed in terms of cold hard cash. For our purposes we need not consider other examples of mathematical expectation.

There are two important applications of mathematical expectation. First, one can use an expectation figure to determine if the price to be paid is fair or unfair, and if so by how much. Let us suppose, for example, that you were required to pay a fee for the right to enter the coin-tossing game described above. The fair price to play this game is $1.50 at every toss; if you pay this price, *in the long run* you will break even. Therefore, if you are asked to pay less, it is favorable for you to make the payment; if you are asked to pay more, it is unfavorable. Furthermore, the amount of difference between payment and expectation measures the extent of the unfairness of the game (in either direction) and indicates how much a person could expect to win or lose if he played it.

The second application is that one can determine from the expectation of *one* trial of the game (e.g., one toss of the coin) what the expectation would be if the game were played more than once. To obtain the expectation for more than one try, *multiply* the expectation for one try by the number of tries.

For example, suppose you are asked to pay $1.60 for the privilege of playing the coin-tossing game we have been discussing. You realize this game is unfair to you, since the expectation of collection is only $1.50. Nonetheless, you decide to enter into this game for the fun, the thrill of tossing the coin, and the chance of winning. But, being an intelligent gambler, you want to know how much you figure to lose. We already know that you can expect to lose 10¢ ($1.50 plus, $1.60 minus) for each toss. Therefore, if, for example, you wanted to play the game 6 times, your expected loss would be 60¢. This does not mean that you will lose 60¢ each time you play the game 6 times; it does mean that *on the average* you will come out 60¢ behind when you try a series of 6 throws. Beware of confusing this number with the necessary capital backing for playing the game 6 times. This amount would be $3.60 — the amount it would cost you if you played the game 6 times and collected $1 each time. (Your loss would be 60¢ per throw, for six throws, or $3.60.) Therefore, to enter into the game, you would need "backing" (a starting amount to guarantee you against running out of money) of $3.60, not 60¢.

However, the expectation allows you to measure what result you can expect, *even though this result may not obtain exactly on any one try, or on any series of tries.* (By the way, this concept is quite a useful and important one in many activities which are not related to gambling. For example, a company might want to know the *expected* number of people who would respond to an advertisement, or the expected number of people who would buy a product at 49¢ compared to the expected number of people who would buy it at 59¢, etc.)

For those who want to be fully in the know, here is the precise formula through which mathematical expectation is computed. Suppose that different results, let us say Result #1, Result #2, Result #3, and so on, can occur when a game is played or when some experiment is run. Observe that while there were only two possible results, heads and tails, in our coin-tossing game, many games involve the possibility of more than two results (roulette, for example). Let us say that the amount of money paid to the player for these results is expressed by the numbers R-1, R-2, R-3, etc., where R-1 is the amount the player receives if Result #1 comes through, R-2 is the amount the player receives if Result #2 comes through, and so forth. To find the mathematical expectation, one multiplies each payoff amount (R-1, R-2, etc.) by the probability that this result will occur and then adds all the products to get the final answer. For example, in the coin-tossing game the expectation of $1.50 would be computed as follows (assuming the coin is fair so that the chance of both heads and tails is one in two):

$$(\$2 \times \tfrac{1}{2}) \text{ plus } (\$1 \times \tfrac{1}{2}) \text{ equals } \$1.50$$

where $2 is the collection for a head and is multiplied by ($\tfrac{1}{2}$), the probability that a head will come up, and $1 is the collection for a tail, again multiplied by the probability of a tail (also $\tfrac{1}{2}$ in this example by coincidence). In many cases, particularly those with many alternative results, the probabilities for the different results will not be equal (horse races, for example, in which the different entries presumably have different chances to win the race).

It is sometimes convenient to express the mathematical expectation in terms of percentage of the money bet so that it can be applied conveniently to any amount bet. Suppose there is a game in which you can bet in multiples of $1 and that your expectation of collection is 85¢, i.e. you expect to lose 15¢ if you bet $1. Thus, *for each* $1 you bet, you expect to lose 15¢. This can be expressed as follows: whatever the amount bet, your expected loss is 15% of the amount bet. This figure will apply to *any* amount and is thus a convenient method of expressing the desirability (or undesirability) of a particular bet. By stating the expectation in terms of the *percentage* of the amount risked one can give both small bettors and big bettors a number with which they can compute their expectation in actual dollars and cents, as well as have a number to compare one form of betting with another.

Before we proceed to the applications of mathematical expectation, a word of caution. The expectation of a game is not always the best method to determine whether or not it is favorable. Other factors, such as the amount you can afford to lose, must enter into the calculation. Suppose a man gives you a coin known to be fair and asks you if you will pay $1,000 to toss it under the following conditions: if it comes up heads, you collect $2,010; if it comes up tails you collect nothing. This game is "favorable" to you inasmuch as you figure to win $5 each time you play. But who wants to risk $1,000 to win $5, even with favorable odds? (It might also be a good idea to use your own coin!)

On the other hand, suppose you have $1,000 and are desperate to have it grow to $2,000 within the hour. (Perhaps your friendly loan shark is coming by at that time with a few "friends" to collect a $2,000 debt.) A holding of $1,000 will be virtually useless to you. In that case you would surely play the game; in fact, you might play it even if you knew the odds were 2 to 1 (or even more) against your throwing heads, because the gain of $1,000 means so much more to you than the loss of the $1,000 you already have.

In short, no gambling proposition can be considered in a vacuum. The odds analyst can reduce things to dollars and cents, and in this role I can tell you what bets are favorable or unfavorable to you and by how much. But I cannot presume to know how much various amounts of money will mean to you as an individual and I implore you to keep this factor in mind before you plunge wildly into a proposition that appears mathematically favorable but which, in fact, involves a potential loss that you cannot afford. Remember that anyone can afford to win at any stake; only *you* know the stakes at which you yourself can afford to lose.

lotteries:

legal and otherwise

PERHAPS THE LONGEST odds you can get for your money are in lotteries. If we disregard the socially-oriented events such as neighborhood bingo games (although the mathematics of these lotteries is the same as all the others), we find there are two types of lotteries in which one can risk money. On the one hand we have the legal lotteries, generally run by a municipal or state organization. Tickets are sold, the proceeds going into the funds of the sponsoring organization, usually subsidies to welfare, education, highways, etc. The winning numbers are drawn from a large drum by a movie star or leading personality. A few people are a lot richer, even after taxes; a lot of people are a little poorer, but may rejoice that the money they lost is going to a worthy cause, presumably accruing at least partially to their own benefit.

State lotteries

The lure of such lotteries is that one can truly get rich quick by winning. For example, in the moderately popular New York State lottery (in which bets usually total between 5 and 10 million dollars every month), the top prize is a cool $100,000. Not a bad return on an investment of $1. I will use the New York State lottery as an example to illustrate how to compute the mathematical expectation in a lottery.

The payoff scheme of the New York State lottery is as follows. Bets are made in units of $1. Each $1 bet gives you one ticket in the bowl when the winning numbers are drawn.

For each million dollars bet each month (each month has a separate drawing) the following prizes are offered:

    1 prize of $100,000
    1 prize of $ 50,000
    1 prize of $ 25,000
    1 prize of $ 10,000
   11 prizes of $ 5,000

Thus, for example, if the total wagered is some 6-million odd dollars, there would be six winners of $100,000, six winners of $50,000, and so on. Since the *chances* of winning a prize in each amount are the same regardless of how many millions are bet (to a close approximation) we can consider the expectation in terms of one million bets. Suppose you buy one ticket, having paid $1. Then your chance of winning $100,000 is 1 in 1,000,000; your chance of winning $50,000 is 1 in 1,000,000, similarly for $25,000 and $10,000 and your chance of winning $5,000 is 11 in 1,000,000. Multiplying each result by its probability of occurrence and adding the products to obtain your expected collection, we find that you can expect to collect $\frac{\$240,000}{1,000,000}$ or approximately 24¢. (The "approximately" is caused by the possibility that the overall amount bet will not be an exact number of millions, which will throw the odds slightly off — but not enough to worry about since any inequity will be divided up among each of the millions.) Thus, for each dollar you bet in the New York State lottery, you can expect to lose 76¢. In other words, you expect to lose 76% of the money you bet in the lottery (not counting taxes!).

It is easy to see that the "house" take is very large. If you remember the discussion of your chances in Las Vegas casinos, I suggested you avoid bets in which the house take was as high as 5%, and search instead for those bets which could be made at approximately a 1% disadvantage. The large "house" take in lotteries is the price you pay for having the chance to win $100,000 at the risk of only $1. In other words, to get such good odds, and have the chance to retire early in life, you must concede quite a bit on expectation. Against this is the compensation that when you lose the money goes to (in this case) the state, not to a private individual or group of individuals as it does when you lose money at a casino. Do realize, however, just how much the chances are against you.

While we have used the figures for the New York State lottery, the numbers are similar for other state and local lotteries. The expected loss is about 75% of the money bet; the benefits are the enormous odds on your money and the chance to hit a really big payoff at little risk, plus the fact that the money you lose presumably works for your benefit; in New York State, for example, lottery proceeds go towards improving educational facilities in the state.

There are other lotteries which may or may not be available to you. These are the illegal lotteries run by "numbers agents," and are usually called "the numbers game" or simply "the numbers."

Private lotteries

Most states (Nevada is a notable exception) have laws prohibiting public gambling. However, exceptions are made for activities run by the state (such as state lotteries, in which the profits go to the state, and horse racing, where the state takes a portion of the "handle" through tax) and also, on occasion, for certain special activities. In particular, religious organizations are permitted to organize and run lotteries which are essentially public. Many churches, for example, run bingo games, perhaps as often as once or twice a week, to help raise funds as well as to provide entertainment.

The important thing to know about the odds in lotteries of this form is that the sponsoring organization is under no (legal) restrictions regarding its profit margin. When you bet at a race track, for example, you are protected by law to the extent that your expectation will be a loss of only 16 cents to the dollar. (See the section on Horse Racing.) In a private lottery, such as a bingo game, the "house" can adjust its margin of profit in any manner it desires. Thus, if $100 is bet in a bingo pool, the sponsoring organization can return $100, $90, $80, $70 or any other amount, to the winner(s), depending on whether it wants no profit, $10 profit, $20 profit, etc.

The methods of adjusting profit margins in lotteries sponsored by individual organizations vary from place to place. If you were interested in maximizing your chances in lotteries of this type (assuming you must enter them), you would, of course, be well advised to search out those in which the profit margins were the smallest.

However, one does not usually play bingo, or participate in similar activities, with such a bloodthirsty attitude. Whatever the "house cut," you have the enjoyment of "gambling," that is, of trying for a big killing, and you know that, even though the odds are against you, the money is going, at least indirectly, to your own benefit or to a good cause.

Nonetheless, many people like to know whether or not any strategy can be applied successfully to bingo, and other lottery games, if for no other reason than that they enjoy getting the best possible deal in all the activities in which they participate. In the bingo family, such strategy is usually limited to the choice of whether or not to buy "extra" cards; that is, whether or not to take more than one chance in the lottery.

The correct attitude towards "extra chances" can be summarized briefly. Assuming all the chances are of equal value (as will be the case, for example, in a carefully run bingo game) there is no advantage in taking an extra card at the same price as your original card. All you are doing is raising your stakes — you will lose faster. If you want to get the extra card so that you will be risking more to gain more, fine; but do not do so because you think it improves your odds.

A simple calculation makes this obvious. Suppose you are one of two players in a game in which the house will pay $8 in prizes for $10 in cards sold. You buy four cards in each game at $2 a card. The other player buys only one card. According to the odds, you are a four to one favorite in every game. But what this really means is that you will figure to win four games in every five. No doubt you will have more fun. But at the end of five games, if the odds work out, you will have paid $40 for four cards in each game. The other player will have paid $10 for one card in each game. You will collect $32. Your loss will be $8. He will collect $8. His loss will be $2. But on every game he had a chance to win $6.

You could, at best, break even.

Obviously, this takes no account of the factor of luck. In a short run, the one card man may win more often. If he wins three times, however, though it might be exceptional coincidence, it would be prudent to inquire whether he is a near relative of the fellow who calls the numbers.

However, if you have the opportunity to buy an extra card at a reduced rate, you gain a *mathematical advantage,* for by so doing you are reducing the average cost of your cards, thus increasing your overall expectation. Thus, if you can get one bingo card for $1.00 or 2 cards for $1.50 (this is an extreme example.), it will be to your advantage to get two cards, even though you are risking more money.

It follows from this discussion that if you yourself are planning to run a "casino night" for your organization, regardless of the nature of the games you choose to run, you can organize your own profit margins. Bingo is the simplest example. All you need do, to establish your rules, is decide what margin of profit you want for the organization. Then, simply deduct that percentage of the amount bet in any one lottery from the total pool (just as the track and state deduct about 16% from the amount bet on a horse race) and return the balance as the prize or prizes. Thus, if you want a 20% profit margin, and $100 is bet in a bingo lottery, make the prize $80 (to be divided in case of ties). Similar adjustments can be made for any lottery-type game you decide to include in your "casino night."

The numbers game

It's a crime to run a numbers game. And from the standpoint of this book, it is also a crime for you to play the numbers, even though it doesn't make you a criminal. The odds against you are 999 to 1. The payoff is 600 to 1 — *if* you are lucky.

Briefly, the numbers game works as follows. Bettors may back one (or more) three-digit number(s). They place a bet that this number will be "the winning number" for the day their bet is placed. Generally, any amount may be bet, the most common bets ranging from a nickel to a dollar or perhaps several dollars. (It is commonly believed that the numbers game subsists by receiving small bets from a large number of people. There is, however, no way I can confirm this.) Each day's winning number is determined according to a preset formula. This formula is often derived from the "handle" (amount bet) on one or more races at one or more racetracks; if you know the formula, you can determine the winning number by obtaining the pari-mutuel handles for the appropriate tracks and races.

If a bettor has picked the winning number, he collects at the odds of 600 to 1 (subject to special exceptions noted below). As far as can be determined, each of the one thousand three-digit numbers 000 through 999 is equally likely to be the winning number. Therefore, the bettor's approximate expectation is a loss of 40% of the money he bets. We see that this expectation is more favorable than that of government lotteries, but not as favorable as can be had by betting pari-mutuels at the horse races.

In certain circumstances, the odds offered will be less than 600 to 1. First of all, there are some numbers which are considered lucky by numbers-game players. The "bank" gives lower odds on these numbers (usually 300 or 400 to 1) to reduce the play on these numbers and to avoid being hit too heavily should one of the "lucky" numbers come in. Second, the nature of betting in the numbers game may cause what is known as a "short slip." Bets in the numbers game are generally made by filling out a betting slip and passing it to a collector, along with the money bet, the amount of which is also indicated on the slip. Since, in many cases, the police frown on the numbers game, it may be inconvenient for the collector to check that the amount indicated on the slip has actually been paid in. If a slip is found to be "short," that is, the amount collected is not equal to the amount listed on the betting slip, lower odds will be offered on a winning number listed on the short slip. Assuming a numbers player wants to get as good odds as possible, he should avoid short slips and avoid betting on the "favorite" numbers of other players, so that he will never receive lower than the standard 600-to-1 odds.

lotteries and sports

Many numbers operators provide their patrons with business cards; these cards will list the numbers which come with reduced payoffs. Below is a sample card:

Beginning APRIL 1, 1967

As of January 12, 1967

NEW YORK CITY

This card is for customers who receive NO commission on their work and pay dollar for dollar only.

Those who receive Commission, old card still stands.

Short slips will be paid 5 - 1

Pay off between 6 & 6:30 Every Day!

Not responsible for arrested work

325 - 3 - 1   125 - 3 - 1
769 - 3 - 1
(Combination)

316	In Combination		
769	"	"	
716	"	"	**400 to 1**
323	"	310	
414	"	205	
212	"	765	
101	"	478	
111	Straight		**400 to 1**
222	"		
100	"		
325	In Combination		**300 to 1**
125	"	"	

Also · TROTTERS · Handle

Obviously, short slips are heavily penalized. "Combinations" (indicated by drawing a box around the number on your slip) are bets that pay off if the winning number of the day is any combination of the three numbers selected. Usually, this bet pays 100 to 1. But if the selected number includes two of the same digits, it offers only three winning combinations instead of six, it is suicide to bet these in combination unless you get better odds.

There are both advantages and disadvantages to this type of lottery betting. One of the drawbacks is that a payoff may be delayed or lost because the numbers operators are jailed. Note the disclaimer: "Not responsible for arrested work," on the gambling card shown. Also, any losses accrue to the benefit of individuals rather than to the state, so that the bettor does not reap a partial profit from his losses. And the maximum payoff is not as high.

However, there are several compensating advantages which explain why the numbers game is so popular — even, according to some police reports, "a way of life" in some areas. First, the bettors' expected loss is lower than in state and municipal lotteries. Second, the odds are not quite as prohibitive, and a regular bettor will occasionally win, which may brighten his life. (In a state lottery, on the other hand, an "occasional person" may win while a regular bettor will lose to the state.) Third, small amounts may be bet — a numbers player can have "action" for as little as 5¢ or 25¢ a day. A government lottery player usually must bet at least $1. Finally, the main lure of the numbers game is action *every day*, whereas in the big-payoff lotteries one must wait a month before the thrill of hoping to have won a big prize. Many people play the numbers so as to take an interest in the activity, not only in the hope of scoring a big victory. These people would rather lose a quarter every day — but have hopes every day — than lose a few dollars once a month, the hope of a life annuity notwithstanding.

The legal positions of these lotteries are, of course, quite different. If you win from $5,000 to $100,000 in a government lottery, the money is taxable and the income will be reported to the good old Internal Revenue Service. Numbers operators will not report your gains (if any) to the authorities, and someone wishing to cheat on taxes would not report such gains. However, it is not a crime to bet in the numbers game. (What *is* criminal is to *run* such a game, collect bets, etc., or not report the income to Uncle Sam.)

The odds in lotteries

Whether you buy tickets in a sweepstakes, participate in a municipal or state lottery, or play bingo at your local social or religious institution, you can determine the odds against you in the same general way.

In this discussion, by a lottery I will mean a game in which skill plays no part whatsoever (or such a small part as to be essentially insignificant), with the winners of the game determined by chance drawings of numbers or other random devices. Furthermore, I will assume that each participant in the game has the same chance to win *in proportion to the amount of money he risks.* Thus, in what I am calling a lottery, a man who buys two tickets, and thus must pay twice as much as a man who buys only one ticket, has exactly twice as much chance to win.

As every lottery bettor knows, consciously or subconsciously, the odds are against you whenever you enter into a lottery arrangement. It is convenient to express the odds in terms of what happens to you on the average. To do this:

1] determine the total amount bet in the lottery;
2] determine the total amount paid out by the lottery organization.

To compute the odds against you, take the ratio of the total amount bet to the total amount paid out (that is, the ratio of *[1]* against *[2]*).

This figure gives you the total odds against you — not the odds against winning on any one particular ticket. For example, using the New York State lottery as we did above, assuming one million dollars bet, we have:

Total amount bet: $1,000,000
Amount returned $ 240,000

Total odds against winning equals the ratio of amount bet to amount returned.

Here, these amounts are 1,000,000 to 240,000, or approximately 4 to 1 against you.

Notice that this answer is given in approximate terms. You could, if you wished, carry out the division to as many decimal places as desired. For most purposes, however, it suffices to get the *approximate* odds to be able to compare bets.

Here are a few other examples of computing the total odds against bets in particular lotteries:

BINGO

The playing of bingo is a popular social activity. Few persons indulge in this activity with a mind towards gambling in the same sense that a casino player does. Nonetheless, it may be of interest to you to discover the total odds against you when you sit down to play bingo. (As we saw before, these odds will not vary with the number of cards you choose to play -- assuming all cards are as good or as bad as all others.)

Bingo, however, is not a standardized game in that the payoffs to the winners are determined solely by the "house," that is, whoever is running the game. (In some places, because lotteries are regulated by local and state laws, it may be necessary for the "house" to abide by certain restrictions. Since bingo games are often run for the benefit of charitable or religious organizations, and since it is presumed that the "gamblers" playing bingo are aware that they are in effect contributing in exchange for an evening's pleasure, these restrictions are not always strict.) If you want to find out the total odds against you when you play bingo, you need only determine how much is bet (altogether) and how much is returned to the winners.

KENO, LOTTO, FASCINATION, ET AL.

Keno is a game similar to bingo. The essential difference between the games is that in bingo the player is given a "free" square in the middle at the outset. This change has absolutely no effect on the odds, because the lottery player is competing against others in the lottery, not against the "house." Keno is so named because (originally, at any rate) the numbers called out, which allow the players to place markers on their own cards, were drawn from a keno goose. A keno goose is a sack arranged so that it will release just one pellet (or other marker) at a time, thus making it suitable for dispensing the numbers to be used in keno (or, for that matter in bingo — but don't let anyone try to sell you a bingo goose!).

Actually, bingo and keno are both forms of a general sort of game called lotto, in which the objective is to place a certain number of pieces (five in the modern games) all in a row, horizontally, vertically, or diagonally. Lotto is played in various forms, of which bingo and keno are just two. There is a board game in which the players alternately claim boxes and attempt to put five of their markers in a row. (This is *not* merely an extension of the popular game of tic-tac-toe because the board is much larger than five-by-five, and many subtle strategies are possible.) This is not a popular gambling game, however.

One form of lotto which is very popular is called "Fascination." Players of this form of lotto throw small balls — of the stickball or handball type — towards a 5 × 5 array of holes at the end of an electrically controlled board. When one hole is claimed, the ball comes back and the player tries again. The first player to get five in a row wins, and payoffs are achieved in much the same way as bingo. This game is not, strictly speaking, a lottery, because there is a certain amount of skill in dispatching the ball. If one assumes that all players are approximately equally skillful at this, it becomes a lottery. "Fascination" is particularly popular along the famous 42nd St. strip in Manhattan, where Fascination parlors can be found in between the dozens of movie theatres just off Times Square.

Another form of this game often found in resort areas is called Pokerino. Pokerino machines are frequently found side by side with pinball machines. This game is non-competitive in that the player isn't trying to be first of a group to win; he throws against the house. He gets five balls to throw on a 5 × 5 square of holes in an electrically rigged board. Each hole corresponds to a card from a standard pack, and prizes are awarded for the formation of various high-ranking poker hands from the cards represented by the five holes into which the contestant's ball drops — hence the name of the game. Naturally, it is very difficult to beat the house at one of these games, no matter how skilled you are at tossing the balls. Few people engage in these activities except for amusement, or perhaps to be able to bring home some trivial prize to show.

In any event, keno, and all these other variations of bingo, require no additional knowledge to be able to compute the odds. In all cases you take the ratio of the total amount bet to the total amount paid to get the total odds against your overall chance of success at the game.

WHEELS OF FORTUNE

Betting on a wheel of fortune is theoretically similar to betting on lotto games. However, it is more difficult to compute the odds because wheels of fortune usually have variable payoffs. For example, a wheel might have 36 numbers. You place your money on a number and you win if that number comes up — that is, if the wheel stops at that number. But the situation is complicated by the fact that there will be, in general, several different forms of win you can achieve. On a typical wheel, there might be 6 slots corresponding to each number: three slots will be colored white, two slots colored red, and one slot colored blue. If the wheel lands on white you win, say, one prize unit; if it lands on red you win two prize units; and if, through your good fortune, it lands on the blue box, you win, let us say, 5 prize units.

Here is how to compute the odds against you on a wheel of fortune which involves this moderate complication. The first thing to do is to compute the *average* collection you achieve if the wheel lands in your box. Let us use the figures given above to do this. Assume the wheel lands in your box. Then out of every six times it does this:

3 times it lands on white; you win 3 units
2 times it lands on red;   you win 4 units
1 time it lands on blue; you win 5 units

Thus, out of six times, your total win is 12 units. This gives you an *average win* of two units.

You can assume, therefore, that you will win two units every time the wheel lands in your box. In other words, if every number were covered exactly once (which will happen, on the average, in the long run) the house would collect 36 fees and pay out 2 units of prizes. Of course, these are *average* results — they will not necessarily occur on any one spin of the wheel. But it is acceptable to use them for computation purposes because it is what happens in the long run that really counts.

Suppose, therefore, that it requires 25¢ to bet on a number on this wheel, and that a prize unit has a cash value of $1 (this is usually in merchandise, so the "house" doesn't pay $1 for it, but that is of no concern to you).

In our example, therefore, the total odds against you are

TOTAL AMOUNT BET *to* TOTAL PAYOFF

which is

$9 (36 slots at 25¢ per slot) to $2 (average prize)

So, in this wheel of fortune, the odds against you would be about 4½ to one. (Notice that this figure is about the same as the one given for the New York State lottery.) Of course, except where subject to local laws, the management can arrange the payoffs of their wheel in any way they like. In effect, they can adjust the odds against you at whim, *even if the wheel itself is completely fair.*

In practice, the management will not totally soak its customers. After all, if no one ever won on the wheel there would be no customers left. In fact, the "blue box" is placed on the wheel so that every so often there will be a jackpot won, and someone will be going around telling a story of how he won at the wheel of fortune, or, just as good, walk around the fair grounds carrying some enormous Kewpie doll as a symbol of his ability in selecting the winning numbers.

The odds against you in slot machines at casinos can be computed in the same way. However, you must be able to determine the payoffs of the machine just as you must be able to figure out the average payoffs in the wheel of fortune.

Short cuts to the odds

Even if it pleases you to be able to compute the odds against you, it may decrease your enjoyment of playing if it becomes a complicated chore. Since you are unlikely to want to enter a lottery for the express purpose of winning (most people are satisfied with the opportunity of playing and the thrill of having a chance of winning, particularly a really big prize such as the $100,000 in the New York State lottery), you probably don't want to get bogged down in too many computations.

In order to simplify your calculation of the odds, you may simplify the numbers involved by approximating. For example, in doing the division to get the ratio for the New York State lottery into lowest terms, I approximated the number $240,000 by the number $250,000 in order to make the division easy. True, my answer was not *exactly* right — you will notice I said that these were the *approximate* odds — but for practical purposes, the figure obtained gives a good picture of the range of the odds.

Similarly, you should simplify the numbers you use to compute the odds. Let the casinos figure their "edges" exactly and to the ultimate decimal point — after all, that's their business! For your purposes, I suggest you try to express the numbers involved as nearly as possible in whole numbers, and to make these numbers as small as possible.

Suppose, for example, you are wondering about the odds in a lottery in which $4,132,564 is bet, and the prizes total $987,637. I once met a man who could do problems like this division in his head, but if you can do this sort of thing mentally you shouldn't be wasting your time betting in lotteries!

Instead, approximate the amounts involved with small whole numbers. The amount bet is *approximately* 4 million and the total payoff is *approximately* 1 million. So the odds against you are *about* 4 to 1. Of course, this is the "wrong answer." You won't pass a mathematics course with answers like that. But neither will you get a headache. These odds aren't off by much — and it is reasonable to assume you will be satisfied with an approximate answer. Time enough to be more exact after you've won one of the prizes.

Finally, if for any reason you need to know the precise odds — to settle a bet, for instance — you know how to find them if it becomes essential. It is just as important, as a practical matter, to know when to do things approximately and when to do things exactly. The time and energy saved by an approximation will be worth much more than any monetary amount you may save by knowing the exact odds.

For the approximate odds will serve just as well.

Some well-known swindles

People very often make "man to man" bets on just about anything. They will bet on facts: which is the largest lake in West Tanganyika, for example. They will bet on the outcome of sports events. And they will often bet on things that just happen to come up in conversation.

Unfortunately, sometimes the things that "happen" to come up in conversation don't just happen. They are planned. There are many real-life situations in which a little advance knowledge can be worth a lot. Not, of course, that I anticipate you taking this knowledge down to your local tavern and depriving the patrons of some of their hard-earned cash. Far from it. But there is no need for you yourself to fall prey to some of the well-known swindles involving "casual bets."

In this chapter, I discuss some of the better known swindles that "just happen to come up." The methods of computing the odds are, in some cases, simple; in other cases, they involve some rather sophisticated mathematics. You need not master *how* to compute the odds, just the results. And these I undertake to provide.

1. THE NEEDLE IN A HAYSTACK

Conversation can easily be brought around to finding a needle in a haystack. And sooner or later someone will be asked to make a bet of the following type. Onto a playing field with equally spaced parallel lines (such as a checkered tablecloth) a "needle" (usually a matchstick) is thrown from considerable height. One player bets that the needle will land on one of the lines; the other bets that it will not.

This is perhaps the best swindle of its kind because it is very difficult to judge, offhand, the exact chance that the needle will land on a line. Of course, the swindler will have ascertained this information well in advance. The chance depends on the distance between the parallel lines (let's call this distance A) and the length of the needle (let's call this length B). Then, the chance that the needle will land on a line (assuming that B is less than A) is

$$B/A \quad \text{times} \ (.6) \quad \text{(approximately)}$$

Thus, if the needle is half as long as the distance between the lines, it will land on a line only about 3 times in 10. (Most people would think it was even money, thus giving the swindler his advantage!)

2. CONSECUTIVE THROWS

People tired of tossing heads and tails may wish to try this game. Two players toss coins alternately, and the first one to throw a head wins. The first player has one chance. If he throws a head, he wins the game. If he does not throw a head, the other player then gets *two chances* to throw a head (and wins if he gets a head either time). If the second player fails with his two tosses, the first player then gets *three* tosses.

Once again it is not immediately obvious what the odds on this game should be. A little thinking will make it clear that the first player has the advantage, because he wins *at least* half the time (when he throws a head at once).

In fact, the odds are 3 to 2 in favor of the first player, and in order to make the game a fair one he should offer these odds to his opposite number.

Slight variations can be made in this game. For example, the second player might be given *three* throws if the first player misses, and so forth. This will, of course, make the game a fairer one, but the advantage will still be with the man who throws first.

3. FAIR GAME?

Suppose someone gives you this offer. You have a stack of chips and must bet a specific unitary fraction (such as ½, ⅓, ¼, etc.) of your chips on each play of a certain game. This game is guaranteed to be a fair one, such as heads-tails in the tossing of a fair coin. And the payoff will be at even money. Furthermore, you are guaranteed that the game will stop only when the same number of heads and tails have come up. So you cannot run into a run of hard luck and be penalized. Would you play this game?

On the surface this game looks completely fair. But appearances can be deceptive, for the odds in this game are stacked very much against you. In fact, *you are guaranteed to lose!*

You don't believe it? Try it and see. Just remember that you must bet the same proportion of your stack on each and every bet. One example to start convincing you: You start with four chips, will bet ½ your stack each time, and will get one head and one tail. Say you win on heads and lose on tails.

For the first toss you bet two chips (half your stack) and, let us say, you win. You now have six chips. You bet three (half your stack) and now lose, evening out the luck. But you are left with three chips, one less than when you started.

Did you say you want to lose first and then win? All right. You bet two chips and lose. You now have two chips. You bet half again (one chip) and win. You now have three chips, again one less than when you began. It's infuriating, but you just can't beat this game!

4. DIFFERENT STACKS

The old game of matching pennies has its variations also. Suppose you and a friend play the following game. You will match pennies, one at a time. If both show heads or both show tails, you win; if they are different, he wins. *But* — here's the twist — you must each commit a specific number of pennies to the game and the game does not stop until one player has lost all his pennies.

If the two players start with the same number of pennies, the game is fair. (By the way, the best way to play it is to put up heads and tails about equally often, without using any special pattern which can be deciphered by your opponent.)

But what happens to the odds if one player starts with more pennies than the other? Suppose you start with 10 pennies and your friend starts with only 5. Do you have twice as good a chance to "clean him out" as he does you?

The answer to this is a doublecross: Yes! In fact, the odds are always in the same ratio as the number of pennies each player starts with. So if you start with 3 pennies and he starts with 7, the odds are 7 to 3 against you.

Here's the swindle. Although the odds are against the player with fewer pennies, *the game is fair*. This is because the man with more pennies is putting up that much more by way of a stake. In the previous example, for instance, while the odds are 7 to 3 against you winning, you are risking only 3 pennies while your opponent is risking 7!

So the swindle comes up when there is a fixed stake that

the game is played for, and the players each contribute to this stake. For the game to be fair, the players must contribute to the total stake in the same ratio as the number of pennies each starts with. If the total stake is $10, and you start with 4 pennies to your opponent's 6, make sure he puts up $6 to your $4 before you play with him. The "skill" in this game is *not* in the arrangement of pennies — in "guessing" which side your opponent will turn up — but in the arrangement of the stakes.

5. CHOICE OF UNFAVORABLE ACTIONS

Sometimes you will be called upon to make the best of a bad bargain. Although you will be at a disadvantage, make sure you don't take any more the worst of it than necessary. Suppose you are faced with a situation in which you must double your money or go broke. You have, say $100, and you must get $200. You are willing to go broke, if necessary, trying to increase your holding to $200. But the situation is such that you can make bets, at even money, only in a slightly unfavorable game, such as crapshooting — in which you have about a 1% disadvantage every time you play.

If you have the choice of betting a small amount many times or a large amount just a few times, *bet as much as possible.* If you bet in very small amounts, you are almost certain to be wiped out. You maximize your chance of winning the amount you want by betting as much as possible at every opportunity (until you reach your desired amount).

The same strategy should be applied to playing games such as roulette, where the house has a small but ever present advantage. Playing slowly is a sure way to lose. Betting boldly is your only real chance to come out ahead.

horse racing

"THEY'RE OFF!"

This announcement of the start of many a horse race might equally well apply to the rush of the millions who pour money into the betting machines at race tracks across the world, and the uncounted horse players who bet uncounted totals with bookmakers. Betting on horse racing is a firmly established custom in many countries, particularly the United States. As many systems have been devised for "beating the horses" as for beating roulette. As is true of roulette, however, the horse player with a system is likely to wind up telling his friends, "I broke even at the track today, and boy did I need the money."

Mathematically there is no way to beat the horses. If we consider the mathematical expectation of betting on the horses, we will see that sooner or later the odds will catch up with a system bettor, or any other kind of bettor, just as surely as they invariably do in roulette (or any other game in which the bettor has a theoretical disadvantage). Let's start with bets made at the track, through "tote" machines. The betting machines that flash the payoffs on track bets are nothing more than small, limited-function computers. They record the total amount bet, *subtract 15–16%* (a portion of which goes to the track, the rest to the state in the form of taxes) and then, on the basis of this reduced figure, compute the odds for a bet on each horse in the race. In the "win pool" (the collection of bets on which horse will finish first) the amount bet on each horse to win is subtracted from the reduced total and the remainder divided by this amount bet in order to get the odds. I'm sure this sounds confusing, but it's really a rather simple process. Let's assume that the state-plus-track cut of the pool is 16%. Suppose that $100 is bet on a race, $21 of that amount on horse number one. (In real life, of course, these numbers would be much higher.) Here is how the tote machine computes the payoff on horse number one — the odds that it flashes on the payoff board. First, it subtracts the 16% "cut" from the total pool, i.e. $16, so the reduced pool is $84. If horse number one wins, the people who bet the $21 will get their bets back and split the balance as winnings. After giving back the $21 there will be $63 left as winnings. This $63 will be divided among winners holding $21 worth of tickets, so each dollar-value in winning tickets wins three dollars. Thus, the payoff odds are three to one.

The place pool (bets that pay off if the horse finishes first or second) and the show pool (bets that a horse will finish first, second or third) are computed similarly, with one twist. Let's consider the place pool. You win a place bet if the horse you bet on finishes either first or second. This means that there will be two different winning tickets — that is, the place backers of two horses will share the winnings. To compute the payoff odds, the machine subtracts the 16% (or whatever) cut, puts aside the money bet on the *two* "winning" horses, and divides the remainder into two *equal* piles — one pile to be distributed to the ticket holders of one horse, a second pile going to the backers of the other horse. For example, suppose that $100 is bet in a place pool with $12 bet on horse number one and $24 bet on horse number two. After subtracting 16%, we have a net pool of $84. Taking away the $36 bet on the two "placing" horses, we remain with total winnings of $48. This is divided into two packages of $24 each, so the place payoff odds on the first horse are two-to-one while the place payoff odds on the second horse are even money.

At most tracks, the place payoff odds are not flashed prior to the race in the same way the win odds are. (This is because the calculation is complicated, because win betting is more popular than place betting, and because the place payoff odds on a horse depend on which other horse comes in in the first two, so many combinations would have to be listed to give all possible place odds.) However, you can figure out these odds — if you like to know what odds you will be getting for your bet — because the amount of money bet on each horse in the place pool, as well as the total, is usually flashed to the crowd.

Of course, any calculation you make in the place pool will involve some uncertainty, for you will not know which other horse will place, even if you assume that yours will. It should be clear from the description of how the payoff odds are computed that you will collect more if your horse comes in with a longshot rather than with a favorite (for the money bet on the other horse, which is subtracted from the reduced pool before the winnings are determined, will be smaller). To avoid painting yourself too rosy a picture, when computing the potential place odds from the numbers flashed to you by the tote machine, I suggest you assume that the most heavily backed horse (other than yours) will be the co-winner. Then, to compute the place payoff odds, deduct 16% (about one-sixth) from the total pool, deduct the money bet on both the horse you wish to back and the betting favorite, take half the remainder and divide into it the amount bet on your horse. (The show pool works similarly, except that the money bet on the three "showing" horses is deducted and the winnings split up into *three* equal groups.)

If one assumes that the betting is in correct proportion to the chances of the horses, betting to win is like playing roulette with the house having zeros practically all over the wheel. The odds against you are enormous and, accordingly, the longer you continue to bet on the horses the greater is the chance you will go broke. Of course, it is not true that the betting is in the correct theoretical proportion. So you can, in principle, beat the horses if you know which bets are worthwhile — in other words, which payoff odds are longer than the actual odds against the horse winning the race. In order to know this, you must know something about the condition of the horses themselves. Usually, such information comes to you in the form of a "tip." It is not my function here to discuss the probable or possible value of such tips. I wish to point out only that even if you have good information regarding which horse figures to win, you still have a long way to go to make up that 16% disadvantage. In short, a bet on the horse races is not, in general, a favorable one. I prefer to consider such bets as methods of increasing the enjoyment of watching the races rather than as cool calculated gambles. Among the possible things on which you might bet, this is one of the least favorable, mathematically speaking.

You have probably heard the tale of the fellow who started with a $2 bet, plowed it all back on each succeeding race, and won seven straight races. In the eighth race, with thousands riding on the result, his horse stumbled in the last furlong and was nipped at the wire. A horrified friend saw him tearing up a huge stack of tickets and asked, "How much did you lose?" The gambler shrugged nonchalantly and said, with absolute truth, "$2."

I fear that I could not have faced this blow as philosophically. However, there are some other truths discernible in this story. The track is one place where there is no betting limit to queer a system, if you are playing one. But the odds are not constant. The more money you put into the pool yourself, the more unfavorable are the odds against you. You get more fun and a better run for your money when you play long shots.

The "sure thing" player isn't as smart as he thinks. Bet an overwhelming favorite to place instead of to win and it may appear that you are getting better odds. But are you really? More often than not, it takes an accident to beat an overwhelming favorite; if accident happens, the favorite may not finish in the money at all.

Human nature being what it is, no one is about to stop betting on the horses just because I tell him it is a losing proposition. Accordingly, I will add one hint that should help your track record. This is hardly an original idea — it has been suggested by many racing observers and its basis is mathematical. If you must bet, *bet to win*. Place and show bets are tempting for their conservatism, but they are really no more than slower and surer ways of disposing of your money.

Special racing situations

There are several special situations which may face the prospective horse bettor and a firm understanding of these may help you get more mileage from your betting dollar.

A common form of bet among regular horse players is a "parlay," sometimes called an "if bet." In this form of betting, the wagerer places a bet on one race with the intention of wagering his winnings, if any, in the next race. If he loses in either race, he has lost his parlay. But if he can pick both winners he will pyramid his money considerably. Parlay betting is an aggressive approach to betting on the horses (or betting on anything else for that matter).

Since betting a parlay is similar to betting on the daily double (you must pick the winners of two races to win), many racing fans wonder whether it is superior betting strategy to bet on the daily double or to bet a parlay on the two horses that would otherwise be bet in the double. The answer is that betting in the daily double is slightly superior, because that 16% that goes to the state and track is taken out of your betting money only once. If you place a bet on each of two races, your money must go through the betting machines twice.

Of course, on any one particular day, the daily double may pay more, less or about the same as a parlay. (This depends on whether the successful horses were backed more strongly by the double players or by the bettors on the individual races.) In the long run, however, at a parimutuel track the double players will do better than the parlay bettors.

"Overlays"

Most tracks provide their own handicapper's evaluation of the horses entered to race by listing the "morning line." These figures represent the "official" estimate of the proper odds for each horse. Of course, no one, not even the track's own handicapper, knows everything necessary to be able to quote precisely the right odds. However, assuming the local handicapper is competent, you can often pick up a good bet by looking for an "overlay," that is, a horse that is quoted at odds significantly higher than those suggested in the morning line.

For example, if horse X is listed at 3 to 1 in the morning line, and you see on the odds board that you can place a bet on horse X at 6 to 1 or 7 to 1, you should consider that this may be a good bet. The track's expert considered the proper odds 3 to 1, so even if his estimate is off by a little you will still have a good bet. Needless to say, horse X will not always win — even the track man thought he would win only about 1 in 4 — but if you consistently get better odds than the horse deserves, you will do better (again, in the long run) than your normal expectation of losing 16 cents of every dollar you bet.

You don't have to rely on your own judgment. There are a dozen or more racing forms or tip sheets that can be bought and many of the newspapers publish the selections of one or more handicappers. Most of this advice costs little in ratio to the sum invested by even a modest bettor, so the price of advice doesn't greatly affect the odds. However, since anybody can buy the dope sheets, neither does the advice. Most of the handicappers wind up on the minus side, along with you.

sports events

THERE ARE no figures on how many people in the United States bet on sports events, but the number must surely run into the millions. Betting on athletic contests, usually accomplished through bookmakers, is in vogue whether the event be professional or amateur. Sentimental betting, on college (or even high school) teams is widespread, and many sports fans find their enjoyment increased when they can bet on their favorites.

With the increase in per capita relaxation time in today's society, the popularity of sports is on the rise. More professional sports are appearing in the United States, and the already existing ones are in a process of wild expansion. This in turn creates more interest in all sports at the preliminary level — usually in schools, colleges and universities. This interest, in turn, creates more betting opportunities and more people interested in betting. I think it can fairly be said that betting on sports events is a part of "the American way of life," just as soccer and rugby pools are part of the way of life in England.

Just as in horse racing, where truly intelligent betting requires technical knowledge about the participants -- in this case, the horses themselves — so also shrewd betting on sports requires being aware of the relative merits of the teams involved in the event on which you propose to bet. Clearly, the more you know about the performances of the teams in the sport you follow, and bet on, the more successful your betting will be.

It is impossible for me to offer advice on which teams to

back in sports bets. You probably have at least as good an idea as I do which team has the best chance to win, let us say, this year's World Series in baseball, or the Super-bowl in football. So you are on your own as far as selecting the teams on which to place your bets.

However, I can tell you what odds you are laying against yourself when you bet on a sports event with a "bookie" and how these betting odds compare with, for example, the odds against you in a gambling casino or at the race track. Consider three types of bet:

Betting on a team

1] "Even-money" bets with a point spread
2] Team against team bets with favorite and underdog
3] Bets on the selection of a team from a "field"

1] BETS WITH A POINT SPREAD

Many sports events are obvious mismatches. For example, West Podunk U. may be a traditional football opponent of Supertropolis State, in a rivalry dating back to the 1880's, when, perhaps, they competed on relatively equal terms; nowadays, however, old W.P.U. is simply out of its league. The true odds against a W.P.U. victory might be as high as 30 or 40-to-1. Under such circumstances, it is unfavorable for the bookmaker to take bets at odds. For one thing, he will get little action. For another, he is open to the always-present possibility of an attempt to "fix" the game. (Fixes are less profitable, and hence less likely, if the odds are low, for the fixers must then have a large amount of capital they are willing to risk in order to show a substantial gain. This will tend to leave them little money with which to affect the result of the game.) Therefore, the odds for such a game will generally be given as a "point spread" – a number of points you can get along with a team. For example, you might have the opportunity to bet on "West Podunk U. plus 28½ points." This means that if the stalwart W.P.U. defenders hold the margin of the S.S. victory to 28 points (or less) you will win your bet. If, however, they are overpowered by more than this number of points, you will lose. The bookmakers attempt to set these point spreads accurately, so as to insure an equal amount of action on each side and to attract as many bettors as possible. These bets are "even-money" bets. This means not that you get even money on your bet but rather that you can take either side at the standard rakeoff for the bookmaker. In the old days, this meant you had to lay 6 to 5 against yourself. Nowadays, however, the standard odds are only $5\frac{1}{2}$ to 5 against you (11 to 10) and this amount measures the odds against you. It should be noted that this disadvantage is mild compared with the potential loss per dollar at, say, the race track. This is perhaps one of the reasons that bookmakers flourish — they offer reasonable odds. Of course, there are other risks, *e.g.* the bookmaker may welsh or may be arrested, but most sports bettors are willing to take this chance.

It is interesting to note that the method of giving a point spread is now employed almost universally in several sports (such as football and basketball) even though many games would not warrant odds of more than about 3-to-2 on one team or the other winning. The reason for this seems to be that the point-spread method increases the amount bet because of added fan interest.

In this regard, there is an anecdote told about the early days of the New York Mets. Although this team is no longer a pushover for the National League musclemen, when it was a new and struggling entity its forces won games only occasionally at random. One day, so it is said, an official observer who knew only the rudiments of the game was watching the Mets batting for the last time during one of their frequent drubbings. In some fashion they managed two baserunners and, although two were out in the ninth and the team trailed by five runs, the huge crowd suddenly came alive with cheers. When the observer asked why the fans were so excited, he was informed that the Mets were $2\frac{1}{2}$ run underdogs and that even though the game was beyond reach, the bets of the fans were not. Whether this story is true or fanciful, it is clear that point-spread betting can increase spectator interest.

I have two observations concerning this form of betting.

First, it is always clear what the odds are against you: the "standard" even-money-less-percentage situation. Second, the point spread has been calculated by people who know quite a lot about the sport. While it is true that you can win at this form of betting by spotting an erroneous point spread, remember that it is in the interest of the people booking your bets to make this spread as accurate as possible, that is, to make it truly reflect the merits of the teams involved. You have to know something special to know more than the professional gamblers.

2] FAVORITE *vs.* UNDERDOG BETS

These are old-fashioned bets at odds. You can bet on either the favorite or the underdog. Once again it is easy to calculate the odds against you and once again the gambling superstructure does best when it makes the odds as close to fair as possible. The only thing that may throw you off is the manner in which these odds are quoted. For example, suppose you see that the Rocketships are 7-9 favorites over the Green Martians. This does *not* mean that you can bet nine dollars on the Rocketships to win seven, or that you can bet seven on the Green Martians to win nine. These numbers are used to express the odds in relation to a "one unit" bet — usually five dollars. In other words, if you want to bet on the Rocketships you must put down nine dollars to win five, while if you want to back the Green Martians you bet five dollars to win only seven.

From these figures you can compute the exact odds at which you are placing your bet and can thus judge for yourself how much of a disadvantage you are at. In general, your *percentage* of disadvantage will be about the same as in the first type of bet we discussed.

3] BETS FROM A FIELD

This is the type of bet where you must pick a winner from a long list of entries, just as you do when you bet on a horse race. For example, the following were the pre-season betting odds for the winner of the 1968 National League pennant race

lotteries and sports

as quoted at Las Vegas. (The odds established at Las Vegas, gambling capital of the world, are usually used throughout the country.)

Cards	eight to five
Pirates	five to two
Giants	nine to two
Braves	nine to two
Reds	six to one
Phils	ten to one
Cubs	fifteen to one
Dodgers	thirty to one
Astros	fifty to one
Mets	fifty to one

These numbers give the exact betting odds. In other words, if you wanted to back the favored Cardinals, you bet five dollars to win eight. You will note that these odds are similar to those quoted for a horse race, and in many ways such bets are similar to those made at a track. It is not clear how to determine how much of a betting disadvantage you would have. One way is to calculate how often out of 100 times a team would win the pennant if the quoted odds were correct. Doing this approximately in this case, we find:

Team	Approx. times in 100 it would win if odds were correct
Cards	38.4
Pirates	28.6
Giants	18.1
Braves	18.1
Reds	14.3
Phils	11.1
Cubs	6.7
Dodgers	3.3
Astros	2.0
Mets	2.0
Total	142.6

Since there will be only 100 true victories every 100 times, and the bettors need 142.6 victories in order to break even if they bet in proportion to the true chances, this gives a measure of the "house" advantage. Of course, it is still true that you might be able to find a favorable (or, at least, not particularly unfavorable) bet if the quoted odds were misguided. In 1967, the previous year, you could have bet on the Red Sox in the American League at 100-1 (with Kansas City and Washington thrown into the bargain). You will recall that this bet would have been rather favorable. It is occurrences such as these that keep the bettors coming back for more.

Whether or not the disadvantage in the odds is worth the increased enjoyment of the bettor and fan I leave to the reader.

The 1969 pennant race introduced a new factor: the two leagues were expanded into two divisions each. Jimmy the Greek's odds for the National League, quoted in *Sports Illustrated* before the season opened, looked like this:

western division		eastern division	
San Francisco	6 to 5	St. Louis	2 to 5
Los Angeles	5 to 2	Chicago	3 to 1
Atlanta	3 to 1	Pittsburgh	4 to 1
Cincinnati	3 to 1	Philadelphia	6 to 1
Houston	100 to 1	New York	25 to 1
San Diego	300 to 1	Montreal	300 to 1

These odds were on leading their divisions. To win the National League pennant, the division winners met. Obviously, St. Louis would be the pre-season favorite to take the playoff as well. But assuming that the San Francisco Giants also topped their division, you could not assume that the odds in favor of St. Louis would be the ratio between 6 to 5 and 2 to 5 (6 to 2) because other factors have been introduced: the strength of the other teams in each division established the odds in relation only to the results in that division; there has been no direct comparison of the two winning teams, etc. Besides, it's a short playoff series.

Bets on other sports events

Most bets that can be placed on other sports events follow the pattern set by horse racing or standard bookie betting. At most tracks (and in some cases, at dog races) in addition to straight win, place or show bets, you can bet the daily double, twin double, exacta and quinella. (Not all of these bets will be available at each individual track.)

The same basic method of computing the odds affects these bets, but they have the theoretical advantage that they are single bets at longer prices; thus, you are following the "lose least when you bet the most" theory in situations where you are at a known disadvantage. However, this assumes that the total amount you will bet (including putting back winnings) would be the same. It takes a truly firm will to stick to this principle; in practice, most bettors won't be able to abide by it. Thus, since bets are now being placed at longer odds, the chance of an eventual loss is greater.

My best advice here is: know what you are getting into. You are aware that you have an inherent disadvantage in any bet you make, but you want to make bets for your enjoyment of the event. Set aside the amount you can afford to lose and determine to bet that amount and no more. If you can stick to this rule, betting on the long-shot possibilities, such as the daily double, offers the best relative odds.

JAI ALAI

Jai alai is one of the few sports involving human participation on which you can bet legally. Betting on this sport is a complex matter, for new odds are quoted after each point is scored. Granting the assumption that the competition is "on the up-and-up," judging bets at jai alai is an extremely complicated and difficult task. Knowledge not only of basic odds and the past performances of the players but also the ability to see how a match is going (is one player tired? etc.) play an important part in successful betting. This is not an area for an inexperienced bettor to try to make some money.

Finally, we come to sports "pools." These are generally run outside the law and thus share with bingo games the quality of having the profit margin uncontrolled. These margins will vary, depending on the size of the organization (which may run from a national syndicate to the boys in your office) running the pool. The only way you can obtain the best deal is to find the pool with the smallest profit margin.

card games

---

luck vs. skill

AMERICAN COURTS have held that poker is a gambling game and bridge is a game of skill. I for one am not about to dispute this. Anyone who knows both games will admit at once that there is more skill involved in bridge. Yet it is paradoxically true that, in any given session, there is less chance that a skilled poker player will lose than that a skillful bridge player will do so. And when an expert poker player loses, it will be comparatively less, as well as far less often.

That is why I begin our discussion of card games with poker. But it is also why there are four times as many pages devoted later to the discussion of going with the odds at bridge. Bridge requires *more* skill. But except at duplicate, where the skilled player "always" wins, bridge does not reward skill with the same *frequency*. The reason is that in bridge a player has no choice of which hands he will play. In poker, the good player drops his bad hands at little or no cost and plays only on his good ones.

Is it true, then, that the rewards of skill are far greater in poker than in bridge? I do not think so. It all depends on what you play for.

The object of the game

Let me illustrate with an incident that occurred in a highly social, high-stake Sunday afternoon auction pinochle game.

In auction pinochle, the high bidder gets the right to use the three cards that are in the blind or the widow. In a way, this is like drawing three cards at poker — except that of course a 15-card pinochle hand will sometimes include many more chances to improve.

Nevertheless, the mathematical chance of improving your hand is usually far less than the odds given by the optimistic bidder. He so thoroughly enjoys the occasional thrill of a lucky buy that he tends to forget about the hands he throws in because he has bid too much.

In pinochle, as in poker, the player who comes to win doesn't count too heavily on what the extra cards will provide. (This is especially true when an overbid not only risks what you will pay out if you don't "buy" but what you would surely win if you bid conservatively because you have a big hand that is cold.)

In this Sunday afternoon game, one of those properly archconservative bidders opened with 350 and allowed himself to be boosted to 370 by a 360 bid from a liberal-bidding opponent. The blind produced three nines, usually the worst possible buy. But one of these was the nine of trumps, with a melding value of 10 points and the additional value of eliminating one losing trick in the play.

The man who had boosted had reason to hope that the buy would bust his opponent, but our conservative friend said, "That ought to be enough." In fact, he was able to show the hand and have it conceded without playing it out.

This so aggravated the booster that he sneered, "Why don't you loosen up a little bit? I'd have bid 400 on that hand right off the bat."

"Why do you play this game?" the conservative answered the question with one of his own.

"For fun," was the reply. "And I'm having it."

"Well," was the retort, "*I* play for money, so we're both getting what we play for."

The tight bidder was right, of course. But it turned out he also was wrong. Since it was primarily a sociable game, the goats grew tired of feeding their tiger and pretty soon he wasn't invited to play any more.

The moral, if there is one, is that if you play to win you cannot also expect to play for pleasure. That is, for any pleasure other than the winning. It is up to you to decide whether that is enough.

poker

The poker-playing frame of mind

You have often read on the sports pages how a coach has spoken admiringly of one of his charges: "He came to play." The desire to play, to get into the action, is an essential attribute of the successful competitor, a quality which has raised many a sportsman of mediocre talents to stardom.

However, nobody who "came to play" ever made it big as a poker player. Poker is, in this respect, similar to hunting or fishing: it is an activity of watchful waiting, interspersed with moments of decisive action. If somebody asked me for a one-sentence formula for success in his poker game, I might say "Bring a good book, and not necessarily a book on poker." In other words, the first lesson in poker is not to throw away your money on poor hands. When you are dealt an unpromising collection, your first reflex must be to turn your cards face down and sit on your chips. There will be another deal soon. Meanwhile you have an excellent opportunity to observe the habits and style of your fellow-players. Your time, therefore, can be put to profitable use.

Although I have spent a lifetime playing and loving the game of bridge, I have often envied poker players for the ability to do just what I have described: to get out of a bad hand. I'd like to have a dollar for every time I have sat helplessly at the bridge table with a miserable collection of tickets, watching as the opponents chalked up huge scores. This need never happen to a poker player. When you have a terrible hand at poker you can just throw it away and watch the player with the strongest hand collect somebody else's money.

In fact, you will never lose much at poker when you hold

very bad cards. Everybody (I hope) knows that when he is dealt, at five-card stud, a six face up and a deuce in the hole, he should get out and not pursue the matter further. (I once knew a man who stayed against me with just such a hand. He caught a straight and beat my three-of-a-kind — to his ever-lasting amusement. His problem was that he tried to repeat this miracle a few times too often. I don't have to say where he finally wound up.) The hands that cause the heavy losses at poker are the second-best hands: hands that are strong except that somebody else's hand is stronger. These hands are the toughest traps to avoid, because you usually don't know for sure that you are beaten. Later on in this section I'll offer some advice in this area.

In this chapter, I will be stressing the virtues of con-servative, "tight" play, because I have found that even medio-cre players, playing "tight" in a "loose" game, have been able to win consistently. But here I must inject a note of mitiga-tion: winning money is not the sole objective of playing poker, at least not when it is played among friends. If you find your-self, therefore, playing poker at a party, for goodness sakes loosen up a bit from the standards I prescribe. Otherwise you may find yourself an unwelcome guest. Play just a bit more conservatively than the others and you are likely to go home a winner; make yourself a conspicuous tightwad and you are likely to lose a continuing source of pocket-money, as well as your friends.

When playing in a club or public game, however, be as ruthless as you wish; social considerations do not apply.

Table stakes, pot limit and limit poker

Poker with rules may seem a bit effete when compared to frontier poker. In the good old days of the West a player bet whatever he owned or could hock, borrow, beg, or steal; the limits were set only by the most informal (and sometimes violent) agreements. Modern America is (theoretically) too civilized for such activities. Hence orderly rules have arisen to govern the maximum amounts that can be bet at any time. The popular sets of rules are known as Limit, Table Stakes, and Pot Limit. Each has strategies of play that differ substantially from those of the other two. While I will describe all three types, I propose to discuss at length only the Limit game, which is by far the most popular version. One compelling reason for the popularity of the Limit game is that the other two types necessarily involve very substantial amounts of money, and are therefore played only by experts who are willing to invest a substantial fraction of their fortune at the poker table, or by lunatics. This book is not directed at either group.

TABLE STAKES

The theory of Table Stakes is that each man puts a certain amount of money (or chips) in front of him at the start of a hand and this is his betting limit for that hand. House rules usually specify that this amount must exceed a certain minimum. If a player is put in the position of having to call a bet that is more than he has on the table, he puts his table amount in the main pot. His opponent's excess then creates a side pot, which is matched by other players who call that bet, and continues in use on subsequent rounds of betting. The player who has put in all his table money thus gets a free ride for the remainder of the hand; he is competing, however, only for those pots in which he has made an investment. There may be several side pots going on one hand, as players successively put all their table money in the middle while a hand is still in progress, but all pots will be "balanced"; that is, each pot will represent an equal contribution from all players active *in that pot*. Each particular pot is won by the active player with an investment in that pot who has the best hand in the showdown, if any. Thus, a player may win certain side pots by default (other players in that pot having folded) but may still have to compete actively for other side pots and the main pot against other players. Needless to say, it can be somewhat confusing for a newcomer to this form of poker to keep track of the pots, let alone the cards.

If this sounds complicated, let me offer an example. In a four-handed game A and B each have 100 chips on the table. C has 60 chips, while D has 20 chips. On the first round A bets 50 chips. B and C can and do call, but D, who would like to call, cannot meet the bet. Therefore a main pot is created in which each player invests 20 chips (D's limit). The remainder of A's bet (30 chips) is put into side pot #1, where it is matched by 30 chips each from B and C. Therefore, at this stage we have:

Main pot = 80 chips
side pot #1 = 90 chips

After the draw, let us say, A bets 30 chips and B raises 10. C only has 10 chips left so he puts them in the current pot, which is side pot #1, along with 10 chips each from A and B. (D goes along for the ride.) Now A and B form side pot #2 with that portion of their bets which C cannot cover. B has bet altogether 40 chips on this round, of which 10 have gone into side pot #1. He therefore puts 30 chips into side pot #2. A meanwhile, has put 10 chips of his 30 chip bet into side pot #1 and the remaining 20 into side pot #2, and he still has to cover B's raise. (C by this time is also along for the ride.) A, after consideration, decides to raise B another 10, so he puts all 20 of his remaining chips into side pot #2, which is the current pot. B, who had been bluffing, decides to fold at this point.

So, before the showdown the pots look like this:

main pot = 80 chips
side pot #1 = 120 chips
side pot #2 = 70 chips

In the showdown it is discovered that A has two pairs, C has three of a kind, and D has a straight. A wins side pot #2 because only he and B were active in that pot and B has folded. C has the best hand of those who were active in side pot #1 and wins that pot. D has the best hand of all and he wins the main pot.

After the hand the wealth is distributed like this:

A has 70 chips
B has 10 chips
C has 120 chips
D has 80 chips.

It doesn't hurt to have an accountant handy to figure out what's going on in a table stakes game.

POT LIMIT

The basic principle of Pot Limit is that the maximum size of a bet at any time is the amount of money in the pot. This scheme provides for an escalating series of bets as the hand develops. For example, the first bet can be no larger than the ante, which may be a half-dozen chips or so, but by the third or fourth round of betting bets may be as large as several hundred chips, and if everybody has his betting shoes on, each bet could be twice the size of the previous one. Mathematically inclined readers will observe that this could lead to a pretty snappy progression.

Usually a table-stakes element will be added to the pot-limit feature: each player will be limited to the number of chips he has on the table as well as to the size of the pot. This is a sensible restriction. Side pots build in the same manner as they do in Table Stakes.

LIMIT POKER

This is the game of millions of Americans who enjoy poker. The point of Limit Poker is that everybody knows in advance what the stakes are going to be and that nobody can attain an advantage by bringing in more money than the others.

A typical social "Friday night" game might establish limits like these:

25¢ or 50¢ on each card (at stud) for the
first three upcards;
50¢ or $1.00 on the final card.

This is enough money so that people will think before they bet but not enough to send anybody home bleeding. Of course, a vast number of players establish much lower limits, and it is interesting to note that in a game where only pennies and nickels are involved, a dime starts to look like a lot of money! Nonetheless, it is my recommendation to establish limits which will be meaningful without being downright painful.

Limit Poker differs drastically in strategy from the Table Stakes and Pot Limit games. The main reason is that the difference between each bet and the preceding one is necessarily small in relation to the size of the pot. In other words, crushing raises are impossible. This factor changes the whole theory of bluffing, because it is impossible to make it really expensive for an opponent to call a bet. There *are* certain types of bluffs which can be successfully "run" at Limit Poker, but it is important to understand their specifics and use them properly. Otherwise bluffing becomes little more than an advertising investment, and *at Limit Poker you are likely to lose your money almost every time you try a bluff.*

In the discussion of the types of games (draw, stud, etc.,) I will make note of certain types of bluffing opportunities with legitimate chances, but I would advise against a strategy of the generalized type of "psychology" bluff which is part and parcel of Table Stakes and Pot Limit.

In the main, then, I shall try to advise in these areas:

1] getting the proper odds for any bet you consider making;

2] the importance of table position;

3] hand evaluation;

4] how to stay out of "traps" with a not-quite-good-enough hand.

Getting the proper odds

It is remarkable that most poker players have no conception of how to relate the odds to a decision on whether to bet. They may know what the odds are against improving their hand, but they do not know how to use this information, or they are too lazy, or too undisciplined. About the latter two traits I can do little, except to note that poker, like bridge, is a game of skill and concentration, and a player unwilling to expend the effort to learn and apply strategy and to concentrate on the game he is playing cannot expect to go home a winner.

I can, however, explain to the willing student how to apply knowledge of the odds. Actually, there is nothing complicated about the mental procedure which the good poker player reviews automatically every time he considers making a bet.

First, the facts you have to keep in front of you at all times:

1] You have to know what the odds are against sufficiently improving your hand to give you a good chance to win the pot.

2] You have to know how much money there is in the pot.

3] You have to know (or be able to make an educated guess) how many other players will call, or have called, this particular bet. In other words, you have to know how much money the pot will contain at the conclusion of this particular round of betting.

This last calculation is sometimes automatic. For instance, if you are the last player with an opportunity to call a particular bet you will know with certainty what the pot will contain after the round of betting is over, because your bet will close the round. On the other hand, if there are several players still to act behind you, you will have to judge how many of them are likely to see the bet, and if any are likely to raise. Granted, this is a bit more abstruse, but it is part of the judgment of the poker player. After all, if the game were altogether a cut-and-dried exercise in the arithmetic of odds, it would have died out long ago.

Now, you marshal your facts as follows:

1] You decide whether you will win the pot if your hand "comes in." Obviously, if the answer is "No," you should fold forthwith, regardless of any other consideration. If, for instance, you are angling for a straight at favorable odds, you would fold rather than continue if you thought somebody else held a flush. Similarly, it is idiotic to draw to a pair of kings when another player is a moral certainty to have three aces. (But I see it all the time.) Three kings is a strong hand, but it is only second best *this time,* and, as I have said, the second-best hand loses the most money of all.

So, let us continue on the assumption that *if your hand comes in it will win.* Then,

2] You divide the size the pot will be at the conclusion of this round of betting by the size of your bet. Note carefully that I said nothing about the amount of money you personally have already contributed to the pot. The minute you put money in the middle it ceases to be yours. One of the great poker crimes is throwing bad money after good. All you should be concerned about is the relation between the size of your bet and the size of the pot.

3] If the odds against improving your hand are greater than the money odds offered by the pot, don't make the bet! It's that simple.

Let's consider a simple example. You deal a five-card draw and pick up a four-flush. The ante was 50¢. The man at your left, who is first to speak, bets a dollar. The other five players fold. The pot thus contains $1.50. Our call (if we make it) will represent two-fifths of the entire pot, or, in other words, the money odds are one-and-a-half to one. The odds against filling our flush are slightly worse than one in four. Thus, even if we assume that we are a sure winner if the flush comes home, the bet would be a losing one in the long run. Remember, if we win we will not win $2.50 for our dollar, because $1 of that money was ours to begin with. We will win only $1.50. Investing $1 to win $1.50 on a three-to-one shot is bad business and bad poker. It is easy enough to see that it is improper to bet a four-flush unless there are at least three other players in the pot with us, because otherwise the money odds will be insufficient. If, on the other hand, two players ahead of us had called the opener, the pot would contain $3.50 when it came to us, and betting a dollar to win $3.50 on a 3 to 1 shot is reasonable. Note that the fact you put up the ante of 50¢ has nothing to do with calculating the odds later. The money no longer belongs to you; it is part of the pot. The mistake of considering money already invested as still yours is what costs poker players a fortune.

Most players, of course, bet on a four-flush because it looks easy to fill and usually wins when it comes in. This is fuzzy thinking, and in fact the four-flush costs these players a lot of money in the long run.

Table position

Table position refers to your position relative to the first bettor of a round. The first bettor may be the first player to place a bet, or may be the first player invited by the rules to bet. In draw poker the player to the left of the dealer is invited to make the first bet on the first round. In stud, the player with the best hand showing is invited to bet first. (If two players have equal values showing the invited player is the one nearest the dealer's left.)

There are no hard-and-fast rules which say which position is most desirable. It depends on your hand and what you are trying to do with it. The significance of table position varies widely from game to game, so its discussion will be deferred until the various forms of poker are discussed individually.

Hand evaluation

It is probably superfluous to list the relative values of poker hands, but for the sake of completeness I will do so. In order of descending strength they are:

Royal flush (A K Q J 10 of a single suit)
Straight flush (5 cards of a suit in sequence)
Four-of-a-kind
Full house (3 of a kind and another pair)
Flush (5 cards of a suit)
Straight (5 cards in sequence)
Three-of-a-kind
Two pairs
One pair
Other hands

When two hands of the same type are in conflict the individual cards are compared from the top down. Thus, if two players have flushes and one flush is headed by an ace while the other is king-high, the ace-high flush wins. If both flushes are ace-high, the second cards are compared, and so on until a discrepancy is perceived. If two flushes are composed of identical cards of different suits the hands are considered equal and the pot is split. (In other words, there is no ranking between suits.) Full houses are compared according to the three-of-a-kind. Thus, three fours and two deuces are better than three threes and two aces.

When wild cards are involved "five-of-a-kind" becomes possible. House rules may vary on the ranking of this extraordinary hand. The standard rule is that it is best of all.

Another area in which house rules may vary is in the use of the ace in forming straights. Some games permit the ace to be used as either part of a high straight or part of a low straight; others restrict it to high straight only. I believe the latter rule is superior. In a seven-card stud game, the sixth and seventh cards are never used as "tie-breakers."

So much for the rules. More interesting is the question: What is a good hand?

The answer depends on the game being played. The stronger hands are considerably less common at five-card stud than at other games. This is obviously so because there is no draw or other chance to improve the original five cards. In five-card stud a high pair, such as kings, will win as often as not. Flushes and straights are most uncommon. In addition to the initial odds against a pat flush (510 to 1) or straight (254 to 1) there is the problem that it is not always feasible to stay around long enough to assemble the hand. After all, a flush or straight, until the fifth card, is just so much garbage. A good player will not normally stay even for a third card simply because his first two cards belong to the same suit. Thus, many potential flushes and straights die aborning in five-card stud. For this reason, and because of the great infrequency of even stronger hands, a high three-of-a-kind will win almost any hand of five-card stud, and a high two pairs are a big favorite as well.

But the real problem in stud is not just to know whether

a certain hand will win most of the time; the problem is whether it will win *this* time. After all, king-high wins a good many pots of five-card stud. In the section on stud I will discuss how to judge from the betting and the visible cards whether somebody has a hand which can beat yours.

In seven-card stud and draw games somewhat stronger hands are needed to win. The point about seven-card is that a player may try for a straight or flush while other things, such as pairs, may give him a fighting chance even if the big one doesn't come in. I would say that in these games it is somewhat uncommon for anything less than a pair of aces to win. A medium three-of-a-kind is a more likely winner, and straights lose a good bit of the time. It is a tough man indeed, however, who can cold-bloodedly fold a hand as good as three aces in any game!

Again, however, the real problem of hand evaluation is a problem of drawing the right inferences from betting, visible cards, and mannerisms. These matters will be taken up in the discussion of the appropriate games.

The trap: the second-best hand

One of the main ideas in winning poker is to stay out of the big pots when you are not going to win. A hand which was hopeless all the way should never have gotten going. The place where the real money is lost is in the vain pursuit of a hand just a bit stronger than the one you hold. You must recognize that some hands, while they are possible winners, are just not worth following through. A common example is a small pair, particularly at draw. I know you hate to throw away a hand and then find that you could have held it and won this particular pot, but this sort of chasing the will-o'-the-wisp will cost dearly in the long run. It is far better to recognize that hands like this are best gotten rid of with a fond farewell. More of this anon.

Five-card draw

The most popular version of five-card draw is known as "Jackpots" or "jacks-or-better." The name derives from the fact the opening bet must be based on a hand which is at least as strong as a pair of jacks. This does not mean that anybody with a pair of jacks is required to open. It is perfectly permissible to check and then play after another player has opened the pot, and in "tough" circles it is equally proper to check and then raise the opener. It is a good idea to find out whether check-raise is favored in the game in which you play. Personally, I say, "Why not? It's part of the game."

The laws allow you to open on jacks, but a seasoned player, sitting directly at dealer's left, would probably not do so. The reason is that sound poker prescribes that you should not open a pot unless you have some reason to believe that you have the best hand. Two jacks should not inspire such confidence with six totally unknown hands lurking about. If you open your jacks and any player raises, for example, you will be compelled to drop and you will have thrown money away. I would not open "under the gun" (*i.e.*, next to the dealer) with less than kings.

However, let us suppose that several players have checked ahead of you. It is now a fair proposition to open some frail reed such as a pair of queens or even jacks. It is true that somebody may have checked a powerhouse, waiting for you to bet into him, but the greater danger is that if you fail to open the hand will be thrown in when you have the best cards. (If a hand of jackpots is thrown in, the pot is sweetened with another ante and play begins again with new cards.)

Suppose that the player in front of you, who was first to speak, has opened, and you are looking at a pair of jacks. What should you do? The answer is that you should fold without giving the matter a moment's thought. Opener has announced that he is at least as good as you are, and unless he is a bit softheaded, he will be better than you. So if you bet you are entering the fray against one known stronger hand, with five unknown quantities yet to speak. It is true that you might stay around and outdraw all of them but whatever odds you have to improve, their odds are even better.

In general, bluffing aside, you have two reasons to make a bet: first, you think you have the best hand at the table; second, you have a chance to improve in the draw to a winning hand. As I explained before, you should always relate the money odds offered by the pot to your chance for improvement when considering a bet which is predicated wholly or in part on "the come."

Here, then, is a table of the odds against improving your hand in draw poker. If there is anything which you, as a poker player, should actually memorize, this is it, for it is information which you will use practically every time you have to make a bet, and other players may not take well to the idea of your keeping the chart in front of you as reference material. Furthermore, referring to such a chart may be taken as an indication that you are betting on futures.

Odds against improving (draw poker)

hand before the draw	cards drawn	improved hand	odds against
one pair	3	two pairs*	2½ to 1
		aces up*	6 to 1
		3-of-a-kind	8 to 1
		full house	100 to 1
		4-of-a-kind	360 to 1
one pair + ace kicker	2	aces up	4 to 1
3-of-a-kind	2	full house*	9 to 1
		4-of-a-kind	22½ to 1
two pairs	1	full house	10½ to 1
four-flush	1	flush	4 to 1
open straight	1	straight	5 to 1
inside straight	1	straight	12 to 1
open straight flush	1	straight*	2 to 1

* means "or better;" i.e., "two pairs*" means "two pairs or better"

KEEPING A "KICKER"

Drawing only one card to 3-of-a-kind slightly increases your chances of landing a full house but substantially reduces the chance of hitting fours. Altogether, drawing just one card to threes reduces your chances of improvement to 10½ to 1; this draw is generally made for tactical reasons, as it conceals the true nature of the hand.

BETTING BEFORE THE DRAW

I have already discussed the considerations determining the soundness of an opening bet. Now I will consider the betting after the opening. If you are playing a sound game (i.e., not bluffing) you do not wish to play unless you think you may have the best hand going into the draw. This means that you should play a pair of kings or better, and rarely anything less (unless the opening bet followed the several checks). A pair of aces is "worth" a raise, but whether such a move is tactically wise is debatable. If the pot has been opened in front of you and you have a powerhouse (high three-of-a-kind or better) you would be best advised to lie low and simply call. You want others in against you, as you very likely have a winning hand, and a raise may drive the customers away. On the other hand, if you are last to speak and hold a powerhouse, and several other players are already in, a strategic raise is in order to increase the size of the pot. Most of the players already committed will stay in. It is important to distinguish this type of strategic raise from a raise designed to drive others out.

Suppose that first hand on your right opens. You have three aces and just call, lying low. Two more players call and the last player to speak raises. Opener calls and it is your turn. What should you do? I would advise a quiet call. If you re-raise you unmistakably announce your strong values and you may drop everybody except the raiser, and maybe him as well. Call as if you were going along with the game and either stand pat or buy one card in the draw. After the draw opener will surely check and you should bet! This bet will drop everybody but the raiser who will try to figure out what you have. He is likely to figure that you went in with two high pairs (if you took one card) and you are trying to persuade him that you hit a full house (or perhaps a straight or flush). This is such an obvious bluffing situation that he will certainly call you and may even raise. Alternatively, if you stand pat the raiser will play you for bluffing and call on the same suspicion.

HANDLING TWO SMALL PAIRS AT DRAW

Two small pairs is the trickiest hand to manage. While it is probably the best hand going into the draw on any given occasion, the chance for improvement is slight; and if a few others are in against you, there is a pretty good chance one of them will outdraw you. Your objective with two small pairs, therefore, should be to have as few players as possible drawing with you. (The odds are that if three other players draw and your hand started out as two pairs, the better of which was tens or worse, you will lose!) Accordingly, if you are seated just over the opener, you must raise to drive others out. This is one of the really clear-cut situations in poker. Directly over the opener is, however, an unpleasant place to be when you hold two small pairs. You would be better placed at the end of the line when you can see how many players are in before you have to bet at all. If there are more than three players in when it rolls around to you, the soundest course of action is to fold. This is particularly true if the pot has been raised. On the other hand, if only one or two other players are competing, it might be wise to push the two pairs and raise strategically, as your chances of winning the pot are pretty good.

Altogether, the handling of this holding will be crucial to your success at draw poker. My advice is that it is dynamite: treat it gingerly.

BETTING AFTER THE DRAW

There are two cardinal rules respecting betting after the draw:

1] *If your betting before the draw has revealed your hand and you have not improved, don't bet.* The reason is simple and much ignored. If everybody knows what you have and you bet, they won't call you unless they can beat you. Thus, the only action you will get will be unwelcome and will leave you in unhappy, losing dilemmas.

2] *Respect pat hands and one-card draws.* If you bet into one of these hands you are inviting the undertaker if it is "for real," so such a bet would indicate that you hold a real crusher (such as a high flush) or that you are staging a not-too-appealing bluff. After all, if any of these short-draws hit he is going to call you; so a bluff is likely to succeed only if none of the shorts hit. In that case you might conceivably drop somebody else. It all depends on how you bet before the draw, and whether there is any inconsistency about your actions which might cause some-body to become suspicious. In general it is *such* a poor bluff that it has a chance to succeed against somebody with something such as a pair of aces.

But unless you laid a good foundation by betting intelli-gently before the draw you are going to find yourself in a poor position afterward. For example, suppose that before the draw A has opened and B has raised. The others have dropped. It is probably silly for you to call without a rather strong hand. Otherwise after the draw you are going to be caught in a squeeze between A and B. (B will probably bet after the draw.) If you could have reraised before the draw, however, your position would be much better. Now B might check to you, and if you have not improved you can attempt a free checkout.

BLUFFING AT DRAW POKER

Sorry — a full discussion of the bluffing techniques avail-able is beyond the scope of this book. Let me make just two observations concerning bluffing:

1] *A good bluff must be planned from the outset.* The sim-plest technique is to imagine that you hold the hand you are trying to project, and then play it as well as you know how. For example, suppose that you are sitting over the opener and wish to bluff a holding of three aces. You should merely call the opener, accept any raises, but then bet vigorously after the draw. If you had raised the opener you might have exposed yourself, since a player with three aces would not raise in this position for fear of driving others out.

2] *A good bluff should be directed at a particular player, rather than at the table at large.* If a certain opponent, for instance, has failed to call you when he might have had you beaten, he should be bluffed as soon as possible thereafter.

An example of a hoary but still effective planned bluff is the pat hand bluff. Sitting over opener you merely call. If anybody raises you continue to call. Then you stand pat and bet the limit after the draw. Opponents will reflect that the odds against a pat hand are 130 to 1, but they will call only with much fear and trepidation.

An overused and usually futile bluff is the betting after the draw of a hand which tried for a straight or flush and failed to connect. This is a bluff which should be employed upon occasion in order to get callers when you hit, but once an evening is enough.

Five-card stud

Five-card stud is the classical skill game. In this game it is possible to calculate the odds with greater precision than in draw poker because you can actually see a great many of the opponents' cards. Thus, it is often possible to form a fairly accurate appraisal of any opponent's hand. If you can judge accurately what the opposition holds, the game reduces almost to mechanical terms (bluffing aside). You ask yourself what the odds are of improving enough to beat the other man, and then compare those odds with the money odds offered by the pot.

If the comparison is favorable, you bet. If it is unfavorable, you fold. Of course, there are always complications. For example, you may bet and improve in the manner you hope but unfortunately, your opponent may improve still further. That is unlucky, but part of your decision of whether to bet should be based on the possibility that your opponent may also improve, and it is possible to calculate his odds as well.

Let us say, for example, that the pot contains 50 chips. You have a king in the hole and you show an ace, a jack, and a ten. Only one other player is left in the game and he shows a pair of nines and a six, and has an unknown hole card which you do not believe is a nine or a six. Your opponent bets ten chips. Should you call?

If you call and draw a queen, you will beat him regardless. Let us say that there are 33 unknown cards left in the deck and one player has already folded a queen. Your chances of drawing a queen are roughly 10 to 1 against. (I say roughly because somebody's hole card might be or have been a queen.) All right, your odds against improving in this manner are 10 to 1, and the pot offers you six to one on your bet. So far, it is a bad bet.

But if you draw an ace, king, jack, or ten you will win *provided your opponent does not draw a nine, six, or a match for his hole card.* Let us say (hypothetically) that on the basis of the cards that have been folded that you and your opponent have roughly an equal chance to improve, and let us say that chance is one in three.

You will win, then, in two cases: 1] you draw a queen; 2] you improve your hand and he does not. Let's figure the odds: You will improve $\frac{1}{3}$ of the time, and $\frac{2}{3}$ of the time your opponent will not improve. For you to win both these things must happen, and the odds that two things will happen together is the product of the odds of each occurrence. Thus, the chance that you will improve while he does not is $\frac{1}{3} \times \frac{2}{3} = \frac{2}{9}$. In addition, you will win outright when you pick up the queen, which will happen $\frac{1}{11}$ of the time. The total chance of your winning, therefore, is $\frac{2}{9} + \frac{1}{11} = \frac{31}{99}$ or roughly $\frac{1}{3}$ (two to one against). Since the pot is offering odds of *six* to one the call is excellent.

Let us say that during the course of the evening you face this same decision three times. Each time you choose to call the ten-chip bet. Two out of those three times you figure to lose your chips, but the third time you figure to win sixty chips. Thus, over the course of the evening (on this decision) you figure to win forty chips (+60 and −20). Divided by the three times that you played in this manner, your win per play is $^{40}\!/_3 = 13+$ chips. This is, most assuredly, a winning play in the long run.

It would be reasonable to ask at this point: "If this bet is such a good one, why merely call; why not raise?" Fair enough. Let's see what would happen if you raised ten chips. Your opponent would presumably call, which would mean that if you won you would win 70 chips, while if you lost you would lose 20. In the course of three such plays you would win 70−20−20 = 30 chips, divided by three plays, which comes to only 10 chips per deal. Not as good as the 13 you had before. Moreover, your opponent can worsen your odds further by raising back.

Does this all sound quite paradoxical? You are in a pot against another player, and the odds favor both of you winning. The answer is simple. This is a situation which occurs late in a hand. The pot has been built up, and some of the money in the pot belonged to you before you put it in. So when I speak of "winning" 60 chips, that will not be your profit on the hand, because you yourself have contributed some of the chips that you will be winning. Put in terms of the game of poker, what I am saying is that this situation is not one which you should avidly seek. If you count all the money you have put into the pot on this deal, the odds favor your losing money in the long run. *But that is not the problem at hand.* Once you have put money into the pot it ceases to be yours. It is community property until somebody wins it. The decision *now* concerns only that last ten-chip bet. *If you have pursued this hand this far* it is worth your while to put up the extra chips. Whether you should ever have come this far with the hand is another matter. Admittedly, A K J 10 is a hard hand to fold under any circumstances.

THE RELATIONSHIP OF THE
HOLE CARD TO THE HAND

Suppose you had an ace and a deuce as your first two cards. Which would you rather have in the hole? The answer,

I think, is clear. The hand is much "stronger" if the ace is concealed. The greater the share of your hand that is concealed, the stronger the hand will play. This is a fundamental principle of stud poker. A simple example will demonstrate why. If you have a pair of aces exposed and you bet them, you will get called only by people with fair odds to win against a pair of aces. That is precisely the kind of caller you can do without! If, however, you have aces "wired" (one in the hole, the other face up) you are as likely as not to have people with things like other high pairs betting against you *because they are not sure what you really have*. Of course, if you break into a cold sweat when you have aces wired, you won't get the callers either. But then, poker is not your game.

Most people understand this principle well enough, but fail to appreciate its simplest extension: that you should not, in general, bet when all the power of your hand is exposed. An example will make this clear. Suppose that all the cards have been dealt and you are high with a pair of kings, which are face up. If you bet, you will be called only by players who can beat a pair of kings. Anybody with less will drop. So if you are called, and you have nothing more than the kings, you are certain to lose. To bet would simply be throwing money away. The correct procedure is to check. If somebody else bets you can decide whether or not to call. If, on the other hand, everybody checks, there will be a showdown. If in fact you are the high hand, you will win just as much as if you had bet, because nobody would have called you anyway. If you are not high hand, however, you have just saved yourself the amount of the final bet that you did not make. It all sounds obvious, but it is amazing how few people realize this. When I first played in a stud game, I understood this principle but almost nothing else about poker. Playing in a game of good players and bad, I was able to hold my own on the basis of this knowledge alone!

Let us return for a minute to the example I gave a few pages back, where you hold A K J 10 and your opponent holds 9 9 6. I said at the time that if your opponent bets it is winning poker to call, but now I must ask you to evaluate how good a poker player the opponent is. If you think he is a poor player, you would do well to call, as his hole card need not be of any value to him. But if he is a good player, you should be wary. It is quite likely that his hand is already stronger than those exposed nines and that you are betting in a virtually hopeless cause. After all, when he bet he could not be certain that you did not already have a high pair. On the other hand, of course, he might be betting on nothing but the nines in order to induce you to drop out and not draw against him. You simply have to decide.

FIGURING THE OPPONENT'S HAND

The only real guide to reading enemy hands is the pattern of the bets. (Only occasionally will you have a "lock" — the opponent cannot have such-and-such a card because you have seen all four of them.) Let us take an example of evaluating a betting pattern.

An opponent shows a king on the first round and makes a strong bet or raise. What do you think he has in the hole? If he is an ingenuous player he probably has another king. That sort of player is (unfortunately) a dying breed. More likely his hole card is an ace, or perhaps the queen of the same suit as the king. If that player picks up an ace or queen, beware.

Another example. Your first two cards were tens "back-to-back" and you have not improved thereafter. The betting has been fairly quiet all around. Finally, after four cards, only you and one other player are left. You have exposed in order 10 Q 6. Your opponent has exposed in order J 4 8. On the last card you catch a queen and he gets a four. You bet and he raises. What do you do?

In my opinion you should raise back, and then call if he raises again. It is most unlikely that he has the three fours. Why? Because his first two cards would have been a four in the hole with a jack up, and he would almost certainly have folded without even buying a third card. Most likely he is bluffing outright with an ace in the hole, or he has a jack in the hole and is inexperienced.

FOLDING AT STUD

If you followed the simple rule of folding whenever you are beat in sight and staying otherwise you would play better stud than half the world's poker players. Fortunately, stud is not quite that simple (or it would rather lack interest).

My rule is not too much more complex, though. Apply it in the early stages of a hand.

Fold when you are beat in sight unless

1] your hole card is better than all but one of the exposed cards, or,

2] you have two cards higher in rank than any exposed or suspected pair, and nothing but the pairs have you beaten at present.

Fold even if you are not beaten in sight if your hole card is particularly poor. In other words, I recommend folding an exposed ace with a deuce in the hole even if nobody else has an ace. Some games require the best hand to bet or fold. I don't care much for this rule. If I have an ace up and a deuce in the hole I believe I should have the right to check and remain active until somebody makes a bet.

In the later stages of a hand you should be able to form a more concrete estimate of the odds against winning vs. the odds offered by the pot and you should be guided by the comparison of these odds.

SEVEN-CARD STUD

In recent years this game has grown rapidly in popularity. It is an exciting game which puts a premium on psychological play and inference. The odds, however, are extremely difficult to calculate in a meaningful way, as an opponent's hand may be radically different from what his exposed cards seem to indicate.

For this reason, a discussion of this game is somewhat beyond the scope of a book whose main theme is the odds. I would observe, however, that most players tend to play this game a bit too "loose." If you bear in mind that two high pairs is generally the *minimum* hand with a chance to win, you will resist the temptation to go on buying card after card in the pursuit of an improvement that will likely as not lose even if it comes in. Unless your hand has prospects for high pairs, straights, or flushes, *fold early*. A slightly defensive attitude will pay big dividends in the average seven-card-stud game.

The expert likes them wild

There is something awry about the dyed-in-the-wool poker player's scorn for anything but straight draw poker or five-card stud and the play-for-fun people who like the wild games best. The fact is that the expert has an even greater advantage in the wild games, because the wilder the game the more difficult it is to figure. Seven-card stud is just one example. Three 9s or three 10s figure to win the pot; after that bit of advice, you're on your own.

High-low is even more difficult to calculate — for one reason because there are so many different ways it is played and each difference may completely alter winning tactics. The basic idea of high-low is that half the pot is won by the high hand and half by the low hand; in effect, there are two pots and half of your bet is contributed to each. The best hand to play is one that provides a chance to win both pots. In fact, it is basic to play along only on such hands as offer a chance to win low. In seven-card high-low, for example, if you have three 10s back to back, far from having a good hand you have one which it might be wise to drop! You have no chance to win low and, if you are playing "cards speak" (where a player need not declare at the end whether he is going for low, or high, or both) you are in danger of being beaten for high by a player who fills a straight or flush while going for low. In the "declaration" variant, you have a bit more protection. The player who fills a straight or flush and has a good low hand may not risk declaring both high and low and possibly losing both if you have bought a pair to your three tens and have a full house.

Three aces are a reasonably good playing hand, because they have a good chance to win high and you are not out of business if the game is ace-low. With aces low, by the way, a 7-low hand should win most pots; with aces only high, 8-low should do it.

If you go with the odds, you won't make the mistake that too many players do: playing a moderately high three of a kind — nines, tens, jacks, queens — to the bitter end. Half of every dollar you bet will be going into a pot you can't possibly win, so you are giving two-to-one odds that your triplets will win the high pot.

A few poker tables

I have left for last some of the mathematical tables about poker to avoid giving the erroneous impression that knowledge of the odds at poker requires memorization of long lists of charts and tables. Nothing could be further from the truth. In order to go with the odds at poker, you need to know how to put to work for you in practice the mathematical principles that determine the fall of the cards. The exact percentages are often irrelevant. Your overall strategy, however, as described in the previous pages, should be guided by the odds.

Nevertheless, particularly if you are an inexperienced player, it may be helpful to examine tables giving the chances of getting particular poker hands, and how high these hands *usually* rank in a particular poker form. It should be carefully noted that no poker table, being an *average* computation, applies to any individual poker deal. The habits of the players and their betting on the deal in question (plus, at stud, the upcards that are showing) determine the chances of any hand being high, or any hand winding up as the winning hand.

You should use these tables only as a general guide to learning the relative strength of different hands at different forms of poker.

1. *The number of possible poker hands*   The table listing the number of possible poker hands is of little value in practical play, except possibly as an indicator of how difficult it is to get a high-ranking hand. (You will notice, for example, that more than half of all poker hands are worse than one pair.) I include this table in answer to a large number of requests for the correct figures.

Many years ago, bridge (and other games) with five suits

TABLE 1 *Number of possible poker hands using different numbers of thirteen-card suits*

hand	1 suit	2 suits	3 suits	4 suits	5 suits
5 of a kind	0 000 000	0 000 000	0 000 000	0 000 000	0 000 013
straight flush	0 000 010	0 000 020	0 000 030	0 000 040	0 000 050
4 of a kind	0 000 000	0 000 000	0 000 000	0 000 624	0 003 900
full house	0 000 000	0 000 000	0 000 468	0 003 744	0 015 600
flush	0 001 277	0 002 574	0 003 831	0 005 108	0 006 385
straight	0 000 000	0 000 320	0 002 400	0 010 200	0 031 200
3 of a kind	0 000 000	0 000 000	0 007 722	0 054 912	0 214 500
two pairs	0 000 000	0 001 716	0 023 166	0 123 552	0 429 000
one pair	0 000 000	0 022 880	0 231 660	1 098 240	3 575 000
no pair	0 000 000	0 038 270	0 306 480	1 302 540	3 984 240
total	0 001 287	0 065 780	0 575 757	2 598 960	8 259 888

instead of the usual four enjoyed a brief vogue. I have received many inquiries asking what would happen if poker were played with five suits instead of the usual four suits. To answer these and similar questions once and for all, I have computed the number of possible poker hands for decks with one to five suits of thirteen cards. Regarding five-suit poker, you can see from the table that a flush, being harder to obtain than a full house, should be rated as higher-ranking than a full house, but that no other changes in the usual order of rank need be made.

In each column, the figure given under TOTAL is the number of all possible poker hands you can hold from the deck being considered. Thus, when a normal deck is used, there are 2,598,960 possible different poker hands.

2. The chance of being high on the deal at draw poker The value of a hand at draw poker depends not only on the card values but also on how many players are in the game.

Obviously, the more players in the game, the less chance any particular hand has of being high.

TABLE 2   *Chance of being high at draw poker (before the draw)*

hand	5 players	6 players	7 players	8 players
nines up	72%	67%	62%	59%
pair of aces	61%	55%	49%	44%
pair of kings	60%	54%	48%	43%
pair of queens	48%	40%	34%	37%
pair of jacks	40%	33%	26%	19%

Most poker games have 5 to 8 players (it is uninteresting to play draw poker with fewer players, impractical to play it with more). The table below gives the chance of particular hands being highest at the table after the 5-card deal. In each case, I consider games of 5, 6, 7 and 8 players. The hands given are typical of those which will give you a difficult decision in a draw poker game. It may be helpful, therefore, to get some idea of approximately how high these hands usually rate (depending, of course, on the number of players). You should bear in mind, however, that particularly active or passive betting will usually be a better indication of the strength around the table than mere figures in cold print.

3. *Chance of having the high hole card at stud*   At stud poker, the crucial factor is often whether or not your hole card is superior to those of your opponents. (Your opponents may have matched pairs, of course, but this is something you can learn only from their betting.)

However, the odds that you have the highest-ranking hole card at stud can be computed with great accuracy. Once again, as in the case of the draw poker table, it depends how many players are in the game. The more players, the less likely it is that any particular hole card is the best hole card.

In the table that follows, the percentages that are given represent the approximate chance that the indicated hole card is *better* (not tied with) than all the other hole cards.

TABLE 3 *Approximate chance of having
the high hole card at stud*

hole card	5 players	6 players	7 players
ace	75%	70%	65%
king	48%	41%	34%
queen	30%	24%	18%
jack	18%	12%	7%

gin

GIN IS one of the country's most popular card games. Yet, because skill at this game is largely a matter of memory and careful following of the odds, rather than occasional brilliant coups, it receives little publicity.

From one point of view, gin is an easy game. That is, you should find the principles of winning play at gin easier to master than those of some of the more complicated card games. On the other hand, gin can be quite a strain. For to play at maximum efficiency it is necessary to remember all the cards that have been played — as well as the order in which they have appeared. Thus, while the *theory* of gin is easy enough (once you know it), it may be difficult to put the winning principles into practice.

It is not the purpose of this book to develop your card memory. That is a matter of training and practice. But however good or bad your card memory may be, a knowledge of the odds at gin will enable you to play with maximum efficiency within the limits of your ability to remember the cards. And that, even for people who "can't remember a card," is quite well indeed. For the fact is that just playing gin regularly will develop your card memory considerably, even if you give it no conscious thought. If you intend to work on your gin game, I therefore suggest you begin by learning the mathematical principles which govern winning play. The memory will, at the beginning, take care of itself. Eventually, if you become a serious gin player, you can concentrate on perfecting your memory. But even a photographic memory will be of little use to you at gin if you do not go with the odds.

I mentioned above that gin is one of the most popular card games. (Any two-handed card game that is at least moderately appealing automatically receives a good deal of attention, for there are few interesting two-handed games.) It is also one of the games most widely played in ignorance of its basic mechanics — of how the odds work. This is surprising, for the mathematics of gin is among the simplest of calculations for the popular card games. It is no cause for wonder that a good bridge player is not familiar with the workings of the odds of his game, for some sophisticated mathematics is involved. But the odds at gin require no more than a little counting, and a little common sense.

Cards in melding combinations

In a gin deal, each card has certain potential values, both to you and to your opponent. The more likely it is that your opponent can use a particular card to form a meld, the greater its potential value to him. In general, the potential value of a card to your opponent will depend on the cards that have been played — in particular, the cards your opponent has thrown and those he has failed to pick from the discard pile.

To take an obvious example, if the nines of spades, hearts and diamonds have been discarded, along with the jack and eight of clubs, the nine of clubs has no potential value to either you or your opponent.

However, it is basic that *even if no relevant cards have appeared in the discards,* cards of some ranks have different potential value, regarding use in a melding combination, than others. In particular:

kings and aces have the lowest potential melding value
queens and deuces have the next lowest potential melding value
all other cards have the same potential melding value.

Of course, melding value is not everything. Aces, deuces and other low cards are useful for reducing the count of a hand. It is generally poor strategy to part with such cards lest they enable your opponent to knock (or, conversely, lessen your own chance of knocking). Similarly, if we are to be 100% technical, a jack has ever so slightly less melding value than a ten because it is less likely to be used in a *four*-card run. However, for practical purposes, such hair-splitting considerations can be disregarded.

The relative potential melding values of different cards can be computed very simply by considering how many ways each card can be used to form a meld. For example, assuming no (relevant) cards have appeared, the king of spades can be used in four ways to make a (three-card) meld:

Groups (3)	♠ K	♡ K	◇ K
	♠ K	♡ K	♣ K
	♠ K	◇ K	♣ K
Runs (1)	♠ K	♠ Q	♠ J

It is obvious that any card in the deck can be used three ways to form a group, in a manner similar to that given for the spade king. Thus, we need not list these possibilities for other cards. Now let us consider the spade *queen*. This card can be used in five ways to make a meld. In addition to the three groups, we have:

Runs (2)	♠ K	♠ Q	♠ J
	♠ Q	♠ J	♠ 10

If we consider the spade jack, we find three runs (the two given for the spade queen, plus J-10-9 of spades) in addition to the three groups. It is clear that the ace will give results similar to those for the king, the deuce will give results similar to those for the queen, and all cards from the ten to the three results similar to those for the jack. Therefore, we can form the following table:

rank of card	number of ways it can be used to form (3-card) melds
king or ace	4
queen or deuce	5
others	6

Two remarks are in order. First, this table itself has certain practical applications. For example, if you are trying to find the safest discard, if all other things are equal you should prefer a king to a queen, a queen to a jack, and so forth. Second, whatever the situation, *the method of counting used to construct this table can be applied to determine the relative safety of discards.*

For example, suppose that for your first discard you wish to throw the *safest* card among the following:

♠ K   ♠ Q   ♡ Q   ♣ J

In order to determine the safest card, you should count the possible ways each can be used in a (three-card) meld. Thus:

card	possible groups	possible runs	total
♠ K	three	none	three
♠ Q	one	one	two
♡ Q	one	two	three
♣ J	three	three	six

The safest card is the spade queen. In fact, it is unlikely you would want to throw the spade queen — for this destroys melding possibilities in your own hand. You would probably want to effect some sort of compromise between safety of discard (defense) and melding possibilities (offense). Again referring to the chart, we find that the spade king and heart queen are equally safe (or "equally dangerous" if you prefer pessimistic terminology). Since retention of the spade king gives you only one melding possibility (spade jack), whereas retention of the heart queen gives you two melding possibilities (diamond queen, club queen), it is probable that your best discard is the spade king.

I would like to point out what may seem obvious: nothing more was involved in determining "the odds" than simply counting the number of melding possibilities — both for your opponent and for yourself. Obvious though this may seem, there are literally millions of gin players throwing away uncounted thousands of points through failure to apply this simple principle.

It is true that the difference between two melding possibilities and three melding possibilities on a particular play represents a very small amount. However, if you consider this difference added up over the long run — on every card you discard, on every deal of a game — the amount to be gained is staggering.

I will now discuss some of the more advanced strategies at gin, with emphasis on how the odds are affected. But all plays boil down to this one basic principle — count the number of melding possibilities. In fact, this is one of the main reasons that being able to remember the cards plays such an important role in successful gin strategy. The more cards you remember, the more accurate the calculation you can make as to the number of melding possibilities of each card later in the deal. And the more accurate these calculations, the more likely it is that you will select the safest discard at every opportunity. And thus, of course, the more you will win.

Early discards: ads, strangers, and zones

Experienced gin players know that the first few discards play a great role in determining the result of a deal. To the amateur, the early discards are virtually meaningless — it seems as if each player simply throws away what he does not want and tries to set up melds in his hand. But it is a fallacy to think that higher strategy in gin begins in the middle game after each player has started to build up his hand. Actually, most gin hands are won or lost in the first few rounds of discarding. An advantage gained during this crucial period is likely to last for the duration of the entire deal. Therefore, it is of the greatest importance to master early discarding strategy.

The overall strategy of your early discards should be determined by the nature of your hand. On those rare occasions when you have a very good hand, and need only one or two favorable picks to enable you to knock, you should throw caution to the winds in your discarding. You expect to win the hand, and you should discard so as to leave yourself the maximum chance of winning as quickly as possible. Selection of the safest card is a secondary consideration. On the other hand — and this case will arise most frequently — if you have an ordinary or poor collection, you should think primarily about defense, that is, preventing your opponent from winning. And to do this you must select the safest possible discard at each stage.

Assuming (as will occur most of the time) that your opening strategy is to be primarily defensive, there are three early-discarding techniques which you must master — advertisements (ads), strangers, and zones.

1. ADVERTISEMENTS

To "advertise" at gin is to discard a card of the same rank as a needed card. For example, the discard of the club seven from a holding of

$$\heartsuit 9 \qquad \heartsuit 8 \qquad \clubsuit 7$$

is an advertisement, or "ad." The idea is to make it look as if a seven will be a safe discard for your opponent. Should he happen to discard the heart seven, you will have completed a run in hearts.

It is relatively standard to offer such "ads." Like any strategy, too much of the same thing is not worthwhile. In the absence of anything better to do, you might well offer an ad. However, do not go out of your way to do so. It is better to play a safer card than an ad which is not as safe. For one thing, it is superior defensively. For another, the less you advertise the more often will your opponent respond to an ad when it is real. A player who does nothing but advertise in the opening rounds is a losing player, for his opponent is sure to get wind of this strategy in short order, and from then on the early discards will be give-aways.

Similarly, you must always be on the lookout for ads. We will see later that the safest cards to throw are not those of the same rank as thrown by your opponent but those of *adjacent* ranks. By following this rule, you will avoid falling for ads. However, whether or not you fall for an ad in the early rounds, it will be important to analyze later whether or not an early discard by your opponent was an ad or not. A situation may well arise later in the play when you must decide whether or not an early discard by your opponent was an ad or not. Therefore, by keeping track of his tendencies in the early discarding, you will be able to reach a more intelligent decision.

In short, the winning philosophy regarding ads is not to overdo them but to expect your opponent to use them. The basis of this technique is experience. The vast majority of gin players — in fact, all but the experts — overuse the ad technique. By observing this, you can obtain an overwhelming advantage — not only in the early rounds, but throughout each deal.

2. STRANGERS

In the early rounds, it is generally a poor policy to break up potential melds. In fact, unless your opponent has been dealt a completely matched hand — no "odd" cards which do not form potential melds — he will rarely discard from a melding possibility for his first few discards. You can take advantage of this by adjusting your counting of melding possibilities accordingly. For example, suppose that your opponent's first discard is the spade ten. Under the theory discussed above, this card is likely to be a "stranger" to other cards in his hand. For example, he is unlikely to hold another ten, the spade jack, or the spade nine. Therefore, *a card of an adjacent rank and a different suit* is a comparatively safe discard. Let us consider, for example, the melding possibilities of the heart jack and heart ten after your opponent has discarded the ten of spades. (Similar calculations could be made for any jack or nine not in spades.)

card	no discard by opponent			opponent has thrown spade ten		
	groups	runs	total	groups	runs	total
♡ J	3	3	6	1 (♡ J ◇ J ♣ J)	1 (♡ K Q J)	2
♡ 10	3	3	6	0	3 [♡ Q J 10 / ♡ J 10 9 / ♡ 10 9 8]	3

If we assume that your opponent, when he throws the spade ten early, does not hold another ten or the spade jack or spade nine, we see that the heart jack (or nine) is safer than the heart ten! And this does not even take into account the possibility that the heart ten is an ad! Notice also that these cards are even safer than a king.

Still another card to be considered is one which matches the one discarded by your opponent in suit, and is adjacent in rank, *e.g.* the spade jack in the above example. This can be used in three groups and one run, for a total of four. Thus, *disregarding the possibility of an ad,* this card is *not* as safe as one of the same rank discarded by an opponent.

Most gin players have a natural tendency to throw a card of the same rank, or of the same suit and of adjacent rank, of a stranger discarded by their opponent. In fact, the safest card to throw is one of an adjacent rank and a different suit — in other words, a stranger to the stranger. Such a card is much safer (less dangerous by half!) than even a king. Although this principle depends on nothing more than counting the various melds in which each card might be used, it is surprisingly little known.

3. ZONES

In practice, most early discarding in gin will be in a zone — high cards, middle cards, or low cards. The reason for this is not hard to find. Once a discard is made, cards in the same zone as that discard become relatively safe. Therefore, any discard is likely to be in the same zone as the previous discard. Because of this, is is often possible to select a zone which is favorable to you and start discarding in that zone. For example, suppose you have a king, two queens, and two tens. Even if the king is not your safest discard, you might well throw it in the hope of establishing a zone of discards in the high range. This will increase your chances of obtaining a queen or a ten from your opponent, for on the face of the discards these will be relatively safe cards.

Conversely, be suspicious if your opponent switches from one zone to another. If it is safe for him to open a new zone, he must have cards near the one he chooses to discard. Accordingly, avoid discarding in that zone until he has broken a meld possibility there. What's good for your opponent generally won't be good for you.

Timing, knocking, gin

In general, you should knock as soon as possible. Therefore, you should keep lower-valued spot cards if at all possible. The mathematics of gin scoring makes it unprofitable to play for gin under doubtful circumstances unless two conditions are satisfied:

1] You have a strong chance for gin. In order to satisfy this condition, you must have at least 5 cards which will enable you to go gin, *and* at least four of these must be unknown to your opponent. (It should be noted that this is a conservative requirement — many experts will play for gin with less favorable conditions — but I have found that conservatism pays off at gin.)

2] You have a very good lead on your opponent and he will be unable to knock and win the hand. Thus, if you are faced with a situation in which you must knock or discard an unsafe card — one which you suspect will help your opponent's hand — prefer to knock. No one ever went broke by salting away a sure profit. By knocking as soon as possible, you give your opponent as little chance as possible to improve his hand and reduce his count. Let the gin hands take care of themselves — if you follow a winning strategy there will be enough of them which arise automatically without your waiting or trying for them.

Getting on the score

There is one time in particular when you should not play for gin regardless of how favorable the prospects may appear. This is when you have not yet scored in the game (or, in the modern form of three simultaneous games, when you are not yet "on" in all three games). The main reason for this is to avoid being "blitzed" or "schneid" on a game — which represents a double loss. Once you have scored on a game, you can *then* afford to take chances. Thus, being on score opens up the field for more speculative play, giving you the chance of sizable gains yet risking only limited losses. This is not true if you are not yet on score, for a large win by your opponent will put you in jeopardy of losing a double game.

When three games are being played simultaneously, it is more important to get on score than to score a large number of points. For one thing, once you are "on" in one game, your score counts twice (similarly, if you score in the first two games your score counts triple). For another, the possibility of a huge loss is multiplied when there are three games. If your opponent gets "on" before you do, he has the opportunity to try for some big hands, and to blitz you on one *or more* games. Your back is to the wall and you must play conservatively, hoping simply to get on score. The position is reversed if you get "on" before he does. Thus, both technically and psychologically it is advantageous to *get on the score*.

Effect of the knock card

Most gin games today are played "Oklahoma" style. When the game is played in this form, the twenty-first card is turned over (the "upcard") and represents the lowest number with which it is permissible to knock. If an ace is turned over, the deal can be won only by going gin; if a spade is turned over all scores are doubled.

Because of the forced gins and doubled scores, it is even more important in Oklahoma than in ordinary gin to get on the score. A gin hand at spades can just about win a game for you! Thus, the dangers of not being on score are magnified.

As far as strategy goes, the size of the knock card is of great significance. If it is a high card (picture card — which counts as ten, ten, nine, eight, and possibly also the seven), you need make little or no change in your strategy. (Except, of course, that you always keep in mind what the knocking number is!) On the other hand, if the knock card is relatively low (four, three or deuce), it is unlikely that you will be able to knock, as you often can in ordinary gin, with two melds and a bunch of lower-valued cards. Under such circumstances, it is best to plan to knock by forming three melds. In fact, it may on occasion be good strategy to give up a low card which is relatively safe in order to keep in hand the possibilities for a third meld. Your opponent is unlikely to be able to make use of this card only for the purpose of reducing the count of his hand and it is more likely that the first player to form a third meld will win. Also, when the knock card is low, and you must choose between two equally dangerous discards, tend to prefer the *lower* one. If you have guessed wrong and your opponent uses your discard to form a meld, he will reduce his count by less (and thus be less likely to be able to knock) if he can use the lower card. If you throw a high card and he uses it to form a meld, his count will probably be reduced enough to allow him to knock. (It should be emphasized that this technique should be employed only when you have no clue whatsoever as to which card is the safer one to throw.)

The odds at gin: knock or try for gin?

Let us assume now that there is no question about getting on score and your primary interest is in giving yourself the best chance to win the current deal, or to maximize your gains. The most important strategical decision you will be called upon to make is whether or not to knock when it becomes possible to do so. It is here that it is most important to go with the odds at gin rummy.

The most important point to remember is that when you knock, you score no bonus points whatever: neither a score bonus nor boxes. You have much to gain by going for gin. Suppose that, to take an arbitrary figure, you can expect to gain 15 points from your opponent's unmelded cards. (This is not an atypical figure. If you are considering a knock, your opponent probably has only two melds at most.) By knocking, you will score 15 points less your knock card. By going gin, you will score (in addition to a "line") 40 points plus two boxes — in effect, 90 points. In effect, then, you are trying for a gain of (at least) 75 points. Your potential loss is that you will lose the hand. If your opponent knocks, and catches you with, say, 5 points, you will have lost 70 points by failure to knock (the 15 points plus a "line" you could have won; the 5 points plus a "line" he wins). In this case, the odds in favor of going for gin are only slightly better than even. If there is danger your opponent will go gin himself if you do not knock, your potential loss is much greater.

Therefore, as a rule of thumb, you should not knock when you consider it a sure win, and should play for gin instead, if you feel you have better than half a chance to gin before your opponent can form three melds. In general, this will require you to have at least five possible gin cards and for your opponent not to have accepted any of your discards. However, if the hand is very young (up to 10 discards) you may take this chance even if your opponent has taken a discard.

The best strategy for deciding when to refuse an apparently "sure win" through a knock can be summarized in this table. This listing is keyed to your estimate of your opponent's potential, since that is the crucial factor in deciding whether or not to play for gin.

rating of opponent's hand	characteristics leading to this evaluation	requirements to try for gin
very good	He has taken two discards; 15 or more discards have been made	Don't. If the knock is certain, take it.
fair to good	He has taken one discard and 10 discards have been made	Play for gin only with outstanding chances (e.g.: 6 gin cards, at least 4 unknown to your opponent)
poor to fair	He has taken no discards or 0 – 10 discards have been made	Try for gin with 5 gin cards

It should be remembered that this table, much as any other chart of guidelines for specific plays, should be taken as a general guide, not as an absolute pronouncement. The exact pattern of discards your opponent makes is the best clue to determining the strength of his hand.

Most of these calculations can be remembered if you keep in mind the basic rule: If you are clearly in the lead, you need better than even money on winning to try for gin. The basic requirement for this is 5 gin cards and (as far as you can tell) a one-meld lead on your opponent.

As we have seen, going with the odds at gin requires primarily caution and counting. The caution comes in remembering the cards and not overlooking sure-fire plays; it comes in getting on score before worrying about anything else; and it comes through taking a sure small win rather than playing for a big gin hand. The counting comes in remembering that the relative potential usefulness of any card, either to you or to your opponent, is the number of ways in which the card can be used to form a three-card meld. It may seem degrading or silly to sit and count possible melds, but that is the road to winning gin. And, as in other games, once you have played for a while and done the mechanical counting, it will soon become automatic, just as it will become automatic that you remember cards, even without conscious effort.

Gin is too easy a game not to go with the odds.

canasta

CANASTA HAS two paradoxical aspects. First, although it is not a complicated game, the skill factor seems to account for as much of the results as it does in any other popular game. Second, it shares with several European gambling games the property that a score can be too good.

As a general rule, the more complex a game, the greater the part played by skill (as opposed to luck). The more aspects to a game, the more different forms of technique to be mastered, the greater the advantage of the expert. For with greater complexity come more ways in which the skill of the superior player can make itself felt. Among games of skill, canasta ranks among the most straightforward. The rules, even for the partnership game, are relatively simple. (Melding, for example, is simpler than in gin!) There are no complicated percentage tables to memorize. In fact, although this is a book about odds, I cannot think of a single odds "table" to present about canasta.

Despite this deceptive simplicity, the superior player will win at canasta as often as he will at any other game. If I were told I could back an expert player against an average player at a game of my choice, canasta would probably be my first or second selection. The only logical conclusion to draw is that strategy, not the luck of the deal, is paramount in canasta. Therefore, to play with the odds at canasta means to follow a sound strategical plan and implement it with proper tactical maneuvering. Thus, my advice on this game will be expressed not in terms of percentages or probabilities (although, of course, matters which are technically mathematical determine which strategies will be successful and which will not) but in terms of technique. The justification for giving this advice will be based not mainly on the odds but rather on the collective experience of successful canasta players.

I will begin the list of canasta stratagems with the second paradoxical aspect of the game — that there can be too much of a good thing. Most canasta deals develop into offensive-defensive battles in which one player (or partnership) attempts to prolong the deal in order to build up a high score in canastas and other melds while the opposition attempts to end the deal by going out as quickly as possible. Obviously the side with more cards under its control will be more interested in prolonging the action, for it has by far the greater chance to form canastas. Furthermore, if one side has more cards than the other, it has an increased chance to grab off any valuable pack which forms in the discard pile.

In almost every instance, the offensive side will be *the side* (whether it be an individual player or a partnership) *which takes the first sizable pack.* If you take the first good-sized pack, you automatically increase your chances of taking subsequent packs (by obtaining more pack-taking ranks), and thus you obtain what should be a lasting advantage for the entire deal.

Hence your first objective on any deal should be the capture of the first sizable pack. Your chances of being able to obtain this first pack depend very heavily on your required initial meld. If you have an advantage in the required count (which implies, of course, that you are behind in the game), as, for example, if your required initial meld is 50 to the opponent's 90 (or 120) you have an enormous edge in the battle for the first big pack. *Some experts estimate this advantage at 2 to 1 in your favor or even higher.*

Canasta is a game of big scores. A big score almost always starts with the taking of the initial pack. Thus, it is worth while deliberately to avoid putting your score over the mark (1500 or 3000) which will require you to have a higher initial meld. Abnormal circumstances excepted, it is usually worth 200 to 300 points to avoid going over 1500 and 300 to 500 points to avoid going over 3000!

Let's see how this fact can be applied in practical play.

When you are about to go out, you can, in general, make minor adjustments in your score. For example, you may have the option of forming a natural or a mixed canasta, or forming a new meld rather than an extra canasta, and so forth. It is good strategy to sacrifice up to the indicated number of points (for simplicity, use the average values of 250 to stay under 1500 and 400 to stay under 3000) in order to keep your score under the limit. Thus, if you can go out and have your score reach either 1400 or 1600 (as in the case of choice of methods of forming a canasta), prefer 1400!

This is the second paradox of canasta — your score can be too good. Of course, the closer you can get to the magic number without reaching it, the better off you are. A score of 1480 must be superior to one of 1450 — at least, at the stage at which you may have the choice between two such scores. Conversely, if you know your score after a deal will be above 1500 or above 3000, it pays to prolong the game to get as far into that melding zone as possible — for you will incur the same disadvantage of initial meld on the next deal regardless.

More plays for the initial pack

There are other basic strategical maneuvers that play a part in the major battle of each canasta deal — the battle for that first big pack. In general, you will try to build your hand into a position in which you will be able to take the pack. Thus, you will preserve pairs whenever possible. Also, you will organize your hand so that you will, if possible, be able to take the pack if a favorable discard is made by your right-hand opponent. Most of the time, the problem of what to keep in your hand will be determined by your required initial meld. Suppose you must make a decision whether or not to break up a potential meld, such as three tens. You have in your hand several other pairs which might enable you to take the pack if a card of that rank is discarded on your right. *You should break up the spread only if you do not need that meld to make the initial count.* For example, if you need only 50, and you have a Joker, any one meld can be used to make the initial count (by adding the Joker if necessary). For purposes of taking the pack, therefore, a third card of a rank is unnecessary. But the extra full meld might be decisive if, for example, your required count was 120.

In planning your early discarding strategy, you should attempt to arrange your discarding in such a way that you will throw dangerous cards early rather than later. The reasoning behind this procedure should be obvious: when you make your early discards, the pack will be of relatively little value. Even if your left-hand opponent can take the pack by using your discard, he might not do so, preferring to wait for a larger pack. If he does take the card, you have sacrificed only a small pack. On the other side of the coin, however, we note that it will eventually become necessary to discard when the pack is sizable, and thus of significant value. At this time you want to have the safest possible discards available. Thus, as a general rule, *part with dangerous cards early*. Save good discards (black threes, low cards matched in your hand, etc.) for the crucial rounds when getting the pack will spell the difference between winning and losing the deal.

Usually, it is inferior play to make the initial meld without taking the pack, particularly if the first big pack has not yet been taken. Sometimes, in the partnership game, one player will make the initial meld in order to help his partner take the pack. If your opponents have made the initial meld without taking the pack, and the pack is sizable, you should play as safely as possible. This means either making a completely safe discard or, if you can afford to do so, by freezing the pack. Suppose, for example, you are South in a partnership game. Both sides need 120 initial meld. Your right-hand opponent (East), makes the initial meld without taking the pack. The pack is large enough to be worth protecting. You should attempt to freeze the pack if you can do so without jeopardizing your chance to make the initial meld. Why? Because East has just made it easier for West to take the pack. West may hold a considerable number of pack-taking possibilities without being able to form the initial meld of 120. *East's meld will give him additional pack-taking power.* Therefore, you must make it as difficult as possible for him to get the pack. If you cannot make a completely safe discard, you should probably freeze.

Later strategy

Later strategy breaks into two completely separate cases, depending, of course, on who has taken the first big pack. If you have taken the pack, withhold melds unless you feel an opponent may go out. You wish to retain control over all later packs, so you will want to keep all pack-taking possibilities in hand. From this point on, you should take packs of even moderate size, simply to prevent the opponents from getting any extra cards and increasing their melding possibilities. You would like nothing better than to have the entire pack run through while you (or your side) gather in pack after pack and form canastas. You should not end the game unless it becomes obvious that an opponent is about to go out.

On the other hand, if the opponents gain the upper hand and take the first big pack, you should play defensively. That is, you should give up all hope of winning points on the deal. Instead, concentrate on making your loss as small as possible. *The best way to do this is to end the hand by going out.* Do not worry about yielding valuable cards to the opponents if, by so doing, you can significantly increase your chance of ending the unfavorable deal. In the partnership game, cooperate with partner's melds in any way possible if this will tend to move your side towards the canastas necessary for going out. By all means do not attempt to cut down on your opponent's profit margin by hoarding cards which you feel he needs (or know he needs) to form canastas, for you are likely to win the battle but lose the war by following such a strategy. The result of such hoarding will be that you can never go out, and the deal will continue to be played with your enemy holding the upper hand. Even if he never completes the canastas you are holding out on him, he will make others based on his overwhelming preponderance of cards and the high probability that he will take all subsequent packs of any value. Instead, cut your losses by conceding to your opponent what is rightfully his, and by getting into position to go out as soon as possible.

pinochle

PINOCHLE, like bridge, involves skill both in bidding and play. Unfortunately, as P. Hal Sims observed, there are too many lay-down hands in pinochle. That is, there are only a few hands on which the contract is really at issue. If declarer has little chance, he will throw the hand in to avoid paying double. If declarer does play, a great proportion of the time he will have no difficulty fulfilling his bid. Finally, although opportunities for spectacular play do occur in pinochle, they are rare.

In general, the play revolves around the bonus of ten points for taking the final trick. It follows that most of the time the best defense is to force the declarer to use his trumps while he still holds losing cards. Similarly, the declarer should plan his strategy to avoid this. A complete description of the various strategies that may be employed in the play of a pinochle deal is beyond the scope of this book. But it will stand you in good stead to remember that *in 90% of the close hands, the side that wins the last trick will triumph.* Therefore, if you are in doubt as to how to proceed, either as declarer or defender, turn your attention to the fight for "last."

This is not to say that the odds do not have a significant role during the play of a pinochle deal — they do. But these odds are subordinate to general strategical rules. However, those who are interested in the probabilities for suit splits in pinochle can learn them easily. They are almost exactly the same as those for suit splits in bridge (see pages 291 to 297). Of course, they are not *exactly* the same, for bridge is played with 13 cards in each suit while a pinochle deck has suits of

12 cards, but this change has so little effect on the odds that for practical purposes they can be assumed to be the same. For example, the chance of five cards being divided 3 to 2 between the two defenders (say) is *approximately* the 68% it would be in bridge. Thus, learning the chances for the common suit splits in bridge automatically gives you the same information in pinochle — at least, to a good approximation. This is convenient for the eager student of the odds.

The odds in bidding

Where the odds *do* play a significant role is in pinochle bidding. In particular, it is impossible to bid intelligently unless you have some idea what your chance is of getting some useful card or cards in the widow. If you need the ace of spades, say, to give you a flush and aces, what are the odds against one of the concealed cards in the widow being an ace of spades?

Because there are two of each card, it is not easy to determine the chances at the table — you must know them in advance. Once you know the odds against finding one of the cards you need in the widow, you can decide whether or not a bid should be made by computing how much you stand to gain and how much you stand to lose by making that bid, then determining whether these odds are higher or lower than those against drawing the card or cards that you need.

Below I present a complete table of odds against finding a favorable card in the widow. This chart takes into account the fact that the face of pinochle is changing rapidly. Until the past few years, the game was always played with three concealed cards in the widow. More recently, some groups have used the variation in which one of the three cards in the widow is exposed, leaving only two cards concealed. This modern form of the game is becoming more widespread and, as you may find yourself playing one game or the other at different times, you should know the odds at both. Accordingly, the chart covers both games.

The chart is constructed on the basis of the number of "favorable cards." In counting the number of cards favorable to you, remember that there are two of each card. Thus, if you need the queen of spades for a flush this gives you *two* favorable cards (there are two queens of spades available). If, however, you have ♠ Q ◇ J ◇ J and the discovery of a second queen of spades in the widow will give you enough points (with a second pinochle) to score your bid, this counts as only one favorable card (for there is only one queen of spades missing). The chart below is more complete than similar charts to be found elsewhere in that it distinguishes "favorable cards" from "places open." The latter is a term used to indicate the number of ranks of card (e.g. queen of spades) which

number of favorable cards	classic game (3-card widow concealed)	modern game (1 exposed, 2 concealed in widow)
1	10 to 1	15 to 1
2	4⅔ to 1	7 to 1
3	3 to 1	4⅓ to 1
4	2 to 1	3¼ to 1
5	1½ to 1	2½ to 1
6	1⅛ to 1	1⅞ to 1
7	1 to 1⅛	1½ to 1
8	1 to 1⅜	1¼ to 1
9	1 to 1⅔	* even
10	1 to 2	1 to 1⅛
11	1 to 2½	1 to 1⅓
12	1 to 3⅛	1 to 1½
13	1 to 4	1 to 2

will give the hand the necessary improvement. As we have seen, an "open place" may mean only one favorable card, not two. As this difference may have a profound affect on the odds, I have included the distinction in the table.

OBSERVATIONS FROM THE TABLE

It will be observed from this table that in the modern game the odds against finding a favorable card among the concealed cards in the widow are very much *steeper* than in the classic game. Therefore, one should not bid as strongly on possibilities in the modern game as in the classic game. (This would seem obvious, for there are only two concealed cards. The chances can be seen to be *approximately* two-thirds in many cases. Mathematical technicalities show why the odds are not exactly two-thirds, particularly when you have many possible winning cards.) However obvious this may seem to the reader, in my experience this advice is not heeded by those players who have adopted the new form of auction pinochle. Thus, "boosting" such over-exuberant persons may pay dividends, as you can expect them to draw a favorable card less often than they expect. However, the most important application of this change to your own game should be to pull in a notch.

Notice that to have about an even chance to draw a favorable card in the classic game you need about 6 possibilities (3 unduplicated cards) whereas in the modern game you must have 9 such possibilities. *Hands with 9 possible fillers are very rare indeed.* This means, in effect, that if no possibility duplicates a card in your hand you must have 4 or 5 places open to have an even chance of filling your hand in the modern form!

The odds against playing

Because of the double *bete* rule (if you play out a hand and fail to make your bid you pay the other players at double the usual rate) the odds seem to be against playing out all but the most certain hands. From the *sound* of the rule, it seems you are losing double if you try to make the hand and fail.

This is not at all the case, however. The discussion which follows will, I hope, clear up this common misconception. Suppose you are playing a normal four-handed game with a kitty. (The "out" player, usually the dealer, pays and collects with the defenders.) Assume you have overcalled a 300 opening with 310, and after melding have a close decision as to whether or not to play the hand out.

If you fail to play, you lose four units (1 to each player and 1 to the kitty). If you do play, however, and lose, you forfeit seven units (2 to each player and 1 to the kitty — the kitty usually does *not* collect double) but you win 3 units (1 from each player; nothing from the kitty for less than 350 under the most common rules) if you make it.

By playing, therefore, you stand to gain 7 units (4 you would lose by throwing in, 3 you win) and to lose 3 units (the difference between a loss of 4 and 7). Therefore, the odds are 7 to 3 in favor of playing, *better than 2 to 1*. Similar considerations apply to other bids.

The effect of this is that it is *not* best to be conservative in your decision as to whether or not to play, the double bete rule notwithstanding. In general, you should play a hand out if just one lucky break (such as a favorable trump division) will guarantee success. Even if the odds are against getting the lucky break, you may still have a good bet going for you. (In addition, there is always the added chance that the defense will not be optimal. Not everyone plays as well as you do.)

Spades double; hearts triple

Most games use the "spades double" rule. This means that a hand played at spades pays or collects double stakes (except those involving the kitty). When spades count double, and you are considering playing a hand in spades, the odds change somewhat. Using the same example as before, if you throw in your 310 hand you will still lose 4 units (you need not name spades trumps, of course, if you do not play it out). If you play and are defeated, however, you lose 13 units (spades are double and the *bete* doubles the stake again, so you lose four units to each player and one to the kitty). If you play and make, you win 6 units. Thus, when you must play with spades trumps, you stand to lose 9 units by playing and stand to gain 10 units. The odds are still in your favor, but now they stand very close to even money. Therefore, when considering playing out a spade hand, you should not play unless you have at least an even-money chance.

Notice the enormous difference in the odds as compared with the case of an "ordinary suit."

The "spades double" rule also has a great effect on the bidding. You can afford to bid more aggressively when you have a potential spade hand, because if you pull it in you collect at twice the usual rate; if you don't, you lose at only the single rate. You should bid with only two thirds as many open places as ordinarily required if your hand will be made in spades if you draw favorably.

Some pinochle groups add even more to the excitement by applying the hearts triple rule in addition to the spades double rule. This tends to place more emphasis on good odds-manship than on good pinochle, for much now revolves around the heart suit and its enormous bonuses. First, let's consider the problem of playing out a hand. Taking the same situation as before (a 310 hand), you still lose 4 chips by throwing in the hand. If you play and are defeated, you lose 19 chips; if you play and make you win 9. You stand to lose 15 chips and to win only 13 chips. Thus, the odds are against playing a hand out when your trump suit is hearts. You should play out a hand based on a heart suit as trumps only when you think the odds are considerably in your favor.

Just as you can take further chances in the bidding when you have spades, you can take even more when you have hearts. Because of the triple score rule, you can bid on only ⅓ as many open places as would ordinarily be required when your trump suit is hearts. You will note that the spades-double, hearts-triple rule therefore opens up the bidding. This rule is therefore preferred by players who prefer a more wide-open game.

When hearts are triple, deliberate boosting can pay off. If you are weak in hearts and spades and an opponent bids strongly, it may pay you to boost him in the hope of getting him too high. The theory behind this is that you will lose little or nothing extra if he would have made his bid in hearts and you lose little if his trump suit was spades.

The odds are greatly in favor of such boosting because of the increased chance of making a profit by driving your opponent too high. However, you should boost only when you are weak in both spades and hearts. Otherwise, there is too much chance you are sacrificing against a "normal" score — and then you will do very badly if you get left in too many boosts.

The perfect time for a deliberate boost is when you have

a long-shot chance of making your bid with an excellent draw in the widow. If you have only 1 or 2 places open, your hand does not justify a speculation on the basis of these possibilities. But if you have these openings for a victory *and* you have a chance to get an opponent with a heart hand overboard, the odds are all in your favor.

As with all good strategies, however, do not overdo it. If you become known as a booster, your opponents will not "take the plunge" and go overboard enough times for your boosting strategy to pay off. The boost against a potential heart hand should be considered in the same light as a bluff in poker. It is a sound strategy and must be done at times — but it loses its value if it is done too often.

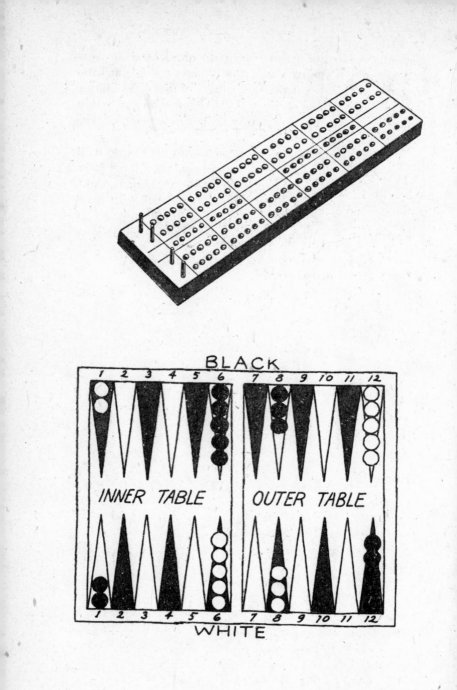

BLACK

1 2 3 4 5 6 7 8 9 10 11 12

INNER TABLE

OUTER TABLE

1 2 3 4 5 6 7 8 9 10 11 12

WHITE

two old favorites

17

cribbage

IT IS with great regret that I report that the popularity of cribbage has decreased during recent years. Perhaps it is that cribbage is traditionally a "parlor" game, and modern society does not emphasize parlor games. Or perhaps recent architectural advances have made parlors old-fashioned. Whatever the cause, cribbage is not nearly as popular now as in the past. This is a shame, for cribbage is a very social game, particularly suitable for children.

Some facets of cribbage strategy are highly complex. Space prohibits anywhere near a complete discussion of this game, but I am including some description of cribbage techniques for those of you who still enjoy this fine game and who, like myself, hope that it will enjoy renewed popularity in the future.

The crib

In general, there are types of cards and card combinations which tend to produce higher scores in the crib. Therefore, when it is your crib you should try to place cards of this nature in it; when it is your opponent's crib, avoid giving him valuable cards.

The best card for scoring in the crib is a five. This will give the opportunity to make fifteens as well as runs. Close behind are "near cards" — those that are close to each other in rank and thus give a chance for a run in the crib. Needless to say, 8–7 is best, for it also produces a fifteen.

Poor cards in the crib are very low or very high cards — some of each. Spread cards such as these have the lowest chance to form fifteens. Also, if you put "far cards" in the crib, the chance of forming a run is greatly decreased.

In choosing the cards to give to the crib, you should be thinking mainly about your own hand. In most cases, you should keep the highest possible score in your hand. The other cases arise when you are playing to the score (which happens surprisingly often), or when it seems to make little difference which cards you play. In close cases, you should *keep low cards in your own hand.* If nothing else, you will be able to score "go" in the play, and low cards have the best chance of combining in one or more ways with the starter to produce a fifteen. If all your cards are in the same zone, keep those cards which give you the best chance to form a run. or, even better, a multiple run. Runs, particularly multiple runs, form the heart of all big scores at cribbage. It is sometimes worth sacrificing a point to keep the chance of developing a double or quadruple run if given a favorable starter.

The play

During the play, there are two key numbers to keep in mind: 15 and 31. Always attempt to play in such a way that your opponent cannot profitably play a ten-point card with regard to one of these numbers. The reason that ten-point cards are so important is that there are so many of them that mathematically your opponent figures to have one or more of them.

Thus, clearly, the best possible starting play is a four. Your opponent cannot score a fifteen and, equally important, he cannot play any card which will guarantee that you yourself will not score one. Equally, avoid playing to a total of twenty-one, for it gives your opponent the golden opportunity to make thirty-one with a "ten-card." Expanding this principle somewhat, avoid playing a card which will allow your opponent to score a "go" with a ten-card. (This extension of the principle may seem obvious, but I have seen hundreds of seasoned cribbage players violate it.)

Counting your hand

Whether or not you use the "Muggins" rule, it is just plain silly to lose points by counting your hand improperly. There is one simple straightforward way to insure that you will never miscount — count in the same order every time you count a hand or the crib. Whatever this order is (and the particular order you select does not matter) stick to it regardless of how obvious the count of your hand may be. Perhaps this advice strikes you as similar to telling a baseball player to run to first base before trying for second, but the odds will never be in your favor if you do not take advantage of the card values you are dealt. Cribbage is one of the few games where miscounting or misreading of the cards is likely to occur — at least, it does seem to occur often. It is presumptuous to assume that you will never fall into this trap if you take no measure to guard against this failing. It may seem like needless trouble, but remember that after you have counted in your established order for a period of time it will become automatic, and you will expend no mental energy in counting. *And you will never miscount!*

backgammon

BACKGAMMON IS a very old game. For a time it waned in popularity, but recently there has been a resurgence. The game deserves its new-found adherents because, despite the relative simplicity of its equipment and rules, there is so much possible variation in the sequence of numbers on the dice and possible positions of the pieces on the board that different styles and strategies can be developed. Just as in apparently more complicated games such as bridge and chess, this tends to create interest in the game.

It is beyond the scope of this book to offer more than a comment on the *odds* in favor of or against following any of the individual general strategies. First of all, it is not clear that a particular form of play — such as conservative or aggressive — is necessarily better than any other. Second, and even more important, it may well be that an individual player will do better if he adopts a style of play with which he is most familiar and comfortable.

For these reasons, I will not attempt to select winning overall strategy. Instead, I will restrict myself to a consideration of those portions of the game which are subject to a fairly rigid mathematical analysis, and show some of the situations in which the odds can be of use in playing backgammon.

The odds of the game

The most important case of knowing the odds for playing backgammon occurs when the pieces of the two sides no longer interlock — that is, when each player has cleared his men past the other's, no more "hitting" is possible, and the game boils down to a race to see who can bear off his pieces first. In such cases, there is no further strategy involved, and it is possible to categorize plays as either right or wrong, depending on whether they give you the best possible mathematical chance of being the first to bear off your pieces.

1] *When your pieces are all in your inner table.* When you are actually in the act of bearing off men, and you have a choice of moves, it is usually best or equal best to remove from the board as many stones as possible. Thus, if you have (perhaps among others) stones on your 2, 4, and 6 points, and you roll a 4-2, it is superior to bear off stones from the 4 and 2 points than it is to take off the one stone from the 6-point.

2] *When your pieces are all in your inner table, or you are about to bring them there.* When making moves within your inner table (i.e., when you are unable to remove stones and must make other moves instead), OR when you are in the act of bringing your remaining stones to your inner table, you should attempt to arrange your stones so that they are spread as equally as possible over different points. In other words, it is *inferior* to have a great number of stones piled up on any one point.

For example, if you have stones on the 4 and 6 points and a roll of 2 to take, it is better to move the stone from 4 to 2 than it is to pile up an extra piece on the 4-point by moving from 6 to 4.

EXCEPTION: An occasional exception to this rule arises when your opponent is about to remove all his stones, or is very likely to do so within *two* rolls. If you have more than two stones remaining, you may be able to compute that you will be forced to roll a double number on your next roll in order to win. In such cases you must take special care to organize your pieces in such manner that the lowest possible double will get you off in one throw — because you anticipate having only one chance.

For example, you have four remaining pieces on your inner table, one each on the 6-5-4-2 points, and you have the misfortune of throwing 2-1. You can bring a man off your 2-point and move the tile on 6 to 5. But this will require that you throw either 6-6 or 5-5 on the next roll in order to get off. If, instead, you take the 2-1 so as to pile both the stone on 6 and the stone on 5 onto the 4 point, it will enable you to get off with 4-4 or better on the next throw.

But it is not always best to move the back man forward. For example, suppose you throw 3-1 with the position, one tile on 6, one on 4, two on 3. Take a man off the 3 and move the 6 to the 5 and you will need 4-4 or better. But if you take the tile off 4, leaving 6-3-3, you can bear off with 3-3 or better.

3] *Choices between moves within your inner table and moving pieces into or towards the inner table.* Assuming you can do so economically — that is, without wasting extra pips on your move — you should generally prefer to move stones into the inner table (to allow bearing off as soon as possible) or towards your inner table rather than interior moves. To take a simple case, if you have a stone 5 boxes away from your inner table, and a five is thrown, it is almost always correct to move the piece into your inner table.

Matters of strategy when the pieces of the two sides interlock depend largely on personal preference. There is a group of players which defies traditional theory by suggesting that a very aggressive game, in which the opposing stones should be hit at almost every opportunity, is the key to success. I cannot state with certainty whether this method of play is more successful than the traditional, conservative style which emphasizes safety; in fact, I am not sure this issue can be determined with certainty — one reason backgammon is so interesting a game. Nonetheless, most experienced players do not make placing opposing stones on the bar a primary objective. The classic theory of when to put your opponent on the bar is that you should do so only when it does not unduly jeopardize your position.

This is not to say one must never take chances. One of the most common mistakes made by beginners is that they attempt to keep all their pieces safe from being placed on the bar at all costs As a result, they often wind up with their pieces placed on very few of the points, and this reduces their flexibility in the later stages, usually with fatal results. In general, it is best to have your pieces occupying as many different points as possible, subject to not leaving blots (unprotected stones) where they are in danger of being placed on the bar by opposing stones, or on your inner table (which will reduce your flexibility in placing your opponent's stones on the bar).

Instead, it is a good idea to take reasonable chances. One almost essential chance-taking procedure is to move down "builders" from their position in your opponent's outer table to positions in your own outer table. And this should be done as early as possible so that you can have stones in position to capture points in your own inner and outer tables, thus preventing your opponent's "runners" (stones beginning on your inner table) from escaping. It is particularly important, if possible, to capture your own "bar point" (the first point in your outer table).

Another common error is to refuse to split up the two runners. Particularly if done very early, this can be done at minimal risk. It is unlikely your opponent will be able to hit these stones profitably (if he doesn't cover on the point where he hits you, he risks having a well-advanced piece sent to the bar), and by splitting your runners you increase the number of rolls which will enable one of your runners to escape. For example, at the beginning of the game, you can bring a runner to safety with a roll of 6-5 ("lover's leap"), taking one to your strong point in the opponent's outer table. If, at some early roll, you have moved one of these up, say, 2 points, you can now escape similarly with a 5-4 (assuming your opponent has not captured his bar point), and perhaps with a 6-3 as well, depending on how your opponent has played. This is another instance in which it pays to have your stones covering different points — it increases the number of rolls you will find useful. And this, of course, is going with the odds.

Forward and back games

A crucial decision of backgammon strategy is the determination of whether to play a forward game (simply try to get your men around as fast as possible) or a back game (keep some men in your opponent's inner table in an attempt to prevent him from taking his own men off). In most cases, a running game will be preferable. Aside from the general difficulty of managing a back game — which requires much more skill than the management of a forward game — there is the risk that you will lose a gammon (or even a backgammon!) if your strategy fails. In general, therefore, you should not look to establish a back game.

Sometimes, however, circumstances will thrust the necessity of a back game upon you. This will occur particularly when you have secured two or more points in your opponent's inner table during the middle game. If the rest of your pieces are not too far advanced, you can hope to trap one of your opponent's pieces on the bar at a time when you have built a strong inner table of your own. You are not likely to do this if you own only one point in his inner table, for it is unlikely that the loss of just one place to move will force him to weaken his position. But if you have two such points, it will be difficult for him to continue moving past your locations without throwing very good numbers.

When you do establish a back game, remember that you do not have enough stones remaining to form a prime on your own side of the table. Therefore, you must take all possible steps not to advance these stones too quickly. If your front stones move too far forward on your own inner table, you will not be able to contain any pieces you are able to place on the bar. As soon as you give up a point in your opponent's home area, your own back game will disintegrate and the game will resolve itself into a race — one which your opponent is almost certain to win if you started with a back game.

Your hope, instead, is to put your opponent on the bar, and keep him in your inner table long enough for you to bring up some stones from your back area to help form a prime (six consecutive points, making it impossible for your opponent to escape) on your own side of the board.

Doubling

The use of the doubling cube is the feature that gives backgammon most of its excitement. It is essential to understand the odds involving the doubling cube in order to be a

successful backgammon player. However, this facet of backgammon strategy is little understood, even among experienced
players, so I will cover it in some detail.

We will assume, at the beginning, that the position is
such that a "gammon" (one player going out before his opponent has taken off any stones — in which case the score for
the game is doubled) is very unlikely. Also, we assume the
doubling cube is at 1 unit, although the arguments will be
identical regardless of the actual value of the cube.

First, let's consider when you yourself should double. To
begin with, you must judge that you have the upper hand, and
are ahead in the race. You wish to double at such a point that
it will be profitable to you whether or not your opponent takes
the double or stops the game and concedes to you at the
previous stake. If he concedes, you win the present stake, and
have avoided the necessity of continuing the game. You might
have run into a series of very unlucky rolls. So by doubling,
you have something to gain if your opponent simply refuses
to play; you have taken out insurance against a very poor run
of luck.

There is danger, however, that your opponent will accept
the double and that he will defeat you. But if he takes the
double you then have a chance to win at double the stakes.
If there were no further action permitted with the doubling
cube, it would be profitable to double the stakes whenever you
had any significant advantage. But this is not the case. If you
double, your opponent then "owns the cube" and he has the
advantage of being able to control the next double. This means
that he can force you out of the game (by doubling again) if
the game should suddenly turn to his advantage.

You are not willing to give your opponent this advantage
unless your position is relatively secure. In fact, as we will see
shortly, by doubling you are giving your opponent 3 to 1 odds
on a "take." When you double, you are really hoping he *won't*
take, so that you can cart off your victory without risking playing out the rest of the game (and possibly hitting that bad run
of luck). Therefore, *you should not double when your opponent can profitably take the double.*

It follows that before we can work out what chance of
winning we need to double, we must know what chance of

winning we need to *accept* a double when one is made. Suppose, therefore, that your opponent doubles, proposing that the stakes be raised from one unit to two units. If you drop out, you lose one unit. If you take the double, however, and the fraction of the time you will win from the given position is X, you will then:

Win two units (the new stake) X of the time;

Lose two units 1−X (the fraction of the time your opponent will win; for example, if X is 9/10, 1−X will be 1/10) of the time.

Your net result, therefore, is the sum of a gain of 2X units and a loss of 2−2X units. These combine to give you a total result of 4X−2 units.

Since you will only take a double when it is profitable to do so, you will accept a double only when 4X−2 is at least as good as a loss of 1 unit (which you could achieve by not accepting the double to begin with).

It turns out that 4X−2 is no worse than a loss of one only when X *is* 1/4 *or more.* Therefore, *you should acc pt a double only when the odds against you are no greater than 3 to 1.* And, from the previous discussion, you should therefore not offer a double unless you feel the odds are at least 3 to 1 in your favor. Actually, it is satisfactory to accept a double with a little worse than 3 to 1 against you because of the possibility of re-doubling.

Against this, however, we must set the possibility of a gammon. When you are so far behind that you are a 3 to 1 underdog, there may be considerable danger that you will suffer a double loss because of a gammon, again doubling the score. If you accept a double on the doubling cube this means you will lose *four* times the original stake. This risk is too great to take, so you should not accept a double if there is a significant chance you will be gammoned. This would be indicated if, for example, your opponent had established a prime (six consecutive points), or if your opponent had a strong inner table and you had a man on the bar, or if you have several men in your opponent's inner table and have not established any points there to form a satisfactory back game.

bridge

the people vs. the odds

I UNDERSTAND that scientists have programmed computers to play a pretty fair game of chess against a human opponent. It might even be possible to set up a bridge game among four computers. But introduce just one real person as a member of the foursome, and fuses will soon start to blow.

Were it not for the somewhat obvious fact that bridge is played by human — sometimes all-too human — beings, the game would be mostly one of odds and percentages. In no other game — not even poker — does the personality of the contestants play so eminent a part, for the "human factor" may change a technically correct action into a losing proposition. That's what makes bridge such a wonderful game — never dull, never predictable.

bridge

Do you ever abandon the "book" bid because of the relative skill of your partner and your opponents? If not, this chapter is for you because the dramatis personae at your bridge table change the odds. A word of caution is in order, however. An individual's bridge personality may be very different from his "real life" personality; Mr. Milquetoast at the office may be a tiger at the table. So reserve judgment about people until you've seen them in action. My favorite partner, Helen Sobel Smith, soft-spoken and honey-haired, was the grateful recipient, in her early bridge days, of countless gifts from opponents who found it hard to believe that such a pleasant young lady could be a demon opponent. After a while, they did catch on that, in her feminine way, she was stealing them blind. Thereafter, Helen still continued to devastate her opponents, but only because of her sheer bridge ability and nerve — opponents stopped actively aiding and abetting her.

In a pivot bridge game, you will change your partner at the end of each rubber. And to some extent, the odds governing various actions will also change, as they are affected by the ability of your partner. You must, therefore, know how to gauge your actions accordingly. With the worst player of the group as your partner, your feeling of gloom and doom is normal, but good oddsmanship will give your side a fighting chance. First of all, you will want slightly better odds for the games you bid. At any vulnerability, you will want to be in a game that offers a 50% or better chance (especially if you will be the declarer), but you will settle for a part score with more doubtful holdings. Of course, if what makes your partner a bad player is his notorious conservatism, you will accept all game invitations — but this is not a matter of the odds, for game will probably be laydown in view of your partner's idiosyncrasy.

For this rubber, forget about all but the soundest of slams. Your object is to get the rubber over with as fast as possible, so that you can play with someone else. If you can win it by scoring up two games, so much the better. Sacrifice bidding is also out, with the possible exception of paying a small penalty (200 at the most) to keep the opponents from making a part-score. This is permissible because you may thus prevent partner from later incurring a much larger penalty to keep opponents from converting a part-score into game. When opponents are in game, go quietly. The one exception should be if you think you might bring home your "sacrifice" contract. The odds in this case are too overwhelming to overlook.

The principle behind this outlook is that you are unwilling to prolong the rubber in order to continue the dubious pleasure of playing with an inferior partner. Giving up a 500-point penalty, for example, to save a vulnerable slam by the opponents is usually commendable practice, but is sheer lunacy in this situation. Who knows what your partner will do on the next hand? And if you argue that it is unfair to treat your partner in this way, you may reflect that you are saving him points, too. The less that you lose when you play with him, the less he also will lose; and if his cards are good enough to win the rubber, so much the better.

All things being equal, you would much rather collect an 800-point penalty than a vulnerable game worth 620 points. Very little is equal here, however, because your partner is not of comparable skill, and you should prefer the game (and a new partner) to the penalty.

Great caution should also be exercised in making low-level penalty doubles. The odds are that partner, knowing that you are his superior in ability, will have so much respect for your double that he will leave it in on the most unsuitable hands; and he surely will not be able to provide the defensive know-how that will be essential to cash in on close doubles. In competitive situations where both sides are bidding to high levels, try to make the decision yourself if you can – don't pass it around to partner, who may not know what to do. Of course, if there is a choice between playing a hand in your suit or his, be a hog unless his suit is clearly better. You would rather play for nine tricks at notrump than let him play four hearts and go down on a hand where eleven tricks are "ice-cold." If the worst happens and you go down while he would (or might) have made his contract, apologize and think up some plausible excuse for your decision, other than the true one: that such actions will save points for both of you in the long run.

Unless you fully expect partner to throw away two tricks

in the defense, you should continue to double the opponents' games when your hand and the bidding indicates they are going down a couple of tricks and maybe more. You are, temporarily, playing at a disadvantage, but you're not a door-mat.

Lead-directing doubles of games and slams should also be made whenever you're lucky enough to have one. The odds of possible gain *versus* possible loss are so immensely favorable that only an emphatic statement from partner, "I don't understand lead-directing doubles," could convince me not to make one.

Now let us suppose that the players have rotated, and you are in the happy position of facing the best player in your game. Excuse me, I mean the second-best player; but partner is *almost* your equal.

Now is the time to don your bidding shoes and accept shorter odds for your games and slams. For one thing, a not unlikely defensive error may let you make an "unmakable" contract. For another, you are less likely to be doubled if suits are breaking badly than if you yourself were on your left. For a third, even if you go down, you will continue a rubber in which you have the advantage.

Normally, one should not bid a small slam that depends for success on anything more than a finesse. In this one situation, however, you should venture a slam that requires both a finesse and a three-two suit break, against nonvulnerable opponents. (Against vulnerable, even if inferior opponents, a slam should still be at least a 50% chance.)

With a partner who will cooperate in producing good defense, penalty doubles of the opponents are very good compensation for game. You should cheerfully accept a 500-point penalty (especially from nonvulnerable opponents) in lieu of a vulnerable game. Although, theoretically, this represents a loss of some 100 points, you are happy to prolong a rubber in which the situation is so favorable, for you fully expect to win the rubber anyway — perhaps picking up another penalty before ending it.

In all such situations, there are hidden bonuses and penalties as real as if they appeared on the scorepad. In one case, you earn the bonus of getting rid of your handicap. In the other, you retain the edge of having a good partner. Set a 200 point minimum on these factors — in many cases you'd gladly pay more -- and the odds become tangible in any situation.

With any partner, a cheerful, confident demeanor can be your greatest asset at the bridge table. Partners are less likely to criticize actions that go wrong, and opponents are more reluctant to double. While it is perfectly proper for the opponents to draw inferences (at their own risk) from your tone and bearing, it is a breach of the proprieties to assume a demeanor for the purpose of deceiving your opponents. Therefore, let me recommend that you make *all* your bids cheerfully and confidently.

Later, I will show how you can manipulate the odds. so that they are more favorable to you: by executing safety plays, by timing your play to give yourself all possible chances to make a contract, and by reaching the safer game or slam. In addition, since there will be times in your bridge life when you will have an inferior player as a partner, you will also wish to employ the tactics recommended to minimize the possible devastation partner can cause and get him to play the best bridge he is capable of so as to improve your odds as much as possible. No special knowledge or technical ability is required of you; all you need is empathy and good manners. If you can't bring yourself to feel friendly, you can at least be sympathetic. If partner goes down in a cold contract, don't bawl him out. Instead, remark that the distribution was unfortunate or that the opponents found the best defense. If he avoids making a terrible blunder, praise him. The poor player is unused to receiving compliments, and he will try his hardest to earn more of yours.

the odds in the bidding

The games people play

Scoring games is the bread and butter of bridge. Taking nine tricks at notrump is not as exciting as landing an elusive slam or as soul-satisfying as sawing off that limb your opponents have climbed out on — to an 800-point penalty tune. But the player who rises from the rubber bridge table a winner at the end of the evening is usually the player who has bid and made game most often.

"But partner, we were vulnerable!"

One of the least understood aspects of going with the odds is echoed in the alibi for missing game: "But partner, I *had* to play it safe. We were vulnerable!"

Being vulnerable should apply a sharp brake to such risky vehicles as overcalls and sacrifice bids. But when it comes to bidding for game, be forward-going in any conditions short of a red light flashing danger. The pre-tournament book that installed the United States Women's team as strong favorites to take their event in the 1968 World Bridge Olympiad might have proven soundly based if our match-point oriented stars had understood that this vagary of the odds applies to International Match Point scoring just as it does to rubber bridge or to four-deal play (Chicago).

The fact is that the odds are more in your favor if you are vulnerable when you bid a one-chance-in-three game than if you are not vulnerable. As you will soon see.

What's a part-score worth?

One of the longest debated bridge questions is: "What is the value of a part-score at rubber bridge?" (In duplicate, making a part-score is automatically awarded a 50-point bonus that is included in the score you write down.) Most experts agree that part-scores are really worth more than 50 points; but no two will agree on just how much more than 50 points is its real, though unwritten, value. Even taking into consideration the plus qualities of having something below the line; of inducing the opponents to sacrifice; of the greater probability of making game — I suggest, nonetheless, that you consider its value to be 50 points. To a large extent this is because the value of a rubber-bridge part-score reverts to zero when it is wiped out by either side scoring a game, whereas the value of a nonvulnerable game persists throughout the rubber, either contributing to your side's rubber bonus or lessening the rubber bonus points scored by the opponents.

. For games, 300 points is the accepted value of the first game scored by either side. A nonvulnerable game now scored by the other side is also worth 300 points — because it *cancels* the value of the first game you scored. Thus, you should always evaluate a nonvulnerable game as worth 300 points. The rubber game scored by either side after both are vulnerable is valued at the full 500 points of the rubber bonus, because the hidden values of the first two games (one by North-South, one by East-West) have been used up in canceling each other out. A game scored when only your side is vulnerable is also worth 500 points, not the 700-point bonus for the rubber that you write down, because the value of the non-vulnerable game already completed has not been canceled and should be taken into consideration. The game scored when only your side is vulnerable is actually worth a shade under 500 points, but its real value is close enough to that figure so that your odds calculations will be substantially correct if you assign 500 points to the value of all vulnerable games.

All good Goren students — in fact, all good bridge players — know that game in a major or in notrump should be bid when the partnership's hand contains a combined total of 26 points, counting both high cards and distribution: (For an odds-on chance in a minor-suit game, a total of 29 points is needed.)

Let me emphasize that *bidding* a good game — 26 points and a fit — is not the same thing as *making* the game. Sometimes — in fact, quite often — the contract will not be made. Nevertheless, it is eminently proper and sound to bid these games always. In fact, it is decidedly wrong not to bid them.

Here's a straightforward example. You, South, deal the first hand of the rubber.

N:	♠ Q 9 8	♡ 9 3 2	◇ A Q 10 4 2	♣ A 3
S:	♠ A J 10 7 6	♡ 7 6 5	◇ K J 9	♣ K Q

THE BIDDING:

S	W	N	E
1 ♠	Pass	2 ◇	Pass
2 ♠	Pass	4 ♠	All Pass

This is an excellent four-spade contract. South has 14 points; North has 13 (adding a promotional point for the queen of partner's suit; no distributional point is counted for the doubleton club because dummy has only three trumps). The duplication in the club suit is unfortunate (because the ace, king and queen of clubs can take only two tricks), but many hands have some flaw in them like this one. The question is, will you take ten tricks?

Of course, if the opponents *never* lead hearts you will make four spades. But hearts is the suit in which defenders have most of their high cards, and the possibility of avoiding three heart losers can be discounted except against the most generous of Wests.

There are millions of ways in which the 26 East-West cards could be divided, but let us consider only two of the possible deals:

```
              ♠ Q 9 8
              ♡ 9 3 2
              ◇ A Q 10 4 2
              ♣ A 3
  ♠ 3 2            N        ♠ K 5 4
  ♡ A K 4                   ♡ Q J 10 8
  ◇ 6 5 3    W       E      ◇ 8 7
  ♣ J 9 7 6 4    S          ♣ 10 8 5 2
              ♠ A J 10 7 6
              ♡ 7 6 5
              ◇ K J 9
              ♣ K Q
```

or

```
              ♠ Q 9 8
              ♡ 9 3 2
              ◇ A Q 10 4 2
              ♣ A 3
  ♠ K 5 4          N        ♠ 3 2
  ♡ Q J 10 8                ♡ A K 4
  ◇ 8 7      W       E      ◇ 6 5 3
  ♣ 10 8 5 2     S          ♣ J 9 7 6 4
              ♠ A J 10 7 6
              ♡ 7 6 5
              ◇ K J 9
              ♣ K Q
```

Basically, making four spades depends on whether the king of spades is held by East or West. Half the time it will be onside, half the time offside. (Playing-card kings, unlike some real ones, stay put and do not shift their courses.)

If you had X-ray vision, of course you would want to bid the first game and not the second one. But as a mere mortal, to whom the opponents' cards unfold only during the play, you will want to bid this game *all* the time. That you should do so is a matter of simple arithmetic. Note that I say arithmetic, not "mathematics." Old-fashioned addition, subtraction and division are all you need to figure the odds at bridge (although the nearest nine-year-old would, in all probability, prefer to work them out for you in the "new math").

bridge

If you bid only three spades, half the time you will take nine tricks and score 90 below the line, plus an unseen 50 points, the standard value of a part-score, for a total of 140 points. The other half of the time, the king of spades will be in the right place for you and you will score an overtrick for a total of 120 points below the line and 50 for the part-score, a total of 170 points. Since you will score 170 half the time and 140 half the time, your average score by bidding only three spades will be 155 points.

Now let us suppose that you have bid four spades on these cards. Half the time you will romp home, scoring 120 below the line plus an unwritten 300 points, the hidden value of a non-vulnerable game, or 420 points total. The other half of the time, with the king of trumps wrong, your opponents will score 50 points for defeating you one trick. To find your average score for bidding four spades, you subtract the 50 your uncooperative opponents score in the one case from the juicy 420 points you will score in the other, leaving 370. Dividing this by two leaves an average of 185.

What all this arithmetic (which you don't have to remember, by the way) means to you is that if you consistently bid non-vulnerable games that have only an even chance of making, you will come out a consistent winner. And if you are vulnerable, the plus for bidding these games is even greater. Your average score for stopping in two or three spades is still the same, 155 points. But here the reward for bidding game is increased; with a trick score of 120 plus 500 above the line for game, half the time you will score 620. Even though the penalty for going down one trick is more, 100 points, your average score now comes out to 260 points, as opposed to the average of 185 points when not vulnerable. So don't be afraid to bid game when you are vulnerable; the penalties are greater if you go down, but the reward for fulfillment is greater still. (You can see from the arithmetic that you don't really need a 50-50 chance to bid a vulnerable game; in fact, the top experts will bid vulnerable games when the chances are somewhat *against* making.)

Even 2 to 1 against may be good odds

We have seen that you should bid all games that have an even or slightly worse chance of making, no matter what the vulnerability is. Knowing the unwritten value of games, vulnerable and not vulnerable, is most useful when the odds against making a particular contract are higher. For example, as South, you deal yourself

♠ A K 5 4 2   ♡ K 6 3   ◇ Q J 8   ♣ 6 5

You bid one spade, and partner responds two diamonds. With your minimum hand, you rebid two spades and North raises you to three spades (while your opponents pass throughout). Do you bid the spade game? It's true you have a minimum for your bidding, but you have a fit for partner's diamonds and he has announced a fit for your spades. You probably have only two minor-suit losers, so, in all likelihood, four spades will depend on whether or not the king of hearts is well placed and how the opponents' trumps behave. If you could see through the backs of partner's cards, you would find that this is indeed the case, for he holds:

♠ Q 9 8   ♡ 5 4   ◇ A K 10 5 4   ♣ J 10 9

You need a three-two break in trumps, which occurs 68% (or just over two-thirds) of the time. And you also need the ace of hearts with East, a 50-50 chance. Combine these chances and you find that you will take ten tricks one time out of three. This is easy to determine: Out of three deals, once you will go down because the trumps don't break; of the remaining two times you will find the heart ace right once (four spades makes) and wrong once (four spades goes down).

Let's figure your average score. If you are not vulnerable and stop in three spades, you will score minus 50 once, plus 140 once, and plus 170 once, for an average score of 87 points. If you bid game, you will score plus 420 once and the opponents will score 100 points once, and 50 points once, for an average score to you of 90 points. Clearly, not vulnerable the odds are about even. It's a close decision, and you should pass three spades because you may be doubled in four if the trumps

bridge

break badly. Vulnerable, your theoretical average score by bidding four is 107 points (plus 620 once, minus 100 once, and minus 200 once), against 70 points for stopping in three spades, and, in actual practice, the odds are even a little better in your favor, for it will be easier for you to play this hand as declarer than for your opponents to defend it, and an occasional layout of the opponents' cards will give you an extra chance of making your game contract. Let us look at three possible complete deals:

```
                ♠ Q 9 8
                ♡ 5 4
                ◇ A K 10 5 4
                ♣ J 10 9
    ♠ 7 6 3          N        ♠ J 10
    ♡ Q J 10 8                ♡ A 9 7 2
    ◇ 9 6        W       E    ◇ 7 3 2
    ♣ A 8 4 3        S        ♣ K Q 7 2
                ♠ A K 5 4 2
                ♡ K 6 3
                ◇ Q J 8
                ♣ 6 5
```

Here you have no problem. After any lead and defense, you simply draw trumps and cash your diamonds, and it is all beer and skittles. Making four spades.

```
                ♠ Q 9 8
                ♡ 5 4
                ◇ A K 10 5 4
                ♣ J 10 9
    ♠ J 10           N        ♠ 7 6 3
    ♡ A 9 7 2                 ♡ Q J 10 8
    ◇ 7 3 2      W       E    ◇ 9 6
    ♣ K Q 7 2        S        ♣ A 8 4 3
                ♠ A K 5 4 2
                ♡ K 6 3
                ◇ Q J 8
                ♣ 6 5
```

· Best defense will defeat four spades. West leads the king of clubs and continues with a club to East's ace. East shifts to the queen of hearts. You cover, West takes his ace and continues hearts. You are down one before you've even begun to play. But — and this is a very large but — West may not lead a club (which is far from unlikely if he has an unattractive holding, such as only one of the three missing honors or ace-queen, in this suit), then you will have no trouble making ten tricks (five spades and five diamonds). Or the defenders may try to cash three rounds of clubs, with the same happy result for you.

```
                ♠ Q 9 8
                ♡ 5 4
                ◇ A K 10 5 4
                ♣ J 10 9
  ♠ J 10 7 3                  ♠ 6
  ♡ J 9 8          N          ♡ A Q 10 7 2
  ◇ 9 7        W     E        ◇ 6 3 2
  ♣ A K 8 3         S         ♣ Q 7 4 2
                ♠ A K 5 4 2
                ♡ K 6 3
                ◇ Q J 8
                ♣ 6 5
```

This time you are not going to make four spades. In fact, if you are not vulnerable and therefore stop in three spades, you will have to time your play carefully to make *that* contract. Suppose the defenders start off with three rounds of clubs. You ruff the third round and play the ace and king of spades. When East shows out, you must abandon spades and lead diamonds until West ruffs. When you regain the lead with either the king of hearts or a club ruff, you lead a low trump to dummy's carefully preserved queen. This will draw West's last trump and, at the same time, serve as an entry to dummy's diamond tricks. Notice that if you play a low spade to the queen early in the hand, you will have no way to reach those good diamonds (of course, if both opponents follow to the second round of trumps, you will draw the third round before starting the diamonds.

These examples show why I believe you should bid a vulnerable game when the apparent odds are *two to one against you*. You are cold for game in one of three cases (example one) and this alone is enough to justify the game bid. And you also have a prospect of making game if with the cards distributed as in the second example, there is a slip in the defense. Nor is this an isolated instance based on a particular hand; you will frequently find that the odds improve in your favor during the course of the play.

Not vulnerable, however, two to one odds against you are too heavy to fight and conservatism will be the winning line in the long run.

Oddly enough (no pun intended), except in the case where both sides are vulnerable, the odds are not much affected by relative vulnerability. With both sides vulnerable, the rubber game is worth 500 points to either side. In other situations, it is worth about 350 — give or take a few points, depending upon who is doing the figuring.

I have presented this discussion of how to calculate the odds in favor of bidding games in some detail, for it is useful to know why it will profit you to bid games freely. And, it may amuse you to indulge in such mental exercise while waiting for a fourth to arrive. But there is no need for you ever to perform all these computations in the middle of an auction. All you need to remember is this:

When making a game appears to depend on one of two or more things being "right" — a finesse, a suit break, etc. — bid the game. It's not even close. The same principle applies to two chances out of three. *

When game appears to depend on just one thing being right rather than wrong, bid the game, vulnerable or not.

But when scoring a game will need success in both of two even money chances, bid the game when you are vulnerable, stop safely in a part-score when not vulnerable.

Following these simple rules will surely boost your bridge winnings.

At sixes and sevens

There is no question about it; bidding and making a slam is the most exciting thing in bridge. At lower levels, there is

---

* *The chance of success in two out of three "right-or-wrong" things (like finesses) is 50%.*

give-and-take, a jockeying for tricks between declarer and defenders. But tension is the chief characteristic of slam plays. You can lose only one trick — sometimes none at all. And when you've brought in a slam, you've landed a big one!

Going down in slam contracts is, as Shakespeare said, "stale, flat and unprofitable." Mostly unprofitable. Your minus score on a slam that fails is not merely the 50 or 100 points you put in the "they" column, but also the full value — trick score plus unwritten game bonus — of the game you would have made had you not bid to a slam. As we have seen, bidding a game with the odds against your making it is sound oddsmanship. Now let's look at some slam arithmetic:

Not vulnerable, you stop in four spades and make six. You score 480 points (180 trick score and 300 for the unwritten value of a nonvulnerable game) and you miss scoring the 500-point slam bonus. Now suppose you bid six and go down. Your minus score is again exactly 500 points (50 to the opponents plus the 450 you would have gained for bidding four spades and making five).

Vulnerable, the odds are exactly the same. If you have not bid a small slam you make, you lose the 750-point slam bonus. If the slam goes down, you miss the 650 points you would have scored for game, plus the 100 points you present to your happy opponents.

So with the gain or loss at stake a tossup, you will want to bid slams whenever they are *at worst* a tossup. Certainly you will want to bid six if it depends on one of two finesses or on a three-two suit break, or on finding the queen of trumps when you and your partner have a nine-card fit, for the chance of success in these cases is considerably better than even money. If a slam seems to depend on a straight fifty-fifty finesse, bid it when you feel lucky, play it safe when things are not going so well. And if the slam appears to depend on more than a card being right or a suit breaking, forget it and start thinking how pleasant it will be to chalk up a game.

| N: | ♠ Q 7 4 | ♡ A Q 10 | ◇ A 7 4 3 | ♣ K J 2 |
| S: | ♠ A K 6 5 2 | ♡ K J 4 3 | ◇ K 8 2 | ♣ Q |

A small slam in spades seems to depend only on a three-two trump break, which will occur more than two times in three, excellent odds in your favor. So you'd like to be in six spades, right? Wrong!

```
                    ♠ Q 7 4
                    ♡ A Q 10
                    ◇ A 7 4 3
                    ♣ K J 2
    ♠ J 10                        ♠ 9 8 3
    ♡ 9 8           N             ♡ 7 6 5 2
    ◇ Q J 10 9 6 5  W    E        ◇ —
    ♣ 7 5 4              S        ♣ A 10 9 8 6 3
                    ♠ A K 6 5 2
                    ♡ K J 4 3
                    ◇ K 8 2
                    ♣ Q
```

Admittedly, Kismet (or, to be honest, your author) has played a dirty trick on you. That six-zero diamond break is less than a 1% chance — and only half of that infrequent time will the hand on lead have the six diamonds. Nevertheless, six spades is *not* the proper contract! The recommended bidding:

1 ♠	Pass	3 NT	Pass
4 ♡	Pass	4 ♠	Pass
4 NT	Pass	5 ♡	Pass
6 NT	All pass		

At the slam level, you should always choose the *safest* slam. Here six notrump is laydown (with the same three-two spade break needed to make six spades), while a ruff will beat the suit slam. North's bidding shows a balanced 16 or 17 points, with no ruffing values. South can tell that there are so few high cards missing that North must have clubs well stopped, and his club queen must be useful. So South wisely chooses the notrump slam.

Sometimes the safest slam will be a suit contract, in which you can establish dummy's side suit by ruffing rather than hunting for mising honors. But the principle is the same. Be choosey . . . choose the best. For example:

N:	♠ 1076	♡ 9832	◇ AQJ	♣ K65
S:	♠ KQJ98	♡ AK5	◇ K7	♣ AJ10

Here the notrump slam is not the best contract. South has only eleven top winners after conceding a trick to the spade ace, and must guess the location of the club queen to make his contract — with a bushel of points riding on his decision. The preferred contract is six spades. South wins the opening lead and knocks out the spade ace, regains the lead and draws trumps, discards a small heart on the third round of diamonds, and cashes the two top hearts (if they have not yet been played) and ruffs a heart. If hearts divide 3-3, South can park the club ten on dummy's good heart; if not, he can still fall back on the club guess. This extra chance greatly improves the odds in South's favor.

Oddsmanship: If it's close whether or not to bid a slam, look at the score. If your opponents have a part-score, settle for the game that erases their partial. If *you* have a part-score, bid the slam; the odds are you'll be able to convert the partial even if the slam goes down. If you are vulnerable and the opponents are not, bid the slam; you're a favorite to win the rubber anyway. But remember, these guidelines apply only to close situations.

A bridge player contemplating bidding a grand slam is, by definition, a man of property. For if he thinks he probably can take thirteen tricks, he can surely make a small slam. But he will have to risk his "money in the bank" small slam to have a fling at the elusive grand slam. Is it worth it?

Not vulnerable, you risk 1030 points (180 trick score, plus 300 for game, plus 500 for a small slam bonus, plus 50 to the opponents) for a shot at an extra 500 points, the difference between the bonus for a small slam and the bonus for a grand slam. Vulnerable, your possible gain is 750 points, the difference between the two slam bonuses, while you stake 1530 points (180 plus 500 plus 750 plus 100 to East-West, who will be trying not to look *too* exultant).

These odds are only slightly less attractive than an angry bull on your side of a fence. Weighing risk against possible gain, I recommend that you never bid a grand slam that depends on the position of a particular card. Restrict your needs to a suit break (three-two with five cards missing; four-two or better with six cards missing; three-one or two-two with four cards out). Of course, a grand slam that can be made with an odds-on break in *either* one of two suits should be bid.

bridge

This is an excellent grand slam:

South dealer
Both sides vulnerable

N: ♠ 4   ♡ A Q 8 7 6 5   ◇ 8 7 2   ♣ 6 4 3
S: ♠ A K Q J 10 9 5   ♡ K 2   ◇ A Q   ♣ A J

THE BIDDING:

S	W	N	E
2 ♠	Pass	3 ♡	Pass
4 ◇	Pass	4 ♡	Pass
4 NT	Pass	5 ◇	Pass
5 NT	Pass	6 ♣	Pass
7 NT	Pass	Pass	Pass

South was surprised but very pleased to hear partner make a positive response to his opening strong two-bid. Before launching into Blackwood, South wisely gave North a chance to describe his hand further by cue-bidding diamonds. Later, when North showed the heart ace but no king, South realized that North must have a pretty fair heart suit for his bidding and therefore contracted for the grand slam. The slam depends on a 3-2 heart break (68%) or on the diamond finesse, a 50-50 proposition that adds an additional 16% to your prospects. There is even the further chance that West may lead a diamond, and there are also some squeeze possibilities. Note that South chose seven notrump, not seven spades, as the final contract; giving up 150 honors is a pretty small price to pay to guard against an opening lead ruff against a grand slam.

How part-scores alter the odds

To me, the one real flaw in duplicate bridge is that I miss all the fun and excitement of part-score bidding. I don't mean jockeying to buy a low-level contract; actually, this competition is somewhat keener at duplicate, and rubber bridge players might borrow a sage leaf or two on the fine art of pushing opponents out of makeable part-scores. What I miss are the

tactics employed after 40 below the line is written down —
encouragingly in the "We" column or menacingly in the
"They" column.

YOU HAVE A PARTIAL

Congratulations! The gods of probability decree that the
odds substantially favor your converting the part-score into a
game before the opponents erase it. And perhaps you will be
pleasantly sidetracked by collecting a penalty from the opponents, while your part-score remains and you remain a
favorite to convert it.

Thus, while it is usually unprofitable to settle for a 300-
point penalty instead of a vulnerable game, *the part-score
situation alters this!* In the first place, the game itself is worth
slightly less, since you have already collected the score for the
partial. In the second place, on the next deal you will still be
odds-on to make your vulnerable game. (Remember that this
optimism should, as usual, be tempered with common sense
when you have a weak partner. Take the sure conversion into
game rather than even a 500 or 800 penalty and hope to cut a
stronger player in the next rubber.)

Possession of a part-score should not alter your opening-
bid requirements. In my opinion, it is a mistake to open the
bidding light when you have 40 or more below the line. Partner will stretch to keep the bidding alive until game is
reached. Also, partner will be eager to double the opponents
if they enter the bidding, and the opening bidder's hand
should be able to pull some weight on defense.

Paradoxically, when the opponents have a part score, you
should open light first or second-hand. This is less a matter
of going with the odds than adopting sound tactics. You cannot afford to lose the tactical advantage of having your side
open the bidding even on a deal where your combined hands
do not offer some hope of game. Third or fourth hand, if
you know your partner will have opened light, you can pass
with anything but a hand that is considerably better than a
minimum.

When you have a partial, small slams can be bid somewhat more freely. (The odds against bidding seven are the

same at any score.) No longer do you need at least a 50 per cent play for a slam contract; six should be bid when you have somewhat less than half a chance of making it. The reason for this change in the odds is that, although you stand to gain the same amount by bidding and making the slam, you are risking somewhat less if you are set, because the value of the game you are foregoing is diminished.

West dealer
Both sides vulnerable
North-South 40 on score

```
                    ♠ A K 8 5 2
                    ♡ K 7 6
                    ◊ A J 5
                    ♣ Q 6
        ♠ Q 9 6            N        ♠ J 10 7 3
        ♡ Q J                       ♡ 10 8 3
        ◊ K 7 3 2     W       E     ◊ 8
        ♣ 10 9 3 2         S        ♣ K J 8 5 4
                    ♠ 4
                    ♡ A 9 5 4 2
                    ◊ Q 10 9 6 4
                    ♣ A 7
```

THE BIDDING:

W	N	E	S
Pass	1 ♠	Pass	2 ♡
Pass	3 ♡	Pass	4 ♣
Pass	4 ◊	Pass	5 ♡
Pass	6 ♡	Pass	Pass
Pass			

On this hand, you should bid the slam when you enjoy a part-score and rest in game when you don't. Slam requires both a three-two trump break (68%) *and* the diamond finesse (50%). In other words, you would expect to make this slam only about one time in three. West leads the ten of clubs to the queen, king and ace. Declarer cashes the king and ace of spades, throwing his losing club, and cashes the king and ace of hearts. Now he is in his own hand, where he wants to be, so he can take the diamond finesse. East can ruff a diamond whenever he wants (with the last outstanding trump), but South can ruff a black-suit return and still have two trump entries to his hand — one to ruff out the king of diamonds and one to get back to cash the established long diamond. Notice that *six diamonds* is not a satisfactory contract even with a part-score. It requires the diamond finesse and three-two breaks in *both* red suits.

Very little has been written about slam bidding when your side has a partial, and this is a good time to get the record straight on which bids are forcing, which are encouraging, and which are signoffs. After all, if the odds favor bidding slams when you have a part-score, you need the machinery to get there.

Any bid beyond what is needed to score game is a slam try *after* a suit has been agreed on. (Except, of course, when your partner has overlooked the score.) South's two-heart response to one spade in the hand above was not forcing, since it was enough for game, and North's three-heart raise showed a good hand, a fit, and mild slam interest. After a suit has been agreed on, bids in new suits are cue-bids, just as they would be without a part-score.

The one exception to the above is a simple raise of opener's one-bid to two, when your side has a partial of 70 or more. This is merely a mild preemptive action, to make it more difficult for the opponents to compete; if responder has a good hand on which he wants to initiate a slam try, he should jump.

When no suit has been agreed on, a non-jump bid beyond game in a new suit is not a slam try but simply an attempt to find the best low-level contract. In the hand illustrated, North showed slam interest by raising partner's suit, *then* cue-bidding. Had he bid three diamonds over two hearts, he would simply have been describing a pretty good hand with spades and diamonds.

A jump shift by responder is forcing and promises that he will make another bid. Therefore, opener can make a minimum rebid over the jump shift, but if he is encouraged by partner's calls, he must take strength-showing action next time around. Note also that responder may have to shade a jump shift slightly. The normal requirement for a jump shift is 19 points, but there is the danger that if responder has 17-18 points and makes some simple response that produces game if made, opener may pass with considerable extra values and slam may be missed. Therefore, you should shade the requirements for a jump shift to about 17 points, or 16 with a very good fit for partner.

Similarly, an opening two-bid in a suit is forcing for one round and promises that opener will make another bid. Therefore, if responder is interested in slam, he must show strength no later than his second turn. If the opener has a real powerhouse, he can jump in a new suit on his second turn; this also forces his partner to keep the bidding open.

Finally, when your side has a part-score, any bid of four notrump by either partner is Blackwood and asks for aces.

Following these simple, logical rules will enable you to reach many good slams when you have a partial. I urge you to discuss them with your favorite rubber-bridge partners.

Having a part-score gives you a little more leeway to deceive and confuse the opponents. If you are first or second to speak, I advocate that you play pretty much your usual game. But once partner has passed, you can "operate" without fear of missing a game or a slam. For instance, you can open one notrump on any balanced hand with from 15 to 22 high-card points when you have 60 or more on score:

North dealer
Both sides vulnerable
North-South 60 on score

```
                    ♠ 10 9 8 7
                    ♡ J 7 2
                    ♢ J 10
                    ♣ K 10 4 2
        ♠ K 6 4           N          ♠ Q 5 3
        ♡ A Q 9 8 5                  ♡ 6 3
        ♢ K 6 3 2     W       E      ♢ 8 7 5
        ♣ 3               S          ♣ J 9 8 7 5
                    ♠ A J 2
                    ♡ K 10 4
                    ♢ A Q 9 4
                    ♣ A Q 6
```

THE BIDDING:

N	E	S	W
Pass	Pass	1 NT	2 ♡
Pass	Pass	Double	Pass
Pass	Pass		

South's reopening double tells partner: "I have more strength than you would normally expect for my one-notrump bid. If you have a long suit, you can safely bid even at the three-level; if you have a weak balanced hand with a couple of high cards, we should be able to beat this contract." Depending on the defense and declarer play, North-South should collect either 500 or 800; if declarer panics, he may even go for 1100. Note that if South opens with one of a suit, his side will be unable to make a penalty double of a low-level heart contract.

In the same way, you can "preempt" in third or fourth seat with a very strong hand.

♠ A 3   ♡ K Q J 10 8 6 3   ◇ A 7   ♣ J 9

In third seat with a part-score, open three hearts; if the opponents compete, double at your next turn to bid. The double indicates more defensive strength than one would expect from a normal three-heart opening. Partner can usually figure out whether to defend or to bid on in hearts. The important thing is that you have lied about the strength of your hand, not about the type of hand that it is. Of course, if partner were not a passed hand you would open one heart, for fear of missing a slam.

With a partial you're in the catbird seat, but there are pitfalls. Opponents who were reluctant to double your overcalls, especially two of a major suit, will double much more freely when their action does not risk giving away a game bonus if the contract makes, since you're at the game level already.

bridge

East dealer
Both sides vulnerable
North-South 60 on score

```
                        ♠ J 10 9 3
                        ♡ 6
                        ◇ J 7 5 4
                        ♣ K Q 10 9
        ♠ 6 2                          ♠ A K 8 7
        ♡ K 9 8 3         N            ♡ Q 10
        ◇ A Q 8      W         E       ◇ 10 9 3 2
        ♣ J 8 6 4         S            ♣ A 7 5
                        ♠ Q 5 4
                        ♡ A J 7 5 4 2
                        ◇ K 6
                        ♣ 3 2
```

THE BIDDING:

E	S	W	N
1 ♠	2 ♡	Double	Pass
Pass	Pass		

West might or might not double you "into game" if you
had nothing below the line; with your 60 on score, his action
is clear-cut. You will be set to the tune of 800 points — and
East-West are unlikely either to bid or to make a game. At any
score your overcall is questionable; with a partial, it's suicidal.
Compete by all means; but make sure that your two-level
overcalls are based on good suits.

THE OPPONENTS HAVE A PART-SCORE

Too often I have seen players permit the opponents to
play undisturbed in a two-level contract on the first deal of the
rubber and then give up penalty after penalty in an attempt
to prevent conversion. The best time to compete, of course, is
during the first deal — it's sounder to give up a small penalty
to prevent the partial in the first place than to try to stop the
opponents from converting it, for they will still be favorites to
score a game after taking the penalty.

Enter the battle, by all means, but be sure your armor is
not tattered. Your best protection, for an overcall, is a very

good suit, even if your hand is slightly weaker in high-card strength than it ought to be. Make slightly shaded takeout doubles, if you like, but make sure your distribution compensates for your shortage of high cards.

Remember that your opponents will be only too happy to settle for a penalty from you instead of their game. And, even more important, once you compete you are inviting your partner into the auction. He will be eager to contest and will be unlikely to consider that you were stretching in the first place. So, except with an ultra-conservative partner, don't stretch.

There is a popular misconception that in these circumstances one should be more aggressive in bidding games, in order to wipe out that obnoxious partial. I am unable to account for such fallacious reasoning. If you stop in a part-score and make it, on the next deal both sides will have a part-score and you will be on equal terms with your opponents. Whereas if you do go down in a thin game, you will be confronted by the same part-score situation all over again. Therefore you should be more, not less conservative in bidding game when the opponents have a partial; don't bid game unless your chances are at least even money.

Should you buy or sell? These odds will tell

Thus far, we have been concerned mainly with the odds as they apply to deals on which your side has the superior force. But, while it's very pleasant to have a bidding "conversation" with your partner, punctuated only by the opponents' meek passes, this doesn't always happen. Unless you are a phenomenally good card holder, about half the time your opponents will enter the auction first. And once the opponents open the bidding, the odds are against your side's holding the balance of high cards (assuming you're not looking at about 20 points yourself).

The key to competitive bidding lies not so much in your high-card strength but in your distribution. Do the opponents' hands seem to "fit"? Then, if you have a long suit or two, your partner p.obably has support for one or both of them. Are the opponents grappling around for a spot in which to play the hand? Then they will be happy to double you if you stick your neck out — and you will often find that they couldn't have made their contract.

Alas, by the time the opponents have finished telling each other all about their hands (with you eavesdropping, of course), the bidding is already too high for you to come in safely. "If it were done, when 'tis done, then 'twere well it were done quickly," Macbeth said. And so should you. Inform partner as fast as you can and as clearly as you can once battle has been joined, and let him carry the attack from there.

Any time you come into the auction after the opponents have bid, you lay yourself open to the possibility of taking a large and costly set. Therefore, while you do not intend always to pass tamely and let the opponents steal you blind, you must have a definite purpose to justify your risk. It might be

telling your partner you have a strong hand, so you can bid a game,

or

attempting to find a fit with partner, so you can reach a game or outbid the opponents for a part-score,

or

pushing the opponents too high, to a contract they can't make,

or

jamming the bidding to help the opponents reach the wrong contract,

or

indicating a good opening lead to partner,

or

(rarely at rubber bridge) suggesting a cheap sacrifice.

To achieve these goals, your weapons are: the overcall, the preemptive jump overcall, the takeout double, and (infrequently) the cue-bid.

THE TAKEOUT DOUBLE

By far the safest attack is the takeout double. The most important message of the takeout double is. "Partner, I have support for the other three suits, as well as a fair hand." Notice I have said "fair," not "good." In the early days of bridge, a takeout double would be based on high cards, with little attention to distribution. All it did was warn the opponents that a lot of high cards were massed against them; and it permitted only infrequent use of a most useful call.

East, the dealer, bids one club, and as South you hold (your side vulnerable):

♠ K 7 3 2   ♡ K 10 6 2   ◇ A J 7 4   ♣ 4

Double! You have only eleven points in high cards, but you have the perfect "shape" for a takeout double. What can happen to you? The odds definitely are highly in favor of North holding a four-card major or diamond suit. Even if he holds no high cards, you will have a good trump fit, so it is unlikely you will be doubled — while East-West have a game. Even if your partner has the very worst possible hand, something like

♠ Q 5 4   ♡ 7 5   ◇ 8 6 5   ♣ 10 7 5 3 2

one of the opponents will have to want to double your partner's bid at the one-level and the other will have to stand for the double. This is possible, and happens once in a while, but it is very unlikely. After all, the greatest experts have taken huge sets every now and then; why not take a small chance at the one-level?

But there is no reason why partner should have that terrible hand above. The full deal might easily be:

```
                    ♠ A 8
                    ♡ Q J 9 8 5
                    ◇ Q 10 2
                    ♣ 9 7 3
      ♠ J 10 6 5          N          ♠ Q 9 4
      ♡ 7 4                          ♡ A 3
      ◇ 9 8 5       W         E      ◇ K 6 3
      ♣ A J 6 2          S          ♣ K Q 10 8 5
                    ♠ K 7 3 2
                    ♡ K 10 6 2
                    ◇ A J 7 4
                    ♣ 4
```

bridge

E	S	W	N
1 ♣	Double	2 ♣	4 ♡
Pass	Pass	Pass	

North has only nine high-card points, but he knows that you will be able to support his heart suit and that you are probably very short in clubs. (If you are not short in clubs, you should have additional high cards as compensation.) North is pleased to have a respectable hand with no "wasted values" in clubs; he knows that the play for game must be excellent and therefore bids it directly. With the diamond king onside, he makes an overtrick and you score plus 650.

Now see what happens if you decide your hand "isn't good enough to double." East bids one club, you pass, and West responds one spade. Your partner passes, East raises to two spades. Having decided you are not strong enough to force partner to bid at the one-level, you are certainly not going to do an about-face now and force him to come in at the three-level. So you and West and North pass and you defend against two spades undoubled. This contract goes a quiet two down for plus 100 to North-South (if you defend brilliantly, you might beat it three tricks). Scoring 100 points, even 150, is inadequate compensation for missing a game, worth 650 points. Notice that I have not even given the opponents a hand — and there are thousands of them — on which they will *make* two spades and you are still laydown for four hearts.

A good rule of thumb for light takeout doubles is: the higher the level at which partner must bid, the better hand you need to double. Therefore, you might double one club or one diamond with only a good ten high-card points and appropriate distribution, but you should set 11 high-card points as the minimum for a double of one heart and twelve for a double of one spade. By "good points" I mean defensive tricks — do not double unless you have two defensive tricks in your hand.

If you and your partner are going to make light takeout doubles, based primarily on distribution, it stands to reason that neither of you should be tempted to pass the double for penalties without a very good reason. That reason must be a very strong trump holding, plus a scattering of outside strength. You would pass a double of one club with

♠ A 5   ♡ Q 9   ◇ 8 5 2   ♣ Q J 10 9 6 2

Here you want to play a club contract, even though partner has only a singleton, or perhaps a void. But with a hand such as

♠ Q 5 4   ♡ Q 10 3   ◇ Q 10 2   ♣ K J 10 8

your proper bid is one notrump, which shows about 9-11 points and the opponents' suit well stopped. Note that here you don't really want to play a club contract, because the opponents are likely to have at least eight and possibly nine clubs between their two hands.

Never pass a double from fright. If you have a bad hand and no four-card suit other than the opponents', bid your cheapest three-card suit. With a hand such as

♠ 6 5   ♡ J 3   ◇ J 8 6   ♣ K 10 7 6 3 2

if your partner doubles one club, your correct call is *one diamond.* Passing one club doubled would be very bad; the opponents are likely to make overtricks despite your six trumps. When you leave in a double at the one-level, you must be able to *draw trumps,* as the opponents will probably take at least seven tricks if they are permitted to score winners via ruffs, and your clubs simply aren't good enough for this purpose. Every once in a while your opponents will be able to double one diamond, but that's life. A small penalty at the one-level is better than allowing the opponents to make a doubled contract, very likely with expensive overtricks, and most of the time you will escape undoubled. In fact, the most likely result is that the opponents will ignore your interruption and bid on, allowing you to retire thankfully from the auction. Remember that your one-diamond bid does not announce any points, distribution, or general values. It merely announces, "partner, you have asked me to bid my best suit regardless of the strength of my hand. The best I can do at this time is to show a diamond suit of (probably) four cards." If partner bids again based on this information, he should have a very powerful hand. If he bids two diamonds, for example, he is likely to have five trumps and about 17 points, in which case you will not be too badly off.

There is another type of hand on which you will want to make a takeout double. That is a hand with a self-sufficient suit and considerable outside strength:

♠ K Q J 10 9 6   ♡ A 6   ◇ A J 7 4   ♣ 4

In the earlier days of bridge, one would announce this type of hand to partner by making a jump overcall of two spades over East's one-club opening. Modern bidders, however, reserve the single jump overcall for preemptive purposes, and use it with hands that contain a strong suit and little or no outside strength. They handle the example hand by doubling one club and then bidding spades over partner's response. This shows a hand too good to make a simple overcall. Remember the hand partner had in response to your first double of one club?

♠ A 8   ♡ Q J 9 8 5   ◇ Q 10 2   ♣ 9 7 3

Partner will again respond with four hearts, which you will correct to four spades, a virtually laydown contract.

Sometimes, of course, you will be blessed with a strong hand in addition to suitable distribution. You tell partner the good news on future rounds of bidding:

♠ K Q 10 5   ♡ A Q J 2   ◇ 2   ♣ A K 9 8

With neither side vulnerable, East bids one diamond and you double. West passes, North bids one spade and East passes. Even if partner has a Yarborough with four trumps, you will have a good play for nine tricks. So you bid three spades, saying "Partner, I think we can make three spades even if you have a terrible hand. With anything that looks useful bid game." Partner accepts the invitation, for the complete deal is:

```
                    ♠ J 9 7 3
                    ♡ K 8 3
                    ◇ 7 6 3
                    ♣ 10 4 3
        ♠ 8 6 4                    ♠ A 2
        ♡ 7 6 5 4      N           ♡ 10 9
        ◇ Q 9 5     W     E        ◇ A K J 10 8 4
        ♣ 7 6 2        S           ♣ Q J 5
                    ♠ K Q 10 5
                    ♡ A Q J 2
                    ◇ 2
                    ♣ A K 9 8
```

North was not discouraged by his "flat" distribution and four points. Very properly, he told himself, "Partner says we can make three spades if I have nothing but four trumps. I also have the king of hearts, which must be useful — hearts is one of partner's suits." If North's king were in diamonds, he would have passed three spades. A king in the opponents' suit is less likely to be useful, and in fact game could not be made as North would not have been able to enter his hand to take heart finesses.

If South's hand were the same except that he had the two of clubs instead of the king, he would bid only two spades; North would then know he needed a bit more for game and would quietly pass. Finally, if South had a minimum double, he would pass partner's non-jump response of one spade.

The takeout double conveys a very specific message to partner:

"I can support your suit, or if not, I have a strong independent suit of my own and a strong hand.

"I have distributional as well as high-card values.

"My hand is better for offense than defense. If we have a fit, we should be able to make a part-score; if you have some working high cards also, we may be able to make a game."

If this message is to come through ungarbled, it is important that you do not make takeout doubles on the wrong kind of hands. You will have plenty of opportunity to use the takeout double on hands when the message is the right one.

bridge

With both sides vulnerable, East deals and bids one spade and you, South, hold:

$$\spadesuit \text{Q 6 4} \qquad \heartsuit \text{A J 3} \qquad \diamondsuit \text{Q J 8} \qquad \clubsuit \text{K 8 7 2}$$

Do you double? Of course not. While you have at least three-card support for any suit partner may bid, your hand possesses no trick-taking potential outside of its high cards. The queen of spades, for example, is more likely to take a trick on defense than offense. If your partner has a distributional hand with some high-card points, he will contest the bidding, trusting your double, and you may be in serious difficulty at the three-level. If the opponents have a fit, they will have been told the location of all the outstanding high cards. The full deal might be:

```
                    ♠ 3
                    ♡ 10 9 7 2
                    ◇ 10 7 6 5
                    ♣ J 10 6 4
     ♠ J 9 8 5          N          ♠ A K 10 7 2
     ♡ K 6 5                       ♡ Q 8 4
     ◇ A 4 3 2     W       E       ◇ K 9
     ♣ 9 3             S           ♣ A Q 5
                    ♠ Q 6 4
                    ♡ A J 3
                    ◇ Q J 8
                    ♣ K 8 7 2
```

THE BIDDING:

E	S	W	N
1 ♠	Double(?)	2 ♠	Pass
3 ♠	Pass	4 ♠	Pass
Pass	Pass		

You lead the queen of diamonds, the only lead that does not cost a trick right away. Without your *information* double, declarer might take the losing club finesse. But on this auction, he knows the club king will be offside, so he looks around for a better line of play. Thus, declarer will ruff out the diamonds and throw you in with the queen of spades to lead a heart from the ace or a club from the king. He will lose a spade and either two hearts and no clubs or one heart and one club, making his game contract.

On this deal, partner was too weak to compete, and therefore you were in no danger of losing a heavy penalty. But your double helped declarer make a contract in which he might otherwise have gone down. That's a gift to the opponents of 720 points. Risks should be taken in bridge only when you have a clear idea of what you may gain as well as what you may lose — and your hand was too poor offensively for any sizable gain to be likely unless partner could bid on his own.

Does this mean you should never enter the auction, once the opponents have opened, with a balanced hand? In general, yes. You will not want your side to be declarer unless your partner can take some action. The exception is when you have enough high-card points so that you may "own the deal."

The one notrump overcall

With a balanced hand of 16-18 points — an opening one-notrump bid — you convey the good news to partner by overcalling with one notrump. Of course, you need the opponents' suit well stopped. For instance, as South, you hold:

♠ A J 5   ♡ K J 3   ◇ Q J 10 3   ♣ A J 10

Over East's opening bid of one spade, you bid one notrump, at any vulnerability. Indeed, you would make the same call over any one-of-a-suit bid by East.

Partner gets an instant picture of your hand, just as he does when you open the bidding with one notrump. Moreover, the playing strength of a one-notrump overcall is usually greater than that of a one-notrump opening bid even though the point count is the same. When you open one notrump, you have no idea how the opponents' strength is divided; but when you overcall, the cards are favorably placed for you, for the opening bidder on your right is marked with most of the missing strength. Therefore, your finesses are going to work!

Partner's responses to your notrump overcall are exactly
the same as though you had opened with one notrump. With
a weak balanced hand, such as

♠ 10 2   ♥ Q 7 4   ♦ K 9 3 2   ♣ 9 5 4 2

he passes, and you will probably just make one notrump. With
a balanced hand and eight or nine points,

♠ 10 2   ♥ A 7 4   ♦ K 9 3 2   ♣ Q 9 5 4

he will raise to two notrump. With your fine 17-point hand,
you will not hesitate to go to game.

With a hand of game-going strength, partner can bid
three notrump:

♠ Q 3   ♥ A 7 4   ♦ K 6 5 2   ♣ K 9 4 2

With a hand such as

♠ 10 3   ♥ A Q 9 4 2   ♦ K 6 5   ♣ Q 9 4

partner should bid three hearts (forcing, as is any jump to the
three-level in a suit). If you have three-card or larger support
for partner, you should bid four hearts, as his bid promises a
five-card suit. Otherwise you will bid three notrump, knowing
that partner has about ten points. Of course, if partner has a
six-card suit, he can take matters into his own hands:

♠ 10 3   ♥ A Q 9 8 4 2   ♦ K 6   ♣ Q 9 4

A jump to four hearts is the correct bid. Partner knows
that you have at least two hearts to provide him with a minimum of eight trumps in the combined hands, since you may
not overcall one notrump with a void or singleton in any suit.
He has no reason to bid three hearts; why give away information to the opponents with an extra round of bidding?

On some hands, bidding the opponents' suit is the best
way of exploring for the best game contract:

♠ 10 3   ♥ A Q 9 8   ♦ K 6   ♣ Q 9 4 3 2

Bidding three notrump on this hand might work out well,
but frequently three notrump is not the best contract on this
sort of hand. As I point out later, bidding is an attempt to
locate a good suit fit if possible. If you have four hearts,

partner will want to play in hearts. He cannot jump to three hearts immediately, because that would show a five-card suit; so he bids *two spades*, the opponents' suit. If you have four hearts, you bid them; if you don't, he will settle for three notrump.

With a weak unbalanced hand, partner will just bid his suit at the two-level, the way he would have over one notrump. On the following hand, his correct response is two hearts:

♠ 3   ♡ Q 10 8 6 5 4   ◇ 9 3   ♣ 9 7 4 2

Of course, if partner has no high cards at all you may be headed for trouble. The opponents will call this to your attention by doubling one notrump. But even when you are doubled, partner may be able to run out to a long suit — he knows he will find support for his suit in your hand. Of course, there will be times when you are doubled and set; if this never happens to you, you are probably not competing often enough and are letting the opponents play too many hands that properly belong to your side. The idea to remember is that you are risking an occasional 500-point penalty in the hope of frequently making games and part-scores. Furthermore, if the opponents choose to bid on, your partner, who knows you have a strong hand with defensive strength, can double for penalties, just as he could have done had you opened one notrump and the opponents competed. But note that it should be the *partner* of the one-notrump overcaller, not the overcaller himself, who should double. The one-notrump bid tells one player's story — his partner can supply the denouement.

Suit overcalls at the one-level

"How many points do you need to overcall in a suit?" is a question I frequently am asked. As far as high-card points are concerned, there are six-point hands that are eminently suitable overcalls and fifteen-point hands on which it is better to preserve a discreet silence. The strength of the suit, not the hand, is the key question.

When an opponent opens the bidding, the odds favor his

side having the preponderance of high cards. When you have a hand suitable for a takeout double, however, your support for all unbid suits puts the odds to work in your favor; it is very likely partner has a fit for one of your suits. With a one-suited hand, however, the odds are not so kind; it is still most likely that this is not "your hand."

Why not "go quietly"? Well, quite often you should. But equally often, you can drive a spoke into the placid progress of the opponents' auction. Sometimes you can bid and make a contract yourself; sometimes you can pay a small penalty to avert a larger loss; sometimes you can direct partner to the best defense; and, most satisfying of all, sometimes you can lead the opponents out of their depth.

Overcalling can be a dangerous business. Good opponents like to make penalty doubles of overcalls. But if you will restrict your interference bids to hands on which attainment of either of two of the above goals seems feasible, the odds favor your doing no worse than breaking even. My own prediction is that you will come out ahead.

As South, you hold:

♠ A K 10 4 2   ♡ 6 5   ◇ Q 9 6   ♣ K 3 2

East, on your right, opens with one club. A one-spade over-call has a lot going for it: You may be able to make a spade contract, you certainly want a spade lead if West is declarer, and West will be unable to bid diamonds or hearts at the one-level. The complete deal:

East dealer
Neither side vulnerable

```
                    ♠ J 9 8
                    ♡ J 8 3
                    ◇ A J 10 5 3
                    ♣ 8 5
    ♠ Q 7 5                      ♠ 6 3
    ♡ A 10 9 7       N           ♡ K Q 4 2
    ◇ 7 4         W     E        ◇ K 8 2
    ♣ J 9 7 4        S           ♣ A Q 10 6
                    ♠ A K 10 4 2
                    ♡ 6 5
                    ◇ Q 9 6
                    ♣ K 3 2
```

THE BIDDING:

E	S	W	N
1 ♣	1 ♠	2 ♣	2 ♠
Pass	Pass	Pass	

Notice the preemptive effect of your overcall. West cannot bid his heart suit — he is not nearly strong enough to bid a new suit at the two-level — and must content himself with a simple raise to two clubs. North, who knows that you have good spades and a fair number of high cards, competes to two spades, and both opponents, with balanced hands and no knowledge of their heart fit, are shut out.

In spades, you will lose two heart tricks and a trick in each of the other suits, scoring up 110 points (60 trick score and 50 for the partial). East-West can easily make three hearts, for plus 140. The overcall gains you a comfortable 250 points.

Let's consider what odds you are giving. Sometimes West will hold:

♠ Q J 9 8 7 5   ♡ A 10 9   ◇ K 4   ♣ J 9

With this hand, he has a clear-cut double of one spade. If your partner has a Yarborough, you will be held to (probably) four tricks and a 500-point penalty. But if partner has no working high cards, the opponents are cold for three notrump, possibly with overtricks. Let's say they will make four notrump on the average. You are risking 70 points (a possible 500-point penalty instead of 430 points for three notrump, making four) in order to gain 250 points. That's odds of almost four to one in your favor. Furthermore, East-West could be cold for *four* hearts — a not-too-remote possibility. In addition, overcalls at the one-level are very rarely punished. If West has enough spades to feel he can take a substantial number of tricks in a trump suit he knows is breaking badly for him, East is likely to have very few spades and not let the double stand.

The preemptive value of a one-spade overcall of a one-club opening bid is so valuable that there are even *four-card* suits on which the overcall should occasionally be made. Take this amusing deal:

bridge

North dealer
East-West vulnerable

```
            ♠ 9 4 3
            ♡ 10 4 3
            ◇ 5 3 2
            ♣ 10 8 7 4
♠ 6 5 2              ♠ J 8 7
♡ K Q 9 8 6    N    ♡ A J
◇ A Q 9     W     E  ◇ K 10 4
♣ Q 3          S    ♣ A J 9 5 2
            ♠ A K Q 10
            ♡ 7 5 2
            ◇ J 8 7 6
            ♣ K 6
```

See how the bidding will go if you tamely pass, with the South hand, over one club:

N	E	S	W
Pass	1 ♣	Pass?	1 ♡
Pass	1 NT	Pass	3 NT
Pass	Pass	Pass	

You will collect your four spade tricks, and the opponents will take five heart tricks, three diamonds and the ace of clubs, making three notrump and scoring 600 points.

Now look what happens if you "borrow" the six of clubs and put it in with your spades.

N	E	S	W
Pass	1 ♣	1 ♠!	2 ♡
Pass	3 ♣	Pass	3 ◇
Pass	3 ♡	Pass	4 ♡
Pass	Pass	Pass	

East·and West have done nothing wrong. With 27 points in high cards alone between them and no apparent misfit, they bid game. Clearly they cannot bid three notrump with no stopper in your suit. And just as clearly they cannot make four hearts. Plus 100 for you, instead of minus 600.

The overcall on a four-card suit is not to be lightly indulged in. Three honors in the suit is a minimum requirement, for if West chooses to double, East may have several spades and be happy to play for penalties. Furthermore, when you do make such an overcall partner is unlikely to raise without at least three trumps, since he will not have an honor in your suit. When it works, the four-card spade overcall collects all the marbles.

Bad overcalls are punished not only by penalty doubles. On the following hand, with neither side vulnerable, East opens with one club, and you hold:

♠ J   ♡ A 6 5   ◇ J 8 5 4 3 2   ♣ K 8 2

If you overcall one diamond, you are not playing the odds. The complete deal may well be as follows:

```
                    ♠ 7 4 2
                    ♡ Q J 9 7 4
                    ◇ K 10
                    ♣ 9 7 3
        ♠ A Q 9 8 5          ♠ K 10 6 3
        ♡ 10 3 2      N      ♡ K 8
        ◇ Q 9 6    W   E     ◇ A 7
        ♣ 10 6        S      ♣ A Q J 5 4
                    ♠ J
                    ♡ A 6 5
                    ◇ J 8 5 4 3 2
                    ♣ K 8 2
```

Since your one-diamond overcall doesn't use up any of the opponents' bidding room, they proceed merrily to four spades. North looks at his hand and very reasonably says to himself: "Well, we'd better cash our diamond tricks before dummy's clubs are set up." After North's lead of the king of diamonds, East-West make five spades (six if you don't cash your ace of hearts when you win the king of clubs). Let's assume you cash, and East-West score 450.

Left to his own devices, North will lead the queen of hearts. If dummy covers, you win and shift to a diamond through declarer's queen. When you win the king of clubs, you lead a second diamond and North cashes the diamond and another heart. Down one, for plus 50.

Your overcall has cost you 500 points. What kind of odds did you get for this minus? Certainly, the one-diamond bid did not suggest the best lead against East-West's contract. Your diamond suit is so weak that partner will need a very good hand for you to make a part-score, much less a game. You haven't preempted the opponents by as much as a single call. Offhand, I would say your overcall *gave* the opponents about 20 to 1 odds in their favor. Such expensive gifts should be reserved for anniversaries and birthdays.

Let's look at another example. Neither side is vulnerable. North deals and passes, East bids one club, and you hold:

♠ 9 3 2   ♡ A K J 10 5   ◇ 10 6   ♣ 8 7 4

With partner a passed hand, you are not going to take many tricks in any contract. Do you overcall one heart? Emphatically yes. You have a golden opportunity to tell partner what to lead. This may stop an overtrick or two; when you're in luck, a heart lead may defeat an otherwise ironclad contract.

North dealer
Neither side vulnerable

```
                    ♠ J 10 7 6 4
                    ♡ 9 6
                    ◇ K 8 7 4 3
                    ♣ A
      ♠ K Q 8 5          N          ♠ A
      ♡ Q 8 7                       ♡ 4 3 2
      ◇ J 9 2     W          E      ◇ A Q 5
      ♣ 9 6 3          S          ♣ K Q J 10 5 2
                    ♠ 9 3 2
                    ♡ A K J 10 5
                    ◇ 10 6
                    ♣ 8 7 4
```

THE BIDDING:

N	E	S	W
Pass	1 ♣	1 ♡	1 ♠
Pass	3 ♣	Pass	3 NT

If North makes his normal lead of a diamond, declarer will make at least three notrump. On the lead of the nine of hearts, however, you play the ten, and now West has no chance for his contract.

At first glance, it would appear that your one-heart over-call stands to lose as much as it has to gain (−500 in 1 heart doubled when partner has a worthless hand and you are set three tricks, as compared to a pickup of 480 points for East-West going down one in three notrump instead of making four as in the above example). But the frequency of gain *versus* loss must also be weighed. It is much more likely that the heart lead will pick up points for your side than that you will be doubled and badly defeated at the one-level, for the opponents will find it very difficult to double when you have a good suit.

Since your partner, by now, knows that you overcall only on good suits, he can raise with three small trumps or a doubleton honor:

East dealer
Both sides vulnerable

```
                    ♠ Q 8
                    ♡ A 4 3
                    ◇ A 6 2
                    ♣ 8 7 6 5 2
    ♠ 6 5 4                          ♠ 10 2
    ♡ J 10 9 6        N              ♡ K Q 7 2
    ◇ 10 9 8 4    W       E          ◇ J 5
    ♣ Q 9            S              ♣ A K J 4 3
                    ♠ A K J 9 7 3
                    ♡ 8 5
                    ◇ K Q 7 3
                    ♣ 10
```

East opens one club, and you call one spade, which West passes. If North fears that you may have scattered high cards and bad spades, he has no option but to pass and you will miss a cold game. If you may have a ragged suit, the most likely result from his point of view is that you will lose control of the trump suit and go down in two spades when the opponents couldn't have made anything. But if you have shown a strong suit, he can raise spades with confidence that the doubleton queen will be good support, and his two aces will be useful.

Suit overcalls at the two-level

The two-level is the danger zone for overcallers. Opponents like to double interference bids of two something, especially when "something" is clubs or diamonds and you will not score a game bonus if you make your doubled contract. Even the structure of bidding makes it attractive for your left-hand opponent to say "double." If he has a fit for his partner, he will raise opener's suit; if not, he needs a fairly strong hand to bid a new suit at the two-level. And if he has a fairly strong hand, no fit for partner, and a few cards in your suit — well, a possibly large penalty will seem more enticing than a questionable game.

At the two-level therefore, lead direction alone is not enough of a reason to enter the auction. You need a hand with sufficient offensive potential to suggest a possible game or inexpensive sacrifice. And, especially if your suit is a minor, your overcall must be based on a strong suit — the kind that will produce tricks at notrump if your partner has scattered highcard values and a stopper in the opponents' suit, for it is most unlikely that your hands will stretch to a minor-suit game requiring eleven tricks. For example:

West dealer
North-South vulnerable

```
                    ♠ K J 9
                    ♡ J 10 7 5
                    ◇ K 10 6
                    ♣ K 4 2
    ♠ 8 4 3 2              N        ♠ A Q 10 7 5
    ♡ 4 3 2                         ♡ A K 9 8
    ◇ Q J 8 3 2     W       E       ◇ 7
    ♣ 9                    S        ♣ 7 5 3
                    ♠ 6
                    ♡ Q 6
                    ◇ A 9 5 4
                    ♣ A Q J 10 8 6
```

THE BIDDING:

W	N	E	S
Pass	Pass	1 ♠	2 ♣
Pass (or 2 ♠)	2 NT	Pass	3 NT
Pass	Pass	Pass	

The same strong club suit that produces the notrump game protects you from a heavy penalty if West, rather than North, has the outstanding high-card strength. Even if partner's hand is useless, you can take six or seven tricks in your own hand. And if you are doubled and go down two, the opponents probably have a game. Therefore, the odds in favor of overcalling are good.

We have all heard a player protest: "But I had an opening bid, partner," as an 800 was being written down in the "They" column of the score sheet. I hope you've never heard yourself say this. If you have an opening bid, by all means open the bidding if you get the chance. But if any opponent gets his bid in first, don't confuse the requirements for an opening bid with the requirements for an overcall.

East dealer
Both sides vulnerable

```
                  ♠ Q 9 6
                  ♡ J 8 7 3
                  ◇ 7 5
                  ♣ J 7 5 2
      ♠ 4                       ♠ A J 8 7 3 2
      ♡ A Q 9 4      N          ♡ 10 5 2
      ◇ K 10 8 3   W   E        ◇ Q 6
      ♣ 10 8 6 3     S          ♣ A K
                  ♠ K 10 5
                  ♡ K 6
                  ◇ A J 9 4 2
                  ♣ Q 9 4
```

THE BIDDING:

E	S	W	N
1 ♠	2 ◇?	Double	Pass
Pass	Pass		

bridge

Unfortunately for South, the defense was very accurate. West led a spade and ruffed the spade return. He played a club to East's king, ruffed another spade, and returned a club to his partner's ace. East shifted to a heart; West won the queen when declarer played low, gave his partner a club ruff with a low trump, and won his ace of hearts. A fourth round of clubs was ruffed by East with the queen, setting up two more trump tricks for the defense. Down 1400!

East-West, with 23 high-card points and no fit, are most unlikely to bid a game, even if they could make one. South, with honors in all suits, doesn't even particularly want a diamond lead. His is the sort of hand that can bid strongly if partner takes action; with a silent partner a discreet silence is called for. The moral should be clear: South's *hand* may have been good enough to overcall, but his *suit* wasn't.

Sacrifice bidding

The close sacrifices, where you take a 500-point set to prevent the opponents scoring 620 points, should be left to the duplicate bridge expert. But the really inexpensive sacrifice, where you go down one trick to prevent a game, is odds-on. Paying out 100 points instead of 620 is five to one in your favor; you can afford to be wrong every so often and discover that you are minus 100 instead of plus 100 because the opponents would not have made their contract. Make the margin of error more than one trick, however, and those favorable odds diminish to unfavorable odds with alarming rapidity.

Let's swing into the North seat, where you hold:

♠ J 7 6 3   ♡ 5 2   ◇ 6   ♣ A 9 7 6 5 2

With East-West vulnerable, the bidding goes:

E	S	W	N
1 ◇	1 ♠	2 ♡	2 ♠
3 ♡	Pass	4 ♡	?

Do you take the four-spade save? The answer to this question is yet another question: "What kind of overcalls does South make?"

If South is a player who bids on scattered values, the full deal is likely to be:

```
              ♠ J 7 6 3
              ♡ 5 2
              ◊ 6
              ♣ A 9 7 6 5 2
♠ 9                          ♠ A K 10
♡ K 9 8 7 3      N           ♡ Q 6 4
◊ A 8 7 3     W     E        ◊ K 10 5 4 2
♣ K J 10         S           ♣ Q 8
              ♠ Q 8 5 4 2
              ♡ A J 10
              ◊ Q J 9
              ♣ 4 3
```

Disaster! East will double four spades and you will be minus 300 instead of plus 100 (or 200, if partner elects to double four hearts). Yes, East would have been better off bidding two notrump rather than three hearts over your two-spade raise. But with no club stopper he can scarcely be blamed for raising partner's known five-card heart suit.

Does partner make intelligent overcalls, with strength concentrated in the bid suit? Then, you will do well to bid four spades, for the complete deal might well be:

```
              ♠ J 7 6 3
              ♡ 5 2
              ◊ 6
              ♣ A 9 7 6 5 2
♠ 4                          ♠ A 8
♡ K Q 9 6 3      N           ♡ J 10 8 7
◊ Q J 7 2     W     E        ◊ A K 10 5 3
♣ K Q 10         S           ♣ J 3
              ♠ K Q 10 9 5 2
              ♡ A 4
              ◊ 9 8 4
              ♣ 8 4
```

On this hand, the opponents will make four hearts (620) and you will be down one (100) at four spades, which is pretty good odds by anyone's standards. But you even have an added advantage. West, with his diamond fit, may choose to go on to five hearts. Now the lead of your singleton diamond will defeat the contract (as long as your partner wakes up when a trump is led, jumps up with his ace, and gives you a diamond ruff). Your four-spade bid will have gained not 520 but 720 points!

In general, sacrificing should be reserved for the fortunate times when you are playing with the best of the other three players at the table. There's no telling what a bad player will do to you on the next hand, should you try to prolong the rubber. Furthermore, you can sacrifice with confidence with a good partner, for he will tend to make intelligent overcalls; while sacrifices based on a poor player's overcalls are likely to prove calamitous.

Preemptive jump overcalls

There was a time when a single jump overcall showed a powerful hand with high card strength and excellent offensive potential. After a one-club opening, a two-heart overcall showed a hand such as:

♠ K Q 2   ♡ A K J 10 9 5   ◇ A 10 3   ♣ 8

This strength-showing jump overcall is a descriptive and useful bid. The trouble with it is that it isn't useful often enough, because the odds are heavily against your holding such a hand. So, many players, myself included, now describe a hand of this strength by first making a takeout double and then bidding hearts. This reserves the single jump overcall for bad hands with good suits. It is purely preemptive in design. With the opponents vulnerable, you would bid three diamonds over an opening bid of one spade on your right with

♠ 3 2   ♡ 7 4   ◇ K Q J 10 9 6   ♣ Q J 9

Your normal trick-taking expectancy is six. If partner's hand is useless to you, you are risking a 500-point penalty. If this occurs, however, it is likely that East-West can make a game, so the odds are a little better than even. If partner has some useful card like the king of clubs, the opponents may still be able to make a game and you will be minus only 100 (if they choose to double you), which will represent a sizable gain.

The big plus value of the preemptive jump overcall, like any other preemptive bid, is that it steals bidding room from the other side. No longer do they have ample time and space to explore their best contract. They must guess.

East dealer
Both sides vulnerable

```
                    ♠ K 7 6
                    ♡ 8 7 6
                    ◇ 7 2
                    ♣ K 10 9 5 4
        ♠ 5 4                     ♠ A 3
        ♡ A K Q 3 2      N        ♡ J 10
        ◇ 10 6 3     W       E    ◇ K Q J 8 5
        ♣ Q 8 7          S        ♣ A J 6 3
                    ♠ Q J 10 9 8 2
                    ♡ 9 5 4
                    ◇ A 9 4
                    ♣ 2
```

THE BIDDING:

E	S	W	N
1 ◇	2 ♠	3 ♡	Pass
3 NT	Pass	Pass	Pass

Your two-spade overcall could conceivably go for 800, but with partner's spade fit and doubleton diamond, you can almost *make* two spades. It succeeds in jamming the opponents into the wrong game. East has a difficult problem over three hearts; it is hard to fault him for not carrying the auction beyond three notrumps with a spade stopper he would get no other opportunity to show. A red-suit game is, of course, laydown; three notrump is defeated.

Preemptive jump overcalls are not restricted to single jumps. The weaker your hand on defense and the longer and stronger your suit, the more you bid. Thus, not vulnerable, with

♠ K Q J 10 8 7 3   ♡ 9 4 2   ◇ 10 3   ♣ 2

bid *three* spades over an opponent's one-diamond opening.

bridge

The chief purpose of preemptive jump overcalls is to deprive the opponents of bidding space and, hopefully, steer them into the wrong contract. Of course, sometimes a preempt will buy the contract, and sometimes it will suggest a game or a profitable save to partner. The important thing for the overcaller to remember is that he has already described his hand — partner is now in charge. A preempter should *never* bid again, but should always leave the decision to partner. Partner should be guided by: 1] a fit in overcaller's suit; 2] distribution — singletons in other suits will probably be very useful; and 3] aces. Minor honors are much more valuable on defense (usually) when partner has made a weak jump overcall.

Cue-bids

All too rarely, "you have your shoes off counting your points," as one of my Ozark mountain friends used to say, and much to your surprise, right-hand opponent opens the bidding. The time has come to bring out the strongest forcing bid — the cue-bid in the opponents' suit.

As most Americans play it, the cue-bid unconditionally forces partner until game is reached. It alerts partner to the possibility of a slam, even if he has very slender values. Thus, you must limit your cue-bids to hands on which game is odds-on, even if partner is completely broke.

In all of the following examples, East opens the bidding with one club, and you are South:

♠ — ♡ A K Q J 10 7 4 ◇ A K ♣ A J 10 3

Cue-bid two clubs and jump in hearts to show a solid suit and a very powerful hand.

♠ A Q J 10 ♡ A Q 10 6 ◇ A K Q 4 ♣ 10

Normally, it is enough with support for all unbid suits to double and then jump to game over partner's response. This hand, however, is so strong that

♠ 8 3 2 ♡ K 8 7 5 2 ◇ 9 3 ♣ 8 7 6

will produce an odds-on *slam* (the opening bidder should have the king of spades, since there are so few high cards missing). Tell partner the good news at once — cue-bid.

East dealer
North-South vulnerable

```
                        ♠ J 3 2
                        ♡ Q J 3 2
                        ◇ K 2
                        ♣ 8 7 3 2
        ♠ —                        ♠ 8 7 6
        ♡ 9 8 7 5 4      N         ♡ A K 10
        ◇ 10 7 6 5 3   W   E       ◇ J 4
        ♣ J 5 4          S         ♣ K Q 10 9 6
                        ♠ A K Q 10 9 5 4
                        ♡ 6
                        ◇ A Q 9 8
                        ♣ A
```

THE BIDDING:

E	S	W	N
1 ♣	2 ♣	Pass	2 ♡
Pass	2 ♠	Pass	3 ♠
Pass	4 ◇	Pass	5 ◇
Pass	6 ♠	Pass	Pass
Pass			

Partner is able to cue-bid the king of diamonds and you reach a laydown slam. Note that the South hand is near-minimum for a cue-bid.

Doubling all bets

Earlier I mentioned that bridge was so absorbing that sometimes one forgets that the object of the game is to score points. I think this mantle of forgetfulness has descended also upon present-day bridge writers. It is the only explanation I can find for the neglect of that score-producing weapon, the penalty (or business) double.

Great attention is paid to a useful tool, the takeout double. (The British call this the "informatory" double — a strange semantic antic for a call that seeks to elicit rather than convey information.) Currently, it is fashionable to stress the "balancing" double with which you enter the auction after two passes following an opponent's bid. This is valuable, too. But the greatest booster of your winnings (second only to bidding and making games) is the double that says, "I don't think you can make your contract, and I'm willing to risk (possibly) giving you more points so I can score more points myself."

DOUBLES OF PART-SCORE CONTRACTS

What odds are you offering? The riskiest double, of course, is one that will give the opponents a game bonus (written or unwritten) if their contract succeeds (such as a double of two spades or three diamonds) in addition to doubling the trick score and adding 50 points for "the insult." Suppose you double two spades and it is made. Vulnerable, your opponents score 670 (60 plus 60 plus 500 plus 50) instead of 110 (60 trick score plus 50 for the partial), a net gain to them of 560 points. You are risking this amount when you double for a gain of 100 for a one-trick set (200 instead of 100), 300 for a two-trick set (500 instead of 200), and 500 for a three-trick set (800 instead of 300). Therefore it pays to double opponents in this situation (part-score converted into game if made) only when you expect them to go down three. Sometimes you will be disappointed and find you've collected only 200 or 300 points instead of the 800 you were hoping for. But rarely will you find that your judgment has been off by a full *three* tricks so that your opponents will make their contract.

The odds in favor of other doubles are much more attractive. The most "winsome" of all are doubles of minor-suit overcalls at the two-level, or of one-notrump overcalls. Here, your risk is 90 points to the opponents if the contract is just made, so that you are getting even odds for a one-trick set and much better odds thereafter. The most profitable doubles are made against low-level overcalls because the opponents are treading blindly when they enter an auction after your side has opened the bidding. On the one hand, if they don't come in, they risk missing a game; on the other, if they over-call, they risk a large penalty. After a few rounds of bidding, the opponents can tell much better their combined strength and fit. Double before they know enough to keep silent.

♠ 6   ♡ A K 10 2   ◇ K 10 4 2   ♣ 9 5 4 3

With both sides vulnerable, North (your partner) opens one spade, East overcalls two diamonds, and your proper action is to double. The full deal is:

```
                    ♠ A J 10 8 2
                    ♡ Q 4
                    ◇ 8 5
                    ♣ A Q 6 2
    ♠ Q 7 5 4 3          N          ♠ K 9
    ♡ J 7 6 5 3                     ♡ 9 8
    ◇ 7            W         E      ◇ A Q J 9 6 3
    ♣ J 8               S          ♣ K 10 7
                    ♠ 6
                    ♡ A K 10 2
                    ◇ K 10 4 2
                    ♣ 9 5 4 3
```

East has a perfectly sound vulnerable overcall of two diamonds with a good suit; if West held your cards, East-West would be near-laydown for three notrump. Yet you chalk up 500 (the hand can be beaten three tricks, but this would require double-dummy defense).

Did you recognize the most important feature of your hand for doubling? The diamond holding is important, of course, but you should double just as promptly with only three diamonds to the king-ten. The critical suit is *spades*. For in doubling it matters just as much what you can score yourself on a deal as what you are risking the opponents making. A 300- or 500-point penalty is very nice, but a vulnerable game is worth more. The worse your holding is in partner's suit, the less likely you are to be able to make a game. If partner has a second long suit, he should remove your double; you have told him you didn't like his first suit, but you haven't heard about the other one.

Another even more important reason for having a short holding in partner's suit is that the defense will work out better for you this way. If you double two diamonds, you are in effect venturing the opinion that, played in a suit in which you have only five or six cards between you, you expect to take more tricks than your opponents. To do this, you have to be able to draw trumps or, alternatively, score a number of tricks by ruffs. If you and partner are long in a side suit, declarer will be short in that suit and you will take few tricks there. Also, length in partner's suit suggests that either declarer has a very long trump suit, in which case you are not going to take very many tricks, or a long side suit of his own, which you are going to have trouble stopping him from establishing and running.

Here is an example. North again deals and bids one spade, East again ventures two diamonds, and you hold:

♠ K 5 4 2　　♡ A 5 3　　◇ K J 10 9 8　　♣ 6

You have four nearly sure trump tricks! Yet doubling is a very bad action: your spades, heart ace, and club singleton will be even more useful to your partner in a spade contract. The complete deal:

♠ A Q J 10 3
♡ K Q J 6
◇ 2
♣ J 10 7

♠ 9 8 6　　　　　　　　　♠ 7
♡ 10 8 7 4 2　　**N**　　　♡ 9
◇ —　　　**W　　E**　　◇ A Q 7 6 5 4 3
♣ A 8 5 3 2　　**S**　　　♣ K Q 9 4

♠ K 5 4 2
♡ A 5 3
◇ K J 10 9 8
♣ 6

Huffing and puffing, you will beat two diamonds *one trick* for plus 200. Partner will not even have to exert himself to take eleven tricks in spades, with 100 honors to boot, for plus 750. Your correct action over two diamonds is to ignore the interference and bid three spades.

Once again let's consider that popular auction of one spade by North, two diamonds by East, and this time your hand is:

♠ 9 4   ♡ 9 8 7 3   ◇ A J 8 7 5 3   ♣ 6

Having been well trained, you look at your spades and find you have an indifferent fit. Next you look at your diamonds. Clearly nobody is going to make two diamonds against your trump holding. Do you double? Let's see:

North dealer
Both sides vulnerable

```
                    ♠ A Q J 10 7
                    ♡ K Q 10
                    ◇ 4 2
                    ♣ A 4 2
    ♠ 8 6 5                        ♠ K 3 2
    ♡ J 6 5 2          N           ♡ A 4
    ◇ —            W       E       ◇ K Q 10 9 6
    ♣ K Q J 10 9 3      S          ♣ 8 7 5
                    ♠ 9 4
                    ♡ 9 8 7 3
                    ◇ A J 8 7 5 3
                    ♣ 6
```

Holding six diamonds, you should realize that someone at the table will not stand for your double of two diamonds. In this instance it is West, who will retreat to three clubs if you double. North, with a balanced 16-count, will (very properly) double. After all, your double of two diamonds has already told him you don't like spades. You will then be well and truly in the soup; either the opponents will play three clubs doubled and make it, or you will be in trouble after retreating to three spades. Partner will surely bid four spades (he doesn't know how weak your hand is) and he will go down. He will very likely get doubled himself. Had you passed two diamonds, the bidding would probably have ended there, and you would have collected a quiet 200.

So remember, a low-level double, to be effective, should show:

1] No fit for partner's suit: A doubleton *at most*.

2] Defensive tricks outside the trump suit.

3] An adequate, not necessarily great, holding in the opponents' suit.

DOUBLES OF
GAME AND SLAM CONTRACTS

Some bridge players who are overly cautious about making low-level doubles seem to feel that a double of a game bid
is a "free" double. While it is true that the extra cost of doubling, say, a four-spade contract that makes is only 170 points,
at this level redoubles and overtricks come into the picture.
Never double a game merely because you hold high cards. The
opponents know they are missing high cards. All it means is
that you have a good hand and your partner is nearly broke.
The time to double is when there are indications that suits
are not breaking and that your honor cards are favorably
located. Here's a case in point:

```
                    ♠ A Q 10 5 4
                    ♡ K 9 5
                    ◇ 9 3
                    ♣ A J 10
     ♠ 7 3                         ♠ K J 9 8
     ♡ A 7 4 3        N            ♡ J 6 2
     ◇ Q 10 8 7    W     E         ◇ 6 2
     ♣ 5 4 3          S            ♣ K 8 7 6
                    ♠ 6 2
                    ♡ Q 10 8
                    ◇ A K J 5 4
                    ♣ Q 9 2
```

You are East, for a change. With both sides vulnerable,
the bidding proceeds:

W	N	E	S
Pass	1 ♠	Pass	2 ◇
Pass	2 ♠	Pass	2 NT
Pass	3 NT	?	

I suggest that with the spade honors behind the spade
bids, and shortness in the suit bid on your left (suggesting

that your partner will win one or two tricks in diamonds), you should double. Don't be frightened because you have "only eight points." On this bidding, the opponents have nothing left over, and may be stretching slightly to get to game. (Actually, they have a full 26 high-card points, but they might have less.) There should be at least six or seven points in partner's hand, and those points should take tricks. The only forcing bid made in the entire auction was two diamonds, so neither opponent will be able to redouble. Your double will keep partner from making a possibly disastrous lead in a red suit; if he doesn't have a good lead, he will know that he can safely play a spade. This is an unlucky hand for North-South; you double because you know it is unlucky. They have 26 points in high cards and all suits stopped; yet they will probably be set two or three tricks because of the location of the spades and diamonds.

Unluckiness is also devastating to the opponents when you can deduce from the bidding that suits are not breaking well. Being the victim of a defensive cross-ruff is bad enough; being doubled in such a situation is much worse.

With both sides vulnerable, you are West and hold:

♠ A 5 2　　♡ A　　◊ 9 8 7 5　　♣ Q 10 8 6 4

The bidding proceeds:

N	E	S	W
1 ◊	Pass	1 ♡	Pass
2 ♡	Pass	3 ◊	Pass
4 ♡	Pass	Pass	?

The double stands out. Since North opened the bidding with one diamond and subsequently raised hearts twice, he probably has four or five diamonds. South almost surely has four diamonds for his raise. Partner therefore has a singleton or void in diamonds. You have two quick entries to give him diamond ruffs, and (this is most important) you have control of hearts, so that declarer will be unable to draw trumps. Even if partner has a Yarborough, four hearts will surely be set one trick, and it might go down much more. The complete deal:

```
                    ♠ K
                    ♡ Q 9 8 6
                    ◇ K Q 10 6 4
                    ♣ A 9 7
    ♠ A 5 2                        ♠ J 10 8 7 4 3
    ♡ A              N             ♡ 7 5 3 2
    ◇ 9 8 7 5    W       E         ◇ —
    ♣ Q 10 8 6 4     S             ♣ K J 3
                    ♠ Q 9 6
                    ♡ K J 10 4
                    ◇ A J 3 2
                    ♣ 5 2
```

You lead a diamond; partner trumps and returns a spade to your ace. You give partner another diamond ruff, and he plays a club. Declarer wins the ace and leads a trump. You win the ace and give partner a third diamond ruff. He now cashes the king of clubs for a tidy 800 penalty. Lucky? Of course. But you doubled four hearts *because* you knew that you would be lucky. Notice that the North-South bidding is quite sound, and four hearts is a good contract.

The worst doubling crime is not that of doubling the opponents into game. Even more heinous is sounding a warning, by an ill-judged double, so that they fulfill a contract that would otherwise have gone down.

With North-South vulnerable, you hold these cards as West:

♠ K J 9   ♡ K 10 6 2   ◇ Q 8 5   ♣ K Q 10

You hear the following bidding:

S	W	N	E
1 ♠	Pass	2 ◇	Pass
2 ♡	Pass	3 ♡	Pass
4 ♡	Pass	4 NT	Pass
5 ♡	Pass	6 ♠	Pass
Pass	?		

You probably have two trump tricks, or perhaps the queen of clubs may be a winner after the king is taken by the ace. Do you double?

No, no, a thousand times no. Unless the opponents are madmen, your fourteen points in high cards tells you they have a fine distributional fit. Your future in defense lies in your trump holding; why tell the opponents about it? Look at all four hands:

```
                    ♠ 10 7 5 4
                    ♡ 3
                    ◇ A K 10 9 6
                    ♣ A 5 4
      ♠ K J 9            N          ♠ —
      ♡ K 10 6 2    W        E      ♡ 9 8 7 5
      ◇ Q 8 5           S          ◇ J 3 2
      ♣ K Q 10                     ♣ J 9 8 7 6 3
                    ♠ A Q 8 6 3 2
                    ♡ A Q J 4
                    ◇ 7 4
                    ♣ 2
```

Without your double, declarer will note with approval that his slam is laydown on a two-one trump break, a 78% chance. Even if East has all three trumps, he still has various chances. So he will properly cash the ace of spades before embarking on a crossruff — and he will go down, unluckily, losing two trump tricks to you.

If you double, however, South will start crossruffing *before* he ever touches trumps. Suppose you lead the king of clubs. Declarer wins the ace, trumps a club, cashes the ace of hearts, and trumps a heart. Another club ruff is followed by another heart ruff; ace, king of diamonds and a diamond ruff puts South in to ruff his last heart in dummy in the following position:

```
                    ♠ 10
                    ♡ —
                    ◇ 10 9
                    ♣ —
      ♠ K J 9            N
      ♡ —          W        E     (immaterial)
      ◇ —               S
      ♣ —
                    ♠ A Q 8
                    ♡ —
                    ◇ —
                    ♣ —
```

South leads the ten of spades from dummy and passes it to your jack; in fact, he can play any card from dummy, as long as he plays the eight of spades from his hand! You win the trick, but have the sad duty of leading into the jaws of declarer's ace-queen of trumps for the slam-fulfilling tricks.

In doubling six spades you were laying very heavy odds against yourself. In order to gain a possible 100 points (or, at the very most, 300 for a two-trick set), you were risking a loss of 1760 points (six spades doubled, making, plus the 100 points you would have scored for down one, undoubled). What you were staking by doubling was not merely the doubled trick score and 50-point bonus for making a doubled contract. By doubling, you permitted the opponents to make their contract, which cost the full value of the game plus the slam bonus plus the trick score. Even when your double doesn't cost the contract, it will in all likelihood present declarer with at least one trick. So you are risking 1760 points to break even! That can't be right.

There is one instance, however, in which it is entirely fitting and proper to double for a one-trick set. That is when you make a *lead-directing* double, guiding partner to what may be the *only* way to set a contract.

The most well-known lead-directing double was invented by Theodore Lightner more than thirty years ago. This brilliant conventional double calls for partner to make an unusual lead against a slam, usually dummy's first bid suit. It warns partner against leading a suit that you or he has bid, or a trump. It also warns against leading the unbid suit, if there is only one. Usually the doubler is void in a side suit.

Here is the Lightner double in action with you in the East seat:

South dealer
Neither side vulnerable

♠ 9 8 7
♡ A Q 10 8 5 4
◇ A Q 3
♣ 7

♠ 4
♡ J 9 7 6 3
◇ J 10 9 8
♣ K Q 9

♠ A 6 2
♡ ——
◇ 7 5 4 2
♣ J 8 6 5 4 2

N
W   E
S

♠ K Q J 10 5 3
♡ K 2
◇ K 6
♣ A 10 3

THE BIDDING:

S	W	N	E
1 ♠	Pass	2 ♡	Pass
3 ♠	Pass	4 ◇	Pass
4 ♡	Pass	4 NT	Pass
5 ◇	Pass	6 ♠	Double!
Pass	Pass	Pass	

Left to his own devices, West would lead the king of clubs against the slam. Your double alerts him to the necessity for an unusual lead, however, and he now leads a heart (dummy's first-bid suit) for you to trump. With any other lead the slam is cold.

If you make a lead-directing double of a slam contract and it is made in spite of your double, you still stand to lose a lot of points. But you are no longer staking against merely increasing your gain from 50 to 100 or from 100 to 200 points. At stake is the *entire value of the slam,* which would be made against an ordinary lead. Thus, the odds are greatly in your favor. The only danger lies in the fact that your double warns the opponents, too, and they may be able to escape into notrump. Usually, however, you can tell from their bidding whether or not it is feasible for them to play the hand in a notrump slam.

The lead-directing double of a suit slam tells partner, "Don't lead a suit we have bid during the auction." Just the

bridge

opposite applies to notrump games and slams. Here the double demands a lead of your suit or partner's.

North dealer
East-West vulnerable

```
                    ♠ J 5 4
                    ♡ 6 5 4
                    ◇ K Q 10 9 8
                    ♣ A K
  ♠ K Q 10 9 8 2         N          ♠ 6 3
  ♡ 3                              ♡ K Q J 10 8 7
  ◇ 6 5            W       E        ◇ A 2
  ♣ J 10 9 7            S           ♣ 5 4 3
                    ♠ A 7
                    ♡ A 9 2
                    ◇ J 7 4 3
                    ♣ Q 8 6 2
```

THE BIDDING:

N	E	S	W
1 ◇	1 ♡	2 ♣	Pass
2 ◇	Pass	2 NT	Pass
3 NT	Double	Pass	Pass
Pass			

Without the double, in the face of North-South's confident bidding, West would choose to lead his own suit instead of partner's, and three notrump would easily be made. After East's double, however, he leads his heart, even though it is a singleton, and East-West collect 500 instead of paying out 600, a very tidy swing.

East's double is obvious on this hand, with his solid hearts and sure entry. The lead-directing double of three notrump is also useful to tell partner you have a high honor in his suit, but you were unable to support because the bidding got too high too fast; in this case, overcaller should lead his own suit despite a broken holding. If you have overcalled one spade on some shabby collection like ♠ J 9 7 6 4 2, for example, lead the suit when partner doubles three notrump. Partner probably has the ace or king of spades and a few high cards in the other suits.

As we saw earlier, a double of three notrump after a

non-competitive auction suggests to partner that he may lead dummy's suit if he does not have a particularly good lead of his own. It is only a suggestion, however. The double of three notrump after your side has bid is a command. Partner knows what he is doing; trust him.

One vs. two: the odds on preemptive bidding

About thirty-five or forty years ago, when contract bridge was a very new game, no one quite knew what an opening three- or four-bid should indicate. One of the leading authorities of the game at that time, P. Hal Sims, was famous for his "Sims three-bids," which were enormous hands that could produce game nearly unaided. If you can open one with an ordinary hand, the logic went, shouldn't an opening bid of two be a good hand, and opening bids of three and four better still? It is possible, although awkward, to bid that way; but experts have found a far better use for high-level opening bids. Since these bids used up bidding space and were at the same time very descriptive, they made life extremely difficult for the opponents. So difficult, in fact, that we are still looking for satisfactory methods of defensive bidding against them. And the odds in their favor are fantastic.

WHEN YOU PREEMPT

Let me give you some idea of the anguish you can create for your opponents. You (South) decide to open with three spades. West's hand:

♠ 5 4   ♡ A K 10 8 5   ◇ A 5 3   ♣ A 4 2

His side is vulnerable. What is he supposed to do? Should he pass?

```
                    ♠ A 2
                    ♡ 7 6 3 2
                    ◇ J 10 4 2
                    ♣ J 10 8
     ♠ 5 4                        ♠ 9 8
     ♡ A K 10 8 5      N          ♡ Q J 9
     ◇ A 5 3        W     E       ◇ K 9 7
     ♣ A 4 2           S          ♣ K Q 7 6 5
                    ♠ K Q J 10 7 6 3
                    ♡ 4
                    ◇ Q 8 6
                    ♣ 9 3
```

If West passes, North will pass, a·d East will probably
pass. You have stolen the hand for thr·e spades, and will go
down one for a paltry −50. In the meantime, East-West are
ice cold for five hearts, worth 650. They will probably spend
the next five minutes arguing about who was supposed to
come into the bidding.

Perhaps you think West should have doubled, or overcalled with four hearts?

```
                    ♠ A 2
                    ♡ Q J 9 3
                    ◇ K 10
                    ♣ K Q J 10 6
     ♠ 5 4                        ♠ 9 8
     ♡ A K 10 8 5      N          ♡ 7 2
     ◇ A 5 3        W     E       ◇ J 8 7 4 2
     ♣ A 4 2           S          ♣ 9 7 5 3
                    ♠ K Q J 10 7 6 3
                    ♡ 6 4
                    ◇ Q 9 6
                    ♣ 8
```

Too bad. This time West found your partner (North)
with a good hand. Four hearts will be doubled and set 1400.
And although North-South can make three notrump, they are
unlikely to bid it; in fact, they might even bid four spades
(without West's intervening call) and go down!

Since you will want to create as many impossible prob-

lems like this as you can, you should open with a preemptive
bid whenever your hand is suitable. I gave point requirements
for three-bids in earlier books, but I found that beginning
players worried too much about points and not enough about
tricks. An opening preemptive (shut-out) bid should have a
long and strong suit with next to nothing outside (there are
a couple of exceptions which I will mention in a moment). If
you open three hearts on:

♠ 5 4   ♡ Q J 10 9 8 6 5 3   ◇ 2   ♣ J 5

nothing much can happen to you, regardless of what your
partner has. Suppose partner has the worst possible hand,
something such as:

♠ Q 8 6 4   ♡ ——   ◇ K 7 6 5 4   ♣ 9 4 3 2

You will still take six tricks and be −500. And your opponents are sure to be able to make three notrump. So you
have actually shown a slight profit (if you didn't bid, your opponents would certainly get to game with a combined high-
card total of 31).

The most important point to remember is: a preemptive
bid is meant as an obstructive bid. It is intended to disrupt the
communications of the opponents, to take precious levels of
bidding away from them. Of course, it also paints a pretty
good picture for partner. He knows that you promise no
defensive strength, but a suit which will take

1] about six tricks if you are not vulnerable (some players
shade this to five tricks if the opponents are vulnerable,
but you won't enjoy taking 700 penalties too often).

2] about seven tricks if both sides are vulnerable.

3] about eight tricks if you are vulnerable and the opponents are not.

To be able to count tricks in this way, you need a long,
solid suit. It is extremely dangerous to preempt with a suit like
♠ K J 9 7 6 3 2, because you have no idea how many tricks you
can take in your own suit. If West has ♠ A Q 10 8 5 behind

you, you may be held to two or three tricks, while if your partner has the ace you may take seven. Preempts need more security than that.

Since your partner knows roughly what kind of hand you have, he can judge fairly accurately how high to go by counting his top tricks. With

♠ 6   ♡ K Q J 10 9   ◇ A Q 10 2   ♣ K 10 2

he should pass an opening bid of three spades; although you may have ten tricks in the combined hands, the opponents will probably take four or five first. But with top tricks, he can be more optimistic:

♠ A 2   ♡ A K 10 6 3   ◇ 6   ♣ A Q J 9 2

If partner opens three spades vulnerable, six spades is a good gamble. Not vulnerable, it may depend on a finesse, but it is still a good shot. If you are conservative, you might bid only five spades. This bid asks partner to look at the quality of his suit in deciding whether to bid six or pass.

An opening bid of three of a minor doesn't shut out quite so many bids as does an opening of three of a major. Nevertheless, three clubs or three diamonds will make the opponents quite uncomfortable, and the bid should be made (nonvulnerable) on a hand such as:

♠ ——   ♡ 5 3   ◇ A J 10 9 8 4 3   ♣ 10 9 3 2

Some people reserve opening bids of three of a minor to show a long, solid suit, inviting partner to bid three notrump. Such hands are rare; in my opinion it is better to preserve the preemptive value of three clubs and three diamonds for weaker hands.

If three-level bids consume space, four-level bids consume more space. The minimum requirements are simply one playing trick more, at the applicable vulnerability, than for three-bids. For example,

♠ A K Q 9 4 3 2   ♡ 5   ◇ 9 8 3   ♣ 10 3

is worth four spades non-vulnerable but only three spades vulnerable. Similarly, with

♠ 4   ♡ Q J 10 9 8 7 4 2   ◇ 2   ♣ A 4 2

open four hearts non-vulnerable but only three hearts vulnerable.

When partner has already passed, you can open four hearts or four spades on quite a strong hand:

♠ A 3   ♡ A Q J 10 9 6 5   ◇ Q 3   ♣ K 8

Slam possibilities are remote, and you want to do all you can to keep the opponents from finding a spade fit should they have one.

WHEN THE OPPONENTS PREEMPT

As we have seen, difficult problems arise when a player opens with three or four of a suit. When the opponents preempt against you, there is no hard and fast defensive principle which will land you on your feet most of the time. Most players act as follows:

1]   double on a good hand with some defense and moderately good support for the unbid suits. A hand such as

♠ 3   ♡ A Q J 4   ◇ A 10 9 4   ♣ K J 8 7

would be an ideal double of three spades. Unfortunately, the ideal hand doesn't come up very often.

2]   overcall with three notrump on a strong hand of about 18 points and opponents' suit securely stopped OR a good hand with one stopper and a long, solid suit, *either*

a)   ♠ A J 4   ♡ K Q 10   ◇ A K 10 4 2   ♣ J 9

or

b)   ♠ A 10   ♡ J 4   ◇ A K Q J 10 7   ♣ K 3 2

would be good examples (over three spades).

3]   overcall with a reasonably good one- or two-suited hand, and hope for the best.

While doubles of three-level bids and of four of a minor are primarily for takeout, doubles of four hearts and four spades show that you expect to beat the hand and partner should remove the double only with a distributional hand and a good suit. After 4 ♡ — Double — Pass, he should bid four spades with

♠ K Q 10 8 3 2   ♡ 5   ◇ J 3   ♣ Q 10 9 6

But if the spades and hearts were reversed and four spades was opened on his left and doubled by you, he should pass; it is too dangerous to venture to the level of five.

The takeout bid over four hearts or four spades is four notrump. This does *not*, contrary to the opinion of many, ask partner to bid a minor suit. The four-notrump bid shows a very powerful hand, usually three-suited. Partner should simply bid his best suit. A typical four-notrump bid over a four-spade opening would be:

♠ ——   ♡ A K 10 8 2   ◇ K Q J 4   ♣ A Q J 3

Partner should bid a slam with a few values in the unbid suits.

A valuable tip to follow when contemplating bidding to dizzy heights in the face of preempt by the opponents is: be conservative. Take a sure game or a sure 300 or 500 set whenever you have a close decision. Don't push to close slams depending on favorable suit breaks. When an opponent preempts against you, he has a very long suit, which means he is very short in one or two other suits. This means that your suits are much more apt to break badly than if the opponents had not bid. A fine slam in, say, a 4-4 fit may be ruined on the rocks of adverse distribution, frequently a 4-1 or 5-0 trump break. The odds in favor of bidding games and slams are now not as good, so take it easy and wait for the next hand.

Great expectations

"How could I know you had such a good hand?" is a war cry often heard at the bridge table. Usually, it is the result of one player not correctly visualizing the great potential of the combined hands, by failing to realize that his partner — on the bidding — was marked with certain values. Another slogan, usually heard after an even more expensive fiasco, is, the odds in the bidding | 213

"How could I know you had a worthless hand for me?"

One of the most important attributes of a successful bridge player is knowing what he can safely count on his partner to hold and what he cannot. And very often, this is simply a matter of gauging the odds. For example, consider the following situation:

S	N
2 ♠	3 ♠
4 NT	5 ◊
?	

South holds:

♠ K Q J 10 6 4   ♡ A   ◊ A K 8 5 2   ♣ 7

What should South bid?

South has determined that North has spade support and that only one ace is missing. But the success of a slam in spades will depend on North's diamond holding. North cannot be expected to cooperate in any way: if South bids five spades, North will pass, trusting South's decision.

It is clear that six spades will be a good proposition for North-South if North has a hand such as:

♠ A 9 7 3   ♡ K 8 7 2   ◊ 7 4   ♣ 9 6 5

But if we make only a slight change and give North:

♠ A 9 7 3   ♡ K 8 7 2   ◊ 7 4 3   ♣ 9 6

then six spades will have less than a ghost of a chance.

How can South determine whether or not a slam bid will be a good bet? The answer is that he can't — not with certainty, at any rate. What he can do, however, is make an intelligent decision based on the odds.

In this case, the main question to be resolved (ignoring the possibility that North may have the queen of diamonds) is whether or not North is short in diamonds. If he has one or two diamonds, the slam will probably have a good chance. If he holds three small diamonds, the chance will be very poor indeed, while if he holds four small, the odds will be three-to-two *against* the slam — not adequate to justify bidding six.

There is nothing in the bidding to this point that gives South a clue as to whether North is long or short in diamonds.

So South must depend on percentages — on the most likely holding for North. Or, to phrase it another way, South must calculate the number of diamonds North could be *expected* to have under normal circumstances. By making this percentage decision, South will not be right all the time. But he will be right more often than not, and being right as often as possible is what makes one a winner.

With this in mind, I strongly recommend that South should, in fact, bid six spades. There is nothing in the bidding to determine the lengths of North's suits in hearts, diamonds, and clubs. But since South has many more cards in diamonds than in hearts and clubs, it follows that *it is likely that North has more cards in hearts and clubs than in diamonds.* This is true simply because, if we take North's cards in hearts, diamonds and clubs from the remaining unseen cards, it is more likely that we will pick for him cards in clubs and hearts because there are more of these cards available to be picked.

Therefore, since South must guess whether North is short or long in diamonds, he should guess him to be short. (Similarly, he should guess him to be long in clubs.) And on this reasoning, South should bid the spade slam in the knowledge that he is going with the odds. This decision is based on a principle which can be generally stated as follows:

All other things being equal, and with no special information being provided from the bidding, you can expect partner to have length in your short suits and be short in your long suits.

Of course, this will not *always* be the case. But it will be true more often than not and you can often take advantage of this principle in making bidding decisions.

A similar principle can be applied in the case of high-card strength, although the method of application is somewhat different from the case of suit distribution. Let's start with the principle this time:

Partner can be expected to hold his share of the unaccounted for high-card strength when there is no indication from the bidding where this strength is.

Here is how this principle can be applied in practice. Suppose you are vulnerable and the opponents are not and the player on your right deals and opens with three spades. You hold:

♠ A Q   ♡ K J 7   ◇ A Q 9 5   ♣ Q 8 7 3

You should bid three notrump! True, you have only 18 points — far short of the 26 required for game. But the opening preemptive has forced you to guess, and if you wait for a full 26 points of your own before bidding three notrump you will probably wait forever. Consider what you can expect from partner: Your right-hand opponent, for his opening preemptive, probably has at most 8 points. This leaves 14 points for your left-hand opponent and your partner, *and partner can be expected to hold 7 of them.* This gives your side at least 25, even assuming that your right-hand opponent has his maximum (he will often have less), and your spade honors are probably well placed, so three notrump becomes a good gamble.

The danger of this principle is overapplying it. Suppose that, as dealer, you pick up a balanced hand with 19 high-card points. There are 21 outstanding high-card points, so partner can be expected to hold seven of them. (This time there are three unknown hands, so partner can be credited with only one-third of the outstanding total.)

You have 19 and partner can be expected to have 7. The total is 26. Should you therefore bid three notrump? Obviously, no. The reason is that you will have the opportunity to discover whether or not partner has as many as seven points. You can open the bidding and see if partner can scrape together a response. If he cannot, then you know he does not in fact have enough points for your side to score a game.

Therefore, a general rule for applying the principles of what partner can be expected to have is the following:

When possible, bid in such a way as to discover what partner holds. When you cannot determine partner's holding (i.e. you are forced into making a decision before you can find out what you want to know) then and only then should you make your decision on partner's expected strength, or expected distribution.

Very often, what partner can be expected to hold can be determined from the previous bidding. The opponents' bidding is often particularly valuable in this regard.

You are South and hold:

♠ K Q 6   ♡ A 10 3   ◇ A J 3   ♣ Q J 8 4

bridge

The bidding has gone:

W: 1 ♠   **N: Pass**   **E: 2 ◊**   **S: ?**

What action do you take?

When I saw this hand played, South decided to bid two notrump. This was promptly doubled and set four tricks — 1100 points. South, of course, complained bitterly about the fact that his partner had not produced any face cards. "How could I know you had such a bad hand?" he asked.

But South *should* have known, for the East-West bidding told a clear story. Even accounting for distributional values in the make-up of their bids, East-West probably had about 21-22 points in high cards in order to open the bidding and respond at the two-level. *At most* North could have 1 or 2 points, and it should have been no surprise to South when he showed up with no points at all.

There is still another reason for passing in positions such as this. Even if the opponents do not stop off to double your bid, your bid will have given them useful information in the play of the hand. They will know where to look for the outstanding high cards.

The point is that South has nothing to gain by bidding. To bid in this situation is commonly known as giving the opponents a "fielder's choice." They can double if they think it will be profitable or bid on, knowing the bulk of the high-card strength opposing them has been located. South can come to the correct conclusion if he thinks about the hand North can be expected to hold. In this case, it is clear that North can be counted on for an average holding of about 1 point (perhaps slightly less). This being the case, South should see that his side will never be able to play the hand — except disastrously in a contract doubled by the opponents.

Alternatively, sometimes the *weakness* of the opponents' bidding makes it clear that partner can be depended upon for fair values. Suppose the bidding has proceeded:

W: 1 NT   **N: Pass**   **E: Pass**   **S: ?**

You, South, hold:

♠ A J 10 9 5 3   ♡ 3   ◊ J 10 5 2   ♣ 8 2

It is clear that N.rth must have some honor strength since East could not try for game after his partner opened with one notrump. Further, that strength will be favorably located behind the opening one-notrump bidder. In this situation, South should bid two spades despite his weakness in high cards. His partner is marked for strength and South has a good suit and good distribution.

Note the difference between the two situations just discussed. In the first instance, South was brimming with high-card values, but had no good suit and had poor distribution to support one of his partner's suits. As he knew his partner had no high-card values, he could not hope to compete on the basis of either high cards or distribution. Thus, as proved to be the case, it was reckless to enter the auction. But in the second case, South realized that his partner was marked with considerable high-card strength; further, this strength was well placed for the North-South team. And South could supply both a good suit and powerful suit distribution to match North's high cards. Observe that it is not enough to know that your partner has certain high-card values. If, in the same situation (1 NT — Pass — Pass) South had held:

♠ A J 10 9   ♡ 5 3 2   ◊ J 10 5 2   ♣ 8 2

it would be foolish for him to bid because even though his partner is known to have considerable high-card values, there is no guarantee that North-South have as much high-card strength as East-West, and South does not have either a good suit or powerful distribution to make up for this potential deficiency. Furthermore, if North-South do outweigh East-West in high cards, South can probably beat one notrump, which will compensate for any part-score contract that South might miss by passing.

When South had six spades and four diamonds, however, he had no reason to believe that a contract of one notrump could be defeated. By passing he would risk the possibility that East-West would make one notrump when he himself could be making two spades (or four spades!).

Just as expected values in partner's hand can be in terms of either high cards or suit distributions, so also the bidding may give you information about either of these factors. We have seen how partner's approximate high-card holding may sometimes be gauged by the opposition bidding. Now let's look at a situation in which his distribution can also be judged to our advantage.

Suppose the bidding has proceeded:

W: 1 ♡   **N:** Pass   **E:** 4 ♡   **S:** ?

and you, South, are thinking about entering the bidding with an overcall of four spades with one of the following:

a)	♠ A K J 7 3	♡ 8	◇ A J 9 5	♣ 10 6 4
b)	♠ A K J 7 3	♡ 8 3 2	◇ A J 9 5	♣ 10

To be sure, a four-spade bid is risky on either hand. It is true that East's four-heart bid is preemptive, and may be an attempt to shut you out of the auction, but West is an unknown quantity. He may be loaded with high-card and defensive values (possibly just short of a two-bid) and may be able to double four spades and defeat you severely. Also, you have considerable defensive strength yourself and may be able to set four hearts, in which case it will be highly undesirable to give up even a moderate penalty in four spades. But it is also risky to pass with hands like this, for if you can find a fit you may be able to make a game, perhaps even when the opponents can make four hearts!

Now, if you must bid four spades on one of these hands or the other, which would you prefer? I would rather have hand *b*). The deciding factor is the three small hearts. The East-West bidding marks your opponents with at least eight hearts, probably nine and possibly ten. North is known to be short in hearts, so there is a good chance he has some spades, which will provide a fit with your spade suit as well as trumps to ruff two or perhaps even all three of your losing hearts. If South has hand *a*), North may have a few hearts and may not contribute any tricks at all to the play in four spades. But opposite hand *b*), South can reasonably expect that North will be able to contribute a ruffing trick or two at the very least.

Thus, a four-spade overcall on hand *a*) is very risky, while the overcall on hand *b*), though still risky is going with the odds.

the odds in the play

A FEW MINUTES after an important tournament ended, a young expert was explaining to some friends how he had played a slam contract. "Just think," he said. "I had to choose between a 4% play and a 3% play. I decided to take the 4% play, and it worked. If I had taken the 3% play, I would have gone down!"

If this were all it took to be a bridge expert, we could just open up our slide rules instead of our convention cards before we started playing and be assured of good results. Bridge would be a mathematician's delight instead of a pastime for everyone. Fortunately, playing your dummies properly requires primarily clear thinking and common sense, not mathematics. All the mathematics in the world won't help you if you are going to block yourself in dummy, forget to take a safety play, miscount trumps, or lead from the wrong hand. In fact, it is not knowledge of the very technical plays that distinguishes the top players from their less successful brethren; it helps, of course, to know how to set up a "blocked-menace squeeze" (there is such a play, by the way), but most tournaments (and money) are won by players who do not make obvious mistakes. Knowing a little about the odds will cut down on those mistakes.

Have you ever played double-dummy bridge? Many newspaper readers and other addicts like this form of the game, which is bridge without odds. You don't have to know the odds against a suit break, because you know that it does break — you can see West's hand. Personally, I do not enjoy this particular offshoot of the game; but if you do, you can avoid any problem with odds. The other alternative is to try to get your opponents to show you their cards after the bidding is over; but I have found from experience that they will seldom oblige.

The odds in the play of the cards usually concern themselves with one question: "What play is likely to succeed?" Let us consider some examples.

N: ♠ 7 5 4 3 2   S: ♠ A Q 6

Without any opposing bidding to help you solve the mystery, a finesse of the queen of spades will work almost exactly half the time and fail about half the time. If you have to take this finesse to make a slam, knowing the percentages won't help you very much; you just shrug your shoulders and hope for the best.

N: ◊ 7 4 2   S: ◊ A K Q 5

This suit will break badly (4-2 or worse) nearly twice as often as it will break evenly (3-3). Knowing that the odds in favor of an even break are about 36% will not help you much; but it will help you to know that the diamond suit is not a good place to try for an extra trick if you can get it somewhere else. Now let us combine these two suits into one hand:

N: ♠ 7 5 4 3 2   ♡ 9 3 2   ◊ 7 4 2   ♣ A 4
S: ♠ A Q 6   ♡ A K Q   ◊ A K Q 5   ♣ J 10 2

With 25 high-card points, you decided to take a chance on the club suit and opened the bidding with three notrump. You were not surprised to hear everyone pass, and West led the five of clubs. Just in case something fortuitous had happened (like West leading from both the king and queen), you ducked in dummy, but East won the trick with the queen and returned the club eight. You are in dummy for the last time; what is your best chance for nine tricks?

Since you have only seven diamonds between the two hands, the chance of a favorable (3-3) break are not too good, only 36%. So you try the 50-50 spade finesse. Here is the complete deal:

```
                    ♠ 7 5 4 3 2
                    ♡ 9 3 2
                    ◇ 7 4 2
                    ♣ A 4
        ♠ J 8              N            ♠ K 10
        ♡ 7 5 4                         ♡ J 10 8 6
        ◇ 6 3        W         E        ◇ J 10 9 8
        ♣ K 9 7 5 3        S            ♣ Q 8 6
                    ♠ A Q 6
                    ♡ A K Q
                    ◇ A K Q 5
                    ♣ J 10 2
```

It is perfectly true that if you took the eight of diamonds and king of spades out of the East hand and traded them for two other cards (not diamonds) from the West hand, the suggested play would lose and the other line, trying for four diamond tricks, would win. But the spade finesse will win more often, and if you go down you can comfort yourself with the knowledge that you have taken the "percentage play." (Note parenthetically that if the spade finesse wins, you can try the diamond suit for an overtrick AFTER you have taken your nine tricks. Also, if the spade finesse loses, there is a chance that East-West can take only three club tricks in all; that is, if the suit had originally divided 4-4. If this happens, the defenders will take four tricks, but then they will have to put you in your hand again and you will still have an opportunity to try for four diamond tricks. But if you try the diamonds first and they don't break, there is nothing more you can do.)

In this hand, your first choice is dictated primarily by the pure mathematics of one chance against another. Later on, however, you will see that often you try first for the chance that has a lesser chance of success but can be taken with greater safety, because you can combine this play with one or more additional chances if the first chance does not work.

Let's look at some of the more common percentages that will help you on numerous hands. You don't have to know them exactly; a rough idea will usually suffice.

Percentages of suit breaks are usually important when

you have more cards in a given suit than the opponents. Let's start with that diamond suit:

◇ A K Q 5   ◇ 7 3 2

When you have seven cards of a suit between your hand and the dummy, the suit will break:

3-3 36% (a little more than one-third of the time)
4-2 48% (nearly half the time)
5-1 15% (about one time in seven)
6-0   1% (about one time in 100)

So when you see a short, stubby suit like that, it is a good idea to make a tentative assumption that it will break 4-2. Usually, however, you are concerned with longer suits, particularly when trumps are involved. (By the way, you haven't lived until you have arrived in a contract of, say, four hearts with seven trumps in the combined hands, played the first round of trumps, and found that one opponent had all six! Fortunately, that won't happen to you often.)

♡ A K 8 5 4   ♡ 6 3 2

This is your trump suit; how many trump tricks do you expect to lose? You may be surprised to find out that, more than two-thirds of the time, you will lose only one trick in the suit. What a difference that eighth card makes! When you had seven cards in the combined hands, the chance of an even break was 36%. Now, with eight cards, the chance of the most even break possible (3-2) is 68%, nearly twice as great.

Notice the enormous difference between a seven- and an eight-card fit. With the former, you can't draw three rounds of trumps immediately without running into the danger of losing control. An opponent may be able to draw your last trump. But with eight trumps, as in the example above, you can safely draw two rounds of trumps. Even if an opponent draws a third round, you still have two trumps left to aid establishing your suits or to stop the opponents from running theirs. It is frequently better to play in a suit like this rather than notrump, as in the following example:

North dealer
Both sides vulnerable

                    ♠ A K 5
                    ♡ 6 3 2
                    ◇ K 2
                    ♣ A 9 5 4 2

♠ J 10 7 3   N   ♠ 8 6 4 2
♡ Q J   ♡ 10 9 7
◇ J 9 6 5 4 3   W   E   ◇ Q 10
♣ Q   S   ♣ J 10 8 6

                    ♠ Q 9
                    ♡ A K 8 5 4
                    ◇ A 8 7
                    ♣ K 7 3

THE BIDDING:

N	S
1 ♣	1 ♡
1 NT	3 ♣
3 ♡	4 ◇
4 ♠	5 ♣
5 ◇	6 ♡
Pass	

This is an excellent slam contract, but a very difficult one to bid unless you realize the value of the eight-card fit. The 33 points usually needed for a good small slam are not quite there, but the excellent "fit" makes up for the lack of high cards. South's three-club bid is forcing and is an attempt to find three-card support for his five-card heart suit. North actually has the values to bid four hearts, since his hand is worth 15 points in support; but since his 6-3-2 of hearts may not be all South expects, he contents himself with a simple bid of three hearts and continues to bid strongly later when South shows interest in slam with his four-diamond and five-club cue-bids.

Six hearts is a somewhat superior contract to six notrump, although greedy duplicate players might strain for the higher-scoring contract and suffer defeat. All you need to make six hearts is a 3-2 trump break. Suppose a spade is led: Win in your hand with the queen, cash the ace and king of trumps and the king and ace of diamonds, and ruff a diamond with dummy's last trump. Your losing club can be discarded on dummy's high spade, and you will lose only to the outstanding high trump. A 3-2 trump break is a 68% chance, so you will make your contract slightly more often than two times out of three.

Most suit bidding in contract bridge is designed so that you can quickly find an eight-card trump fit if there is one. One of the reasons for this is that the suit is very likely to break well for you.

When you have eight cards of a suit between your hand and the dummy, the suit will break:

3-2   68% (more than two times out of three)
4-1   28% (a little more often than once in four times)
5-0   4% (once in twenty-five times)

Not only is an eight-card fit better because the suit is likely to break, it also may be better even when it doesn't break, as in the following example:

```
                  ♠ A 7 3 2
                  ♡ Q 10 8 7
                  ◇ K 9 6
                  ♣ A 6
     ♠ K 10 9          N          ♠ Q J 8 5 4
     ♡ 6 5 4 3 2                  ♡ ─
     ◇ J 7         W     E        ◇ Q 8 4 2
     ♣ Q 8 5          S           ♣ K 10 9 7
                  ♠ 6
                  ♡ A K J 9
                  ◇ A 10 5 3
                  ♣ J 4 3 2
```

THE BIDDING:

	S	N
	1 ♡	3 ♡
	4 ♡	Pass

Even if North-South do not open four-card major suits, four hearts should still be reached:

S	N
1 ◇	1 ♡
2 ♡	2 ♠
4 ♡	Pass

Most of you would reach four hearts on these cards; but you can note in passing that the notrump hogs will have a terrible time taking nine tricks if a spade is led. In four hearts, the one in twenty-five shot has come in and the trumps are 5-0. Horrors! But even with a trump lead, North-South are cold for eleven tricks! Spades can be ruffed in the South hand, with North's high cards used for entries. This illustrates one of the big advantages of the 4-4 fit: its flexibility. Either hand can be used as the master trump hand. Besides the advantage of favorable odds (68% in favor of a 3-2 break) you can have the best of all possible worlds: it may be conceivable either to crossruff, or set up side suits by ruffing, or make dummy the master trump hand as in this hand. Here is another example:

North dealer
East-West vulnerable

```
                    ♠ K 8 7 5 2
                    ♡ A Q 4 2
                    ◇ A 3
                    ♣ 5 4
    ♠ J 10 9 6              ♠ A Q 3
    ♡ 9 8 7       N         ♡ 6 3
    ◇ 4        W     E      ◇ 9 8 7 5
    ♣ K Q 10 9 8     S      ♣ J 7 3 2
                    ♠ 4
                    ♡ K J 10 5
                    ◇ K Q J 10 6 2
                    ♣ A 6
```

THE BIDDING:

N	S
1 ♠	2 ◇
2 ♡	4 NT
5 ♡	6 ♡
Pass	

This is an easy slam to reach, whether you play for matchsticks or for something more valuable; but did any of you old-time rubber bridge players bid six diamonds because of the 100 honors? If you did, you will see why the 4-4 fit is superior. In hearts, trumps can be drawn and dummy's losing club can be thrown on a long diamond. Then South can ruff his low club. In diamonds, there is just no place to put that annoying losing club.

This leads us to a maxim that is by no means always true, but which applies often enough to be important:

When choosing a trump suit, it is usually better to select the suit that is more evenly divided between the two hands.

Most of the time, when you are playing a suit contract, you will have eight trumps, and you can be comforted by the knowledge that your trump suit will break favorably for you much more often than not. You would suppose, therefore, that when you have more than eight cards in a suit between declarer's hand and dummy, you will be more fortunate still. Let us consider the following suit:

♣ A K 9 4 3   ♣ 7 6 5 2

How often do you expect to take all five tricks in this suit? In the example below, you would have to know your chances before being able to choose the right play:

South dealer
Both sides vulnerable

```
                    ♠ A J
                    ♡ 5 4 2
                    ◇ 10 9 5 2
                    ♣ 7 6 5 2
   ♠ 9 8 7 6 5 2          N      ♠ K 4 3
   ♡ J 9 8                       ♡ K 10 7 6 3
   ◇ 8            W         E    ◇ 7 6 4 3
   ♣ Q J 10             S        ♣ 8
                    ♠ Q 10
                    ♡ A Q
                    ◇ A K Q J
                    ♣ A K 9 4 3
```

THE BIDDING:

```
        S        N
       3 NT     Pass
```

Cover up the East-West hands and see how well you play this one. The opening lead is the six of spades. You play the jack from dummy, but unfortunately East wins with the king and returns the spade four. You have to win in dummy with the ace. Now what?

If you banged down the ace and king of clubs, you were wrong. The odds of clubs breaking evenly are three to two against you. The odds in favor of the heart finesse are still the same old 50-50.

When you have nine cards of a suit between your hand and the dummy, the suit will break:

> 2-2 40% (two times out of five)
> 3-1 50% (half the time)
> 4-0 10% (once in ten times)

So, perversely enough, a nine-card suit is less likely to break evenly than an eight-card suit.

Rather than try to remember all these percentages, it is better to keep a simple rule in mind:

If you have an odd number of cards in a suit, the chances are that the remaining cards will break "oddly."

If you have an even number of cards in a suit, the chances are that the outstanding cards will break evenly (or, as evenly as possible).

A complete list of all possible suit splits will be found on page 295.

Let us test a suit fit to see if it conforms to our rule:

♠ A K 9 5 2   ♠ J 8 7 4 3

Do you expect to lose a trick in this suit? The answer is no. In fact, you will be quite unlucky if you do lose a trick to the twice-guarded queen. The spades will break 2-1 for you nearly four times out of five (78%). By the way, the correct way to play this particular spade suit has nothing to do with odds or percentages: If the jack is in the dummy, lead it! You are going to play the ace from your hand anyway, but the player with three to the Q-10 might get sleepy and cover. If he makes that mistake, you get back to dummy in some other suit and take the proven finesse against his ten.

This odd-even rule is a great help in remembering percentages. The only exception to the rule is with eleven-card suits. The only time you have to worry about eleven-card suits is when you are missing the king, *e.g.:*

$\diamond$ A Q 9 8 7 6   opposite $\diamond$ J 10 5 4 2

Here the odds are slightly in favor (52% to 48%) of the king dropping when you play the ace. But this is such a close one that if you have the slightest contrary indication, such as a tell-tale quiver, take the finesse.

The percentage play

Fortunately for you, the right way to play a hand is not neatly sealed and stoppered in a bottle. Many of the hands in the previous chapter probably struck you as somewhat artificial or unusual. They are, because most hands you will get to play will involve several different kinds of plays at once. On the same hand, for example, you may have a hold-up play, a successful finesse, an unsuccessful suit break, and an endplay. By now you probably have some idea of when a suit is likely to break and when it isn't — but can you use your knowledge in figuring out the best way to play the hand? See how you play this one, making sure to remember what you have learned about odds.

```
                    ♠ 3 2
                    ♡ A K 9 4
                    ◇ 10 7 3 2
                    ♣ K Q 9
   ♠ Q J 9 5 4          N          ♠ A 10 8 6
   ♡ J 8 7                         ♡ 10 6 5
   ◇ K            W         E      ◇ 6 5 4
   ♣ 8 7 6 5          S           ♣ J 4 3
                    ♠ K 7
                    ♡ Q 3 2
                    ◇ A Q J 9 8
                    ♣ A 10 2
```

THE BIDDING:

S	N
1 NT	2 ♣
2 ◇	3 NT

North's two club response is the Stayman convention, asking South to bid a four-card major suit if he has one. This convention is extremely valuable for purposes of seeking out 4-4 major fits, the merits of which we have already seen.

West leads the queen of spades; East encourages with the eight, and you win with the king. What is the best chance for your ninth trick?

Obviously the diamond finesse is the best chance, since a finesse will succeed 50% of the time and a 3-3 break in hearts will work only 36% of the time. But it would be foolish to take the diamond finesse until you have availed yourself of both opportunities. You can't afford to let your opponents into the lead, because they will surely be able to cash enough spade tricks to defeat you. So cash the queen, king and ace of hearts to see if the suit happens to break luckily for you. Hurrah! Hearts break 3-3, and you won't have to take that diamond finesse after all. You have won one spade trick; along with three clubs, four hearts and the ace of diamonds, this will add up to the nine tricks you need. You are even luckier than you realize, for when you take your ninth trick with the ace of diamonds, the king drops and you find that you have all thirteen tricks. Just taking your tricks in the right order here made a five-trick difference in the play. Had you carelessly taken the diamond finesse before testing the hearts, you would have taken only eight tricks instead of thirteen.

This was an easy one; the "percentage play" is not always that simple to determine. On the next hand, you are in a slam; see if you can play so as to take advantage of all possibilities.

N:	♠ 6 3	♡ A Q 3 2	◇ A Q J 9 8	♣ A Q
S:	♠ A J	♡ K J 10 8 7	◇ 10 5 4 3 2	♣ 6

bridge

N	S
1 ♢	1 ♡
4 ♡	4 ♠
6 ♡	Pass

The bidding has been brief but effective, and you have reached an excellent slam contract. Making the slam, however, will be more difficult than bidding it. West leads the king of spades, and you win with the ace and draw two rounds of trumps, which happen to break 2-2. What now?

You can see that you could always make your contract if you knew that the diamond finesse was going to work. In this case you could just finesse diamonds and give up a spade trick at the end. On the other hand, if the diamond finesse is going to lose, you will have to take the club finesse first: if this wins you can discard your losing spade on the ace of clubs and give up a diamond trick.

Which finesse, clubs or diamonds? Is it a toss-up?

No, because here you have an extra chance. If you cash the ace of diamonds, about once in four times someone will have the singleton king, and you won't have to worry about the other finesse. There is no point in deciding whether to take the diamond finesse (50%) or the club finesse (50%) when you have the chance of the singleton king of diamonds dropping (about 25%) *plus* the club finesse. It won't work the other way, of course; the chance of dropping a singleton king of clubs is astronomically against you. Someone would have to have a nine-card suit, for one thing, and you would surely have heard about that in the bidding. But with ten diamonds between your hand and the dummy, there is quite a respectable chance of dropping the king.

Let me warn you that this is not the right way to play the diamond suit if that were all you had to worry about. I have seen many inexperienced players, faced with a diamond suit like this one, lead low toward dummy. When West plays a small card, they go up with the ace. Upon being asked why they did not take the finesse, they answer, "Why take the finesse? If East has a singleton, isn't it just as likely to be the king as a small card?" Very true; but they have forgotten that

East may very well be void. If you consider this possibility, you will see that the finesse is by far the best play of the suit, *but not on this hand!* Here is the whole layout:

```
                    ♠ 6 3
                    ♡ A Q 3 2
                    ◇ A Q J 9 8
                    ♣ A Q
  ♠ K Q 10 4              N         ♠ 9 8 7 5 2
  ♡ 6 5                             ♡ 9 4
  ◇ 7 6          W          E       ◇ K
  ♣ J 10 8 7 3             S        ♣ K 9 5 4 2
                    ♠ A J
                    ♡ K J 10 8 7
                    ◇ 10 5 4 3 2
                    ♣ 6
```

Combining your chances in this way is often referred to as "echeloning" your plays; the word "echelon" comes from an Old French word which originally meant "ladder." If you echelon your plays whenever you can, you will be climbing the ladder of bridge success.

Let's try another example of this type of play. This time you have arrived in three notrump:

N: ♠ 6 4 3 2	♡ A K 8	◇ K Q 7 3	♣ 9 7
S: ♠ A K J	♡ 7 6 4 2	◇ A 9 2	♣ A 10 6

THE BIDDING:

S	N
1 NT	2 ♣
2 ♡	3 NT
Pass	

Opening lead: ♣ K

Since you have 28 points in high cards between your hand and the dummy, you probably don't expect much trouble in three notrump. The difficulty is that clubs are stopped only once and you may be set if you have to give up the lead. So you duck the king of clubs to see what happens (if you win, you have only eight tricks on top if nothing breaks favorably). West, as expected, continues with the queen of clubs, and you duck again. On a third club lead, you discard a small spade from dummy and win with the ace while East discards the five of spades. What now?

Remembering about echeloning your plays, you see that you have the chance of a 3-3 diamond break for your ninth trick, and if that doesn't work, a spade finesse. So you cash the ace of spades, just in case West has the singleton queen, and play three rounds of diamonds ending up in dummy. When West discards the three of hearts on the third round of diamonds, you shrug your shoulders and finesse the jack of spades. West wins with the queen and cashes three more clubs, setting you two tricks. Can you spot where you went wrong? Or were you just unlucky?

Since West had six clubs and would take five of them if you let him into the lead, you certainly didn't want to take a finesse into his hand until everything else had failed. But you were in too much of a hurry. *East* could do nothing harmful if he won a trick, and you missed an additional chance. (The ladder had more rungs than you thought.)

There are seven hearts between your hand and the dummy. If the suit breaks 3-3, you can set up your ninth trick in that suit. You will have to lose a heart trick in order to do this, but this is all right if you can lose that trick to East. After winning the club ace, lead a low heart. If West plays a low heart, "finesse" the eight. East is now on lead and can do nothing to hurt you. He will probably return a spade. Win with the ace and cash the ace and king of hearts. Good play is rewarded; the hearts break, and now you don't have to take any finesses. Return to your hand with the ace of diamonds to take the thirteenth heart, on which you throw another spade from dummy (not a diamond; that suit might break, too, and an overtrick will do you no harm). You cash the high diamonds; when they don't break, you take your king of spades for the ninth trick (two spades, three hearts, three diamonds and one club). You get an unexpected bonus when West's queen of spades drops, and you make four notrump. Here is the complete deal:

```
              ♠ 6 4 3 2
              ♡ A K 8
              ◇ K Q 7 3
              ♣ 9 7
♠ Q 9              N          ♠ 10 8 7 5
♡ 9 5 3                       ♡ Q J 10
◇ J 4         W      E        ◇ 10 8 6 5
♣ K Q J 8 5 2      S          ♣ 4 3
              ♠ A K J
              ♡ 7 6 4 2
              ◇ A 9 2
              ♣ A 10 6
```

West could have made things somewhat more difficult for
you by putting up the nine of hearts on the first round. You
would have to play the king, for if you duck, there would
be the danger of West being able to win the trick and cash
his clubs. In this case, your best play would be to take the
king of hearts and come back to your hand with the ace of
diamonds (not the ace of spades) and lead another low heart.
This time, it so happens that West could only play a small
card, so you would "finesse" the eight, with the play then becoming the same as before.

Note that you would not have echeloned your plays
properly if you used the ace of spades as the re-entry to lead
hearts a second time. East would have returned a spade when
he got in, and you would have had to guess whether to take
the spade finesse or to play for hearts to break evenly. The
other way, you retained all your chances.

Playing for luck and playing for safety

When the opening lead is made and the dummy goes
down, you will nearly always have to make one or more assumptions as to the distribution and position of the opponents'
cards. Even if you are just cashing your nine top tricks in a
contract of three notrump, you have probably made the assumption that the opponents could cash five tricks if they got
in; or even that they would get annoyed if you spent a lot of

time working out how to get a tenth trick. When you take a finesse, you make an assumption that a key card is placed where you want it; when you refuse a finesse, you refuse to make an *unnecessary* assumption. *Bridge is a game in which you have to make exactly the right number of assumptions, and no more.* The trouble with many bridge players is that they make either too many assumptions or not enough of them.

To a greater or lesser degree, all hands can be classified as "lucky" hands or "unlucky" hands. On the "lucky" hands, something nice has to happen or you will be in trouble. So you play on the assumption that the cards are lying well for you. On the "unlucky" hands, you are in such a good contract that only extremely bad luck can beat you, so you go about trying to cope with that bad luck. The following hand is a good example:

N: ♠ 3 2	♡ 10 9 4	◇ A K Q 6 4 2	♣ 10 7
S: ♠ A 10 7 6	♡ A K	◇ 10 5	♣ A J 9 8 6

You are in six notrump, with the opening lead of the heart five. How do you play it?

Someone in your partnership has gotten carried away during the bidding (partner, no doubt), because the contract is a very bad one; a simple three-notrump contract is far preferable. Therefore, you have to be lucky. How lucky? Well, the diamonds have to break 3-2, or you have no chance at all. That gives you one spade, two hearts, six diamonds and one club for a total of ten tricks, so you need two more tricks in the club suit. For this to happen, either East has to have both club honors, or the club honors must be divided between East and West with East having no more than three clubs. So you win the heart lead with the ace, cross to the ace of diamonds, and run the ten of clubs. If it is covered, all you need is a diamond break. If it loses, you run the diamonds (assuming they will run), take a deep breath, and repeat the club finesse. When it wins and a club honor drops under your subsequent play of the ace, you score up your ambitious slam and reflect to yourself that you have been moderately lucky. The full deal might be like this:

```
                    ♠ 3 2
                    ♡ 10 9 4
                    ◇ A K Q 6 4 2
                    ♣ 10 7
   ♠ K J 5 4            N        ♠ Q 9 8
   ♡ J 8 6 5                     ♡ Q 7 3 2
   ◇ 8 3          W        E     ◇ J 9 7
   ♣ Q 5 4            S         ♣ K 3 2
                    ♠ A 10 7 6
                    ♡ A K
                    ◇ 10 5
                    ♣ A J 9 8 6
```

But let's forget the East-West hands for a moment and suppose that instead of six notrump, you are playing the correct contract of *three* notrump. As before, the opening lead is the five of hearts. Do you play the same way?

Let's see. You have one spade, two hearts, six diamonds and one club, for a total of ten. So it's just a question of overtricks . . . wait a minute! You might not have six diamond tricks. Suppose the suit breaks 4-1?

You don't need *six* diamond tricks; you need only five. You can guard against an "unlucky" diamond break. At trick two, lead the ten of diamonds from your hand and duck the trick, whether or not West plays the jack. As long as diamonds are not 5-0, you will be sure of five diamond tricks. (If diamonds are 5-0, you still have a chance if West shows out. Win the diamond in dummy. Now it is a lucky hand again, like the previous example, for the clubs have to be favorably located for you.) But if you carelessly won the first diamond trick with the ace, this might be the layout:

```
                    ♠ 3 2
                    ♡ 10 9 4
                    ◇ A K Q 6 4 2
                    ♣ 10 7
   ♠ K J 5 4            N        ♠ Q 9 8
   ♡ J 8 6 5 2                   ♡ Q 7 3
   ◇ 8            W        E     ◇ J 9 7 3
   ♣ K Q 5            S         ♣ 4 3 2
                    ♠ A 10 7 6
                    ♡ A K
                    ◇ 10 5
                    ♣ A J 9 8 6
```

bridge

You can see that if you played greedily, you would go down in three notrump. West would get his hearts set up before you could set up your club suit. This hand, in *three* notrump, is an "unlucky" hand where you have to resort to a "safety play" to make your contract. In *six* notrump, you needed luck and therefore could not afford to indulge in such luxuries as safety plays.

A "safety play" is the concession of one or more tricks to guard against potentially unfavorable distribution. If the diamond suit had been normally divided, you would have given up an unnecessary trick. But the odds in favor of doing this are extremely high. You have given up a paltry 30-point overtrick to insure making a game worth (vulnerable) 600. Twenty to one in your favor!

Of course the real odds are nowhere near as high as that. The diamond suit will break 4-1 only about 28% of the time and you may be able to bring in the clubs anyway. But the odds are still heavily in your favor.

The worse your contract, the more assumptions you have to make. When you were in six notrump, you had to assume that diamonds were breaking 3-2. You also had to assume that the club suit was divided in such a way that you could take three tricks while giving up the lead only once. In three notrump on the same cards, you were in such an excellent contract that the only assumption you had to make was that West did not have all five outstanding diamonds.

Sometimes your contract will be so bad that you will have to assume that your opponents will make an error, for there will be no legitimate way of taking the necessary number of tricks. And some contracts will be so good that you can increase your chances to 100% by taking an elementary precaution or two. But on all hands you must make a decision at some point as to whether or not you have to be greedy, make a lot of assumptions, and play for luck.

North dealer
North-South vulnerable

N:	♠ K 9 6 5	♡ K Q	◇ A J 9 7	♣ A J 10
S:	♠ A J 8 4 3	♡ A J 6	◇ 4	♣ K Q 7 3

THE BIDDING:

N	S
1 NT	3 ♠
4 ♠	4 NT
5 ♡	6 ♠

Opening lead: ♡ 9

During the bidding, you were mildly worried about missing a grand slam. When the dummy came down, you were glad North had the queen of hearts instead of the queen of spades, which would make the grand slam a laydown. So, still thinking about that grand slam you didn't bid, you led the king of spades from dummy . . . and East showed out. Six spades down one.

You made the mistake of being greedy when you didn't have to be. You could afford to lose a spade trick; all you had to do was make sure you didn't lose two.

The correct play is a low spade from dummy. If East follows suit, go up with the ace. Now if West shows out, you can lead a spade to the king and a third round toward your jack. East can take his queen whenever he wants it. If East shows out on the first lead (as he did here), it is just as easy. Put up the ace of spades and lead a low spade toward the king-nine. Whether West plays his ten or not, he will get only one spade trick.

This is a 100% safety play; there was no way you could be set if you played the trump suit correctly. I agree that you were unlucky when West turned up with all four spades; this happens only about 5% of the time. But why give up that 5%? Note also that you will still make an overtrick if the trumps divide evenly, or if the queen is singleton. The whole layout:

```
                    ♠ K 9 6 5
                    ♡ K Q
                    ◇ A J 9 7
                    ♣ A J 10
    ♠ Q 10 7 2          N          ♠ —
    ♡ 9 8 7 5 2                    ♡ 10 4 3
    ◇ Q 8        W         E       ◇ K 10 6 5 3 2
    ♣ 9 8              S           ♣ 6 5 4 2
                    ♠ A J 8 4 3
                    ♡ A J 6
                    ◇ 4
                    ♣ K Q 7 3
```

bridge

There are a great number of suit holdings, like the spades in the previous example, which you can guard against unfavorable distributions by playing them the right way. With many of these suits, you are not necessarily giving up a trick you don't have to; you are just making bad luck work for you. Consider, for example:

> N: ♠ A J 9 7 5
> S: ♠ Q 8 6 4 3

If you can't afford to lose any tricks in this suit (let us say you are in seven spades!), you have to assume that West has the king. But make sure to lead the *queen*. There is no reason why you have to make the assumption that the spade suit is breaking evenly. If you lead low to the jack, East may show out and you will discover that you can't pick up West's remaining K-10 of spades. If you lead the queen first, West can cover, but you can get back to your hand in some other suit and play a low spade toward the jack-nine to take the proven finesse.

> N: ♡ A K 8 4 2
> S: ♡ Q 9 6 3

Here, there is no earthly reason why you should not play the queen first, just in case West has ♡ J 10 7 5.

With suits like the preceding ones, you really had to make no assumptions at all; all you had to do was play them correctly. More frequently, you will be faced with suits like this:

> N: ♣ A J 3 2
> S: ♣ K 5 4

Suppose you are in three notrump, and the only question is how to play this suit. What's the best way of tackling the clubs?

Given only this information, there is no way to tell. It is necessary to know exactly how many tricks you need to take. You would play one way for four tricks, another way for three.

| N: ♠ J | ♡ A 9 8 6 | ◇ K 7 6 5 | ♣ A J 3 2 |
| S: ♠ A 10 | ♡ K 4 3 | ◇ A 9 8 3 2 | ♣ K 5 4 |

You are in three notrump (five diamonds is a better contract, but let us say that partner bid his hand incorrectly). West leads the five of spades, and dummy's jack is covered by East's king. How do you play the hand?

Of course, if the diamonds break there will be no problem; you will have ten tricks which you can cash immediately. But if East or West should turn up with a diamond stopper, you will have to make two assumptions about the club suit, because clubs will have to provide you with two additional tricks. You have no time to set up your diamonds, because your opponents (unless they make some terrible mistake) can immediately take at least four spades and a diamond.

You lead a low diamond to the king, and East plays the jack. On another diamond lead from dummy, East discards a low spade. Too bad — you now need luck, and you have to be greedy with the clubs. West has to have the queen, and the suit has to break 3-3. So you cash the king of clubs and lead a low club to the jack. More than four times in five you will go down, but an 18% chance is better than no chance at all.

Let's put that club suit into another three-notrump contract:

```
N:  ♠ K 9      ♡ K Q J 8    ◇ J 6 2     ♣ A J 3 2
S:  ♠ A 10 6   ♡ A 10 7     ◇ Q 8 5 4   ♣ K 5 4
```

THE BIDDING:

	N	S
	1 ♣	2 NT
	3 NT	Pass

West leads the deuce of spades, and you play the nine from dummy. East plays the jack, and you duck the trick. East continues with the three of spades; West plays the four, and you win with the king. What now?

You have eight tricks off the top — four hearts, two spades and two clubs. You might be able to get a trick in the diamond suit if you knew which opponent had a doubleton honor (or both honors); but your chances there are not very good. So it will have to be the clubs.

In the last hand, you had to take four club tricks or suffer immediate defeat. Here, three club tricks will do. But if you play the king, then low to the jack, there is the danger that

East may have the doubleton queen. Do you see how you can avoid this unpleasant possibility without decreasing your odds?

Cash the ace and king of clubs first; if the queen drops on either the first or second round, fine. If West has a singleton or void, there is nothing you can do. But if both opponents follow to two rounds, lead a third club toward the jack. Now you will get three club tricks:

- *a*)   If East is void (about ½ of 1%)
- *b*)   If either East or West has the singleton queen (about 2½%)
- *c*)   If either East or West has the doubleton queen (about 16%)
- *d*)   If West has five to the queen (more than 5%)
- *e*)   If West has four to the queen (about 16%)
- *f*)   If the suit breaks 3-3 (about 36%)

You would probably have done almost as well by cashing the king first, then leading low to the jack. But why throw away an extra 8% chance when you don't have to? On this hand, you didn't care about the overtrick which would have been available if West held three clubs to the queen; you wanted to make your contract and were able to increase your chances to 76% — pretty good odds.

Apropos of this discussion of percentages, it might be wise to recall that diamond suit from the first hand in the chapter. It's the sort of suit that crops up all the time, as in this deal:

N: ♠ 9 7   ♡ 7 6   ◇ A K Q 6 4 2   ♣ 10 7 3
S: ♠ A 3   ♡ A K 5   ◇ 10 5   ♣ A 9 8 6 4 2

You are, once again, in three notrump.

Should you play for this to be a "lucky" or an "unlucky" hand? As yet, you cannot tell, for it depends on what opening lead was made. If the full layout is

```
              ♠ 9 7
              ♡ 7 6
              ◇ A K Q 6 4 2
              ♣ 10 7 3
♠ K 10 2              N              ♠ Q J 8 6 5 4
♡ Q J 10 8 3                        ♡ 9 4 2
◇ J 9 7 3     W           E         ◇ 8
♣ Q                  S              ♣ K J 5
              ♠ A 3
              ♡ A K 5
              ◇ 10 5
              ♣ A 9 8 6 4 2
```

and the opening lead is the queen of hearts, then you can
afford to play this as an "unlucky" hand. Needing only five
diamond tricks for your contract, you can safely duck a diamond, guarding against a bad break in the suit, and bring in
five diamond tricks even though they are four-one.

. But suppose the full deal is:

```
                ♠ 9 7
                ♡ 7 6
                ◇ A K Q 6 4 2
                ♣ 10 7 3
♠ K Q 10 8 6 5        N              ♠ J 4 2
♡ Q 9 8 3                            ♡ J 10 4 2
◇ J 8         W           E         ◇ 9 7 3
♣ Q                  S              ♣ K J 5
                ♠ A 3
                ♡ A K 5
                ◇ 10 5
                ♣ A 9 8 6 4 2
```

and the king of spades is led. Now you can still guard against
a four-one diamond break by ducking the first trick in the
suit. Unfortunately, however, you won't begin to enjoy your
diamond suit until after East-West have cashed enough spade
tricks to defeat your contract. The opening lead has forced
you to hope that this is a lucky hand. Fortunately, you have to
be only moderately lucky, and make one assumption — that
diamonds are breaking three-two. Even though there may be

a "right" way to play a suit, it must take a back seat to the right way to play the hand.

Of course, there are frequently obviously correct ways in which to play suits. You can easily misplay them if you are not familiar with the combinations involved. For example:

♠ A Q 10 6   in dummy opposite   ♠ 9 8 5 4 2

Many players faced with this trump suit lead the deuce to the queen the first time. When this loses to the king, they now have to guess whether to finesse the second time. But as long as you can afford to lose a trick in this suit, there is no need to finesse at all:

Lay down the ace first; if you are lucky enough to drop the king or jack, your problems are over. If nothing happens, enter the South hand in another suit and lead toward dummy, just in case West was dealt ♠ K-J-x.

Another suit combination you have to be careful with is ten cards missing the king and queen:

N: ◇ A J 10 9
S: ◇ 8 7 6 5 4 2

Don't cash the ace. The likelihood of the suit not breaking evenly is small (22%), but why take unnecessary chances? If the suit breaks 2-1, it does not matter how you play it. It also doesn't matter if East has all three outstanding diamonds; you will always lose two tricks. But if West has all three diamonds, you can save a trick by entering the South hand, leading a low diamond, and covering whatever card West plays. East may win the trick, but the diamond ace will clear the suit on the second round. This is about an 11% chance; why throw it away?

Similarly, with

N: ♣ 10 2
S: ♣ A K 9 7 5 4

you can cash the ace, all right, but don't get careless if either West or East drops an honor. Enter dummy in another suit and lead the ten; this way you will lose at most one trick in the suit. If you banged down the ace and king, you might find West grinning at you with ♣ J-8-6-3.

A good general principle to follow with these suit combinations is to make opponents' honor cards fall on your low cards whenever you can. With this suit,

N: ♡ A J 10 5 4
S: ♡ Q 7 3

don't lead the queen unless you are short of entries to the South hand. A low heart lead will save a trick if West has the singleton king. If you had led the queen, East would have irritated you with his ♡ 9-8-6-2 stopper.

You might have occasion to play this funny-looking suit sometime:

N: ♠ ——
S: ♠ J 10 9 7 5 4 3 2

No matter how this suit is distributed between the opponents' hands, you will lose at least three tricks. If the suit divides 3-2, you don't have to worry; you will lose only three tricks no matter how you play the suit. It is the 4-1 breaks you have to worry about. So *think* before you lead the jack!

Here leading the jack will lose you four tricks instead of three. A low card is correct to guard against someone holding a singleton honor. Of course, a low card will lose an unnecessary trick if one opponent holds the singleton eight, but that is only one possibility as opposed to three possibilities the other way (singleton ace, king or queen).

A frequent holding in a suit you wish to develop is:

N: ◇ K 5 3
S: ◇ Q J 7 4

bridge

If you want three tricks in this suit, how you play it when it breaks 3-3 doesn't matter. The only 4-2 break that is important is when East has the doubleton ace. Lead low to the queen; when this holds, lead low from dummy again when you next have a chance. This will make East's doubleton ace "fall on air." Of course, you could play West for the doubleton ace by leading toward the king first, then ducking the next round of the suit completely, but this would be a strange way to play; you would be giving up the chance of all 3-3 breaks.

Sometimes you can take more tricks than you are really entitled to by giving your opponents awkward guesses. It does you no harm to increase the odds in your favor by playing for a defensive error. Some years ago, a friend of mine was in a grand slam, and this was his trump suit:

N: ♠ J 5 4   (dummy)
S: ♠ A 10 8 6 3

Needless to say, he had no losers in the side suits! Rather than give up and concede down one or down two (you have to be lucky to lose one trick in this suit, let alone none), he calmly led the jack from dummy. Poor East covered with the queen, and this was the layout:

♠ J 5 4

N

♠ K W   E ♠ Q 9 7 2

S

♠ A 10 8 6 3

As you can see, East's cover was not a success. Declarer could enter dummy twice subsequently to finesse the six and eight and take five spade tricks!

There are other less spectacular ways in which you can induce the defenders to help you. For example, an old chestnut is the following (it still works):

N: ♣ Q 7 4 3
S: ♣ J 10 8 6 5 2

The lead of the queen from dummy may persuade East to cover with the doubleton king, crashing his partner's singleton ace. Sometimes this works even with only nine cards instead of ten in the combined hands.

We have seen that you can sometimes induce a cover by leading the jack with ◇ J 8 7 5 4 opposite ◇ A K 9 6 3. A more complicated suit in which you may be able to work wonders is:

> N: ♡ J 5 4 2
> S: ♡ A 9 7 6 3

You will lose one trick in this suit if it breaks 2-2, or if East has a singleton king or queen. If you are convinced, however, that East has more than one card in the suit (perhaps he opened the bidding with one notrump, for example), lead the jack from dummy. This gains a trick legitimately if East has ♡ K Q 8 and West has the singleton ten. It also steals a trick if East makes the mistake of covering with ♡ Q-10-8 or ♡ K-10-8.

The defenders can sometimes help you out of difficult guesses. Suppose this is your trump suit:

> N: ♠ A 4 2
> S: ♠ Q J 10 7 5

You will lose no tricks in the suit if West has the doubleton or tripleton king. If he has the singleton king, however, he will cover your queen (because he has no choice), and you *could* take five tricks by playing low from dummy and finessing the seven. You would feel silly, though, if the suit was breaking normally all the time and West had covered from ♠ K-8.

It may help you to lead the *ten* the first time. If West covers, the odds are that he has the singleton king. He would not normally cover the ten with two or more spades in this situation; he might run into

> N: ♠ A 4 2
> S: ♠ J 10 9 8 6 5 3

or

> N: ♠ A 4 2
> S: ♠ Q 10 9 8 5 4

In either of these cases, West's cover costs him a trick. So if West covers with ♠ K-9 and you finesse the seven on the second round, just congratulate him on having made a very nice play.

Acting on information received

While the *a priori* odds that a missing honor will be in one hand or another are exactly 50-50, once the opponents have entered the bidding this is no longer the case. An opponent who opens the bidding will hold more than an average allotment (10 points) in high cards; a takeout doubler is also marked with strength. A player who makes a preemptive opening bid or overcall sho·ld have very little in high cards outside of his long suit.

Any information the opponents give you during the auction can be put to good use. For example, if you hold a hand with several tenaces and are deciding whether or not to bid a close game, you should take the opponents' bidding into account. Are you sitting over or under the opening bidder? If the opponents have remained silent, holding a fair number of points, then it is likely that missing honors are divided between them.

Sometimes one of the opponents will make a bid that exactly limits his hand in high cards, such as an opening bid of one notrump. This information can help you in the play of many hands.

East dealer
Neither side vulnerable

```
                    ♠ A Q 10
                    ♡ Q 9 8
                    ◇ Q 9 7
                    ♣ A J 9 4
      ♠ 9 8 7 5          N          ♠ K J 6 4
      ♡ 6                           ♡ K 5 4
      ◇ J 10 8 4 3   W       E      ◇ A K 2
      ♣ 10 6 5           S          ♣ Q 8 3
                    ♠ 3 2
                    ♡ A J 10 7 3 2
                    ◇ 6 5
                    ♣ K 7 2
```

THE BIDDING:

E	S	W	N
1 NT	Pass	2 ◇	Pass
Pass	2 ♡	Pass	4 ♡
Pass	Pass	Pass	

When dummy comes down, you can see that East-West have a total of 17 high-card points between them and, since West has led the jack of diamonds, his high card is immediately made known to you. You cover the jack of diamonds with the queen, hoping to keep West off lead so he can't play a spade through dummy's tenace holding, but East wins the king and plays a diamond to partner's ten. West now does exactly what you feared he would do and shifts to a spade. You put on dummy's ten — perhaps East's one notrump opening was shaded — but East's jack wins and a third diamond is led, which you ruff with the ten.

Now you play a spade to the ace, lead the queen of hearts, which holds, and the nine of hearts. Again East refuses to cover and West discards a low diamond. It's now time to take stock. East clearly has the queen of clubs, so a straightforward finesse of the jack won't work. Can East have a doubleton club? West certainly has at least five diamonds, leaving East with at most three, and you know East has three hearts. If he has only two clubs, then East has at least five spades, and he might well have opened the bidding with one spade with a five-card suit. Is there any hope for this hand? Yes, if East has the queen of clubs *and West has the ten*. So you lead the jack of clubs from dummy, winning with the king if East covers, draw the outstanding trump, and finesse the nine of clubs. Making four hearts.

Note that lack of entries to dummy, combined with East's refusal to cover the first two heart leads, made it necessary for you to tackle the clubs before pulling the last trump. Incidentally, suppose East had had a five-card spade suit all the time, and only two clubs. The odds would still be in favor of the finesse of the nine of clubs succeeding, for West would have more clubs than East.

The opponents' bidding is also a guide as to how suits will break. With an eight-card suit holding between you and dummy, it would be foolish to assume that there is a 68% chance of a three-two break if the suit has been bid by one of your opponents. If one of your opponents preempts it is unlikely that the other suits will break according to the *a priori* odds. After all, when one opponent is known to hold a seven-card (or longer) suit, there is very little room left in his hand for cards in other suits. That's why I advise bidding cautiously after an opponent preempts.

West dealer
Neither side vulnerable

```
                         ♠ K 8 7 4
                         ♡ J
                         ◇ Q 9 7
                         ♣ K Q 10 7 5
        ♠ 5                              ♠ J 10 9 2
        ♡ K Q 10 9 8 7 6      N          ♡ A 2
        ◇ 10 3 2          W       E      ◇ J 6 4
        ♣ 4 3                S          ♣ J 9 8 6
                         ♠ A Q 6 3
                         ♡ 5 4 3
                         ◇ A K 8 5
                         ♣ A 2
```

THE BIDDING:

W	N	E	S
3 ♡	Pass	Pass	Double
Pass	4 ♡	Pass	4 ♠
Pass	?		

At this point North might think about making a slam try. I recommend that he settle for game, despite his fit for partner, useful club suit, and good distribution. This would be an excellent six-spade contract if the opponents had not opened with a preempt, depending only on a three-two spade break. With the preempt, there is too much chance of a trump loser (as in the actual case).

Another inference you can make from the opponents' bidding is that any time they compete as high as the three-level with only moderate high-card values they probably have distributional compensation. So after a competitive auction, time your play to guard against bad suit breaks.

Not only can you gather information from the opponents' bidding, sometimes their silence can be as eloquent as speech. Take this deal:

East dealer
North-South vulnerable

```
                    ♠ Q 10 7 5
                    ♡ Q 6 5
                    ◇ Q 6
                    ♣ A Q J 4
    ♠ K 3                           ♠ 8 2
    ♡ J 8           N               ♡ A K 9 7 4
    ◇ J 9 7 5 3 2   W     E         ◇ K 10 8 4
    ♣ 8 7 2             S           ♣ 5 3
                    ♠ A J 9 8 4
                    ♡ 10 3 2
                    ◇ A
                    ♣ K 10 9 6
```

THE BIDDING:

E	S	W	N
Pass	1 ♠	Pass	3 ♠
Pass	4 ♠	Pass	Pass
Pass			

West leads the jack of hearts. East cashes the ace and king of hearts and West trumps the third round with the three of spades. He exits with a diamond, and you slyly put up dummy's queen. Knowing whether East has the king of diamonds is going to be very helpful. East falls for your little trap and covers, and you win with the ace and start thinking. East has already shown up with five hearts to the ace-king and the king of diamonds. Surely if he had the king of spades as well, he would have opened the bidding. Therefore West must have the spade king, and your only hope is that it is now singleton. So you eschew the trump finesse and bang down the ace of spades, and your calculations are justly rewarded.

Even if West had not led a diamond, you might have done well to win his alternative shift of a club in dummy and lead the queen of diamonds yourself. An expert East would wonder why you were messing around with diamonds instead of drawing trumps, but there are very few players who could decide not to cover the queen without giving you some hint that they had a problem.

Counting on the odds

Some of your most educational bridge lessons may have been learned from watching, or "kibitzing," famous players. Perhaps you have had an experience similar to the following one that befell a friend of mine. One sleepy Saturday afternoon he wandered into his favorite club and spotted the well-known Mr. X, winner of countless Regional and National championships, playing at the table in the corner with three other good players. He pulled up a chair and decided to watch for a while.

After watching several hands, he noticed something rather unusual. Mr. X seemed to guess everything right. If he had a two-way finesse for a queen, he always seemed to know who had it. If it was a choice of finesse or drop, he finessed when it was necessary to finesse and played for the drop when the missing honor dropped. After a while my friend went away, saying to himself, "I guess I'm just not as lucky as he is." Of course he knew that Mr. X was a good player, too. But why did he get all the luck?

Too many players have battled at bridge for years without realizing that they could be just as lucky. All they had to do was learn how to count to thirteen! If you haven't already found out how to do it, let me illustrate one of those hands in which Mr. X was "lucky."

South dealer
East-West vulnerable

N:	♠ A 9 2	♡ K 10 9	◇ J 5 4 2	♣ Q 7 3
S:	♠ K 5 4	♡ A J 8	◇ K Q 10	♣ K 8 5 2

THE BIDDING:

S	N
1 NT	3 NT
Pass	

The opening lead was the queen of spades. Mr. X played

low from dummy, and East discarded the deuce of hearts. Declarer won the king of spades and led the king of diamonds. East won with the ace and returned a diamond; declarer won with the queen and cashed the ten of diamonds, all following suit. He continued with the deuce of clubs; West played the six, dummy the queen and East the ace. East persisted with the four of clubs; declarer played the eight; West won with the jack and shifted to the jack of spades. Declarer won with the ace, East discarding the three of hearts, and led a club to his king, West discarding the three of spades. Mr. X laid down his hand, making the announcement, "I go over to the king of hearts, cash the diamond and finesse East for the queen of hearts. The ace of hearts makes nine tricks."

How did Mr. X know that East had the queen of hearts?

When you look at your hand and the dummy, you know how many cards of a suit you have, just by adding. For example, the three clubs in dummy plus four in your hand make seven. The opponents have the other six, but you don't know how they are divided. As the play continues, however, you will get clues, and sometimes absolute certainties, as to how the suits divide.

Let's go back to Mr. X's hand. After the first trick he already knew a great deal. When East discarded a heart, Mr. X immediately had "a count" of the spade suit; West had seven, East none.

By the time Mr. X had played the third round of diamonds, he knew about that suit, too; East and West each had started with three.

The count of the club suit came later in the hand, when Mr. X cashed the king of clubs and West threw the three of spades. West had only two clubs, and therefore East had started with four.

All Mr. X then had to do was to add up what he knew about the other three suits to find out about the hearts. West had seven spades, two clubs, three diamonds and therefore only one heart. Mr. X therefore led a heart to the king, and when West didn't have the singleton queen, the finesse through East was as sure as if he had looked at East's hand. Which he had, in a way. Because by that time he knew every card in both hands. Here is the complete deal:

```
                    ♠ A 9 2
                    ♡ K 10 9
                    ◇ J 5 4 2
                    ♣ Q 7 3
    ♠ Q J 10 8 7 6 3          ♠ ──
    ♡ 7            N          ♡ Q 6 5 4 3 2
    ◇ 7 6 3     W    E        ◇ A 9 8
    ♣ J 6          S          ♣ A 10 9 4
                    ♠ K 5 4
                    ♡ A J 8
                    ◇ K Q 10
                    ♣ K 8 5 2
```

I must admit that this deal is unusual in that the distribution of both opposing hands could be figured out by the
declarer with absolute certainty. Most of the time this doesn't
happen. But on nearly all hands, you will have something
to go on. Frequently you find out a lot because of the opponents' bidding. In other cases, you can reason that because
the opponents did not bid, they must have so-and-so rather
than something else. Here is a good example of an "inferential
count":

N: ♠ K J 3 2	♡ A J 9 8	◇ A K 5 4	♣ 2
S: ♠ A 10 9 4	♡ K Q 10 5 4	◇ 2	♣ A 10 3

West opened the bidding with three clubs, and, as happens frequently when the opponents jam you with preemptive
bidding, you bid a little more than you should and arrived
in the shaky contract of seven hearts. The sixty-four dollar
question is, "Who has the queen of spades?" Let's see if we
can figure it out.

West leads the king of clubs and you play the ace and
draw two rounds of trumps, which split evenly. You cash the
ace and king of diamonds, discarding a spade from dummy,
and trump a diamond, West and East both following suit.
Next, you trump a club, and both opponents again follow.
When you ruff dummy's last diamond, both opponents ob-
stinately continue to follow suit, as they do when you ruff
your last club.

What do you know about the East-West hands? West

started with two hearts and four diamonds. He opened the bidding with three clubs, which means that unless he is an extremely wild player, he has six (he can't have more than six because East followed to three rounds). Two hearts, four diamonds, six clubs, and therefore only one spade. Cash the king of spades, and if the queen does not drop, finesse the ten and claim your thirteen tricks.

From the lofty reaches of a grand slam, let us proceed to a quiet two notrump contract:

South dealer
Neither side vulnerable
North-South 30 on score

| N: | ♠ K 10 4 | ♡ A 5 4 2 | ◊ 10 6 | ♣ A 10 9 5 |
| S: | ♠ A J 6 | ♡ K 9 3 | ◊ J 8 4 2 | ♣ Q J 3 |

S	W	N	E
Pass	Pass	1 ♣	1 ◊
2 NT	All Pass		

With a part-score of 30, I do not think North's skimpy third-hand opening is particularly good tactics; but your partner has already made the bid, and you are left to struggle in two notrump. West leads the seven of diamonds. East wins the trick with the queen and shifts to the heart jack. You win with the king and lead the queen of clubs, which wins the trick, and follow with the jack of clubs, which East takes with the king. East continues with the eight of hearts; you cover with the nine and let West's ten hold (just in case the suit breaks evenly, and also to get a count). West continues with the queen of hearts and you have to win this or lose six tricks (three diamonds, two hearts and one club). On this heart trick, East discards the five of diamonds. You cash two high clubs, East following suit and West throwing the deuce and three of spades. What now?

Unless East-West are being extremely tricky and unusual in their bids, it is odds-on that West has the queen of spades. You *know* he has four hearts and two clubs, and you *assume* he has no more than two diamonds because of East's one-diamond overcall. Therefore he has at least five spades, and percentages definitely dictate that he holds the queen.

bridge

Of course, East *could* hold the doubleton queen of spades, but this is not particularly likely. Suppose you take the spade suit out of a deck of cards and deal one card face down. You then ask, "Is the ace of spades more likely to be the card I have dealt, or is it more likely to be in the pack of twelve spades?" Obviously, the odds are heavily in favor of your *not* having dealt yourself the ace. Similarly here, if you were to take out the queen, nine, eight, seven, five, three and deuce of spades, shuffle them and deal two cards face down, the odds would be that a specific card, the queen, is in the group of five rather than in the group of two. The odds here are not nearly as high as you might wish, but they are still in your favor, and taking the spade finesse through the five-card holding will see you a winner more often than not. A five-to-two proposition is certainly better than an even bet!

If you get into the habit of trying to count the defenders' hands whenever you can, you will frequently be able to avoid plays based on careless thinking. The next hand is rather difficult, but it illustrates some of the problems you can surmount by counting out your opponents' hands:

East dealer
Both sides vulnerable

| N: | ♠ K 10 9 | ♡ A J 9 2 | ◇ K 4 3 | ♣ Q 9 2 |
| S: | ♠ A Q J 8 4 3 | ♡ 4 3 | ◇ A J 8 2 | ♣ 8 |

THE BIDDING:

E	S	W	N
Pass	1 ♠	Pass	2 NT
Pass	4 ♠	Pass	Pass
Pass			

Opening lead: ♡ K

You see that ten tricks appear easy to take; you will lose one heart and one club and perhaps one diamond, but you can ruff your fourth diamond in dummy

You get a rude shock. When you put up the ace of hearts, East ruffs and shifts to a trump. What now?

Your ten tricks have suddenly turned into nine unless you can think of some way of getting rid of your losing heart. Or, perhaps the diamond finesse is right.

So far, so good; but what's the hurry? You draw a second round of trumps ending in your hand, and West follows. You lead a club, and West puts up the king and leads another club. You ruff, enter dummy with the king of diamonds, and — no, don't take that diamond finesse!

You know that West started with seven hearts, because East ruffed the first lead (unless he revoked, and then you don't have to worry!). West also followed to two rounds of clubs, two rounds of spades, and one round of diamonds.

He has one more card you don't know about, either a club or a diamond. Whichever it is, you can ensure your contract. Ruff dummy's last club; it so happens that West discards a heart. Lay down the ace of diamonds, and if the queen doesn't drop, lead a heart. With nothing but hearts left, he is faced with a Hobson's choice. He can either duck and let you win your ninth trick (later ruffing a diamond), or he can win and give you two heart tricks in dummy by his forced heart continuation into dummy's jack-nine.

The full hand might be:

```
                    ♠ K 10 9
                    ♡ A J 9 2
                    ◊ K 4 3
                    ♣ Q 9 2
      ♠ 5 2                          ♠ 7 6
      ♡ K Q 10 8 7 6 5      N        ♡ —
      ◊ 10 6           W       E     ◊ Q 9 7 5
      ♣ K 10               S        ♣ A J 7 6 5 4 3
                    ♠ A Q J 8 4 3
                    ♡ 4 3
                    ◊ A J 8 2
                    ♣ 8
```

In this case, you would make the hand by finessing the jack of diamonds, but suppose West had the queen of diamonds instead of the ten? Since you can find out that West had exactly two diamonds and no more, the diamond finesse can gain nothing and might lose.

special odds

The odds at four-deal bridge

ALTHOUGH FOUR-DEAL BRIDGE (sometimes called "Chicago" after the place where it gained its first popularity) has been played for over 20 years, it is only recently that it has become a serious threat to old-fashioned ordinary rubber bridge. This may sound like a revolution in the card-playing habits of the world's bridge players, but actually the two games are not so different as to warrant any such description. In fact, four-deal play is best considered as a refinement of rubber bridge – one which has so many advantages that it is easy to see why it is becoming so popular. (Some advocates of four-deal bridge claim that 90% of all non-duplicate games played in bridge clubs are now the four-deal variety. Although the evidence is anything but conclusive, some surveys have been made and these seem to back up this claim.)

Four-deal bridge is played like rubber bridge but with some changes in the scoring. Each "rubber" (sometimes called a "chukker") consists of four deals, one dealt by each player. Arbitrarily, on the first deal, neither side is vulnerable; on the second and third deals, one side is vulnerable and the other is not (there are two ways to interpret this rule and I will discuss them below); on the final deal both sides are vulnerable. When a game is scored, the team achieving it is awarded 300 points if it is not vulnerable and 500 points if it is vulnerable. Furthermore, a part-score made on the final deal is worth a bonus of 100 points. This award is made on the theory that there must be compensation for the value of the part-score which, because of the rules, cannot be converted into a game. If a hand is passed out, the same dealer deals again.

For the vulnerability conditions on the second and third deals, one may play either that the dealer is vulnerable and his opponents are not, or that the dealer is not vulnerable and his opponents are vulnerable. Although, in the opinion of this writer, the second variation is superior (it avoids the "vulnerability-killing opening" — described below — which leads to dull contracts, and increases the number of preemptive bids and competitive auctions), the first is by far the more popular. Thus, in this discussion, it will be assumed that the rules specify that on the second and third deals of each chukker the dealer and his partner are vulnerable while their opponents are not.

Although, for the most part, sound rubber-bridge strategy will be equally effective at four-deal bridge, certain modifications must be made because the odds change as the scoring methods do. For example, you need not worry about prolonging a rubber with an unfavorable partner, because all "rubbers" end in four deals, regardless of what scoring has been achieved. By the way, this is one of the major advantages of four-deal bridge — you need not get stuck with a poor partner for a long and financially disastrous (as well as esthetically displeasing) rubber.

While we are on the subject, here are some of the other advantages of four-deal bridge. You will want to know these in case you are faced with the problem of convincing your regular bridge group, or the players at your club, that four-deal bridge is for the best.

Four-deal bridge shows a marked advantage when there are more than four players at one table. When one is "out" it seems that the rubber in progress always takes an eternity. And sometimes it really does. In four-deal bridge, the "out" player need not wait more than four hands before getting back "in." Similarly, the problem of "just one more rubber" can be avoided. Somehow, whenever it is agreed to play just one more rubber, that rubber is prolonged beyond the limits of endurance. In the four-deal variation, you can agree to play another chukker without fear of being delayed later than you anticipated.

bridge

Before we go into winning strategy at four-deal bridge, it should be noted that the scoring system has another effect which may not be obvious at first glance. *The stakes are greater at four-deal bridge than at ordinary rubber bridge.* The reason for this is that the two partnerships, between them, are vulnerable more often at four-deal than at ordinary rubber bridge. Thus, scoring bonuses and penalties are increased (because of the vulnerability) more often than they are at rubber bridge. Experts differ on their estimates of the magnitude of the change in stakes. Most guesses are that the stakes are increased by a margin of between 20% and 50%. Thus, if you are considering switching from ordinary rubber bridge to four-deal bridge, bear in mind that you will be playing at a somewhat higher stake, and make sure the stakes do not thereby become too high for you.

Now let's get down to a discussion of what changes in strategy should be made at four-deal bridge to have the odds working for you. The necessary changes can be divided into two categories: revised action based on the different values of part-scores, and action necessary in special situations peculiar to four-deal bridge.

THE VALUE OF PART-SCORES

In general a part-score is not as valuable in four-deal bridge as it is in standard rubber bridge. This decrease in value stems from the fact that in four-deal bridge you have less of a chance to convert into a game, while the opponents can still wipe out the game-producing value of a partial by scoring a game of their own. Therefore, except under special circumstances, you should push to game rather than settle for a part-score.

However, under certain circumstances you should value a part-score *higher* than you ordinarily would. It is this paradoxical situation which makes calculating the odds at four-deal bridge so difficult.

Consider the following situation. You deal the first hand (neither side vulnerable) and a game is made or a contract is defeated — in other words, no part score is carried to the second deal. Your left-hand opponent deals the second hand

and, according to the rules, his side is vulnerable and your side is not. Suppose that during the course of this second deal you face a decision as to whether to bid a close game or settle for what appears to be a sure part-score. In our previous discussion of the odds at rubber bridge, we saw that it would be profitable, in the long run, if you bid game whenever the chances of making it were more or less even. But you need a better chance to bid game profitably in this situation because you are trying to make a nonvulnerable game whereas your part-score will carry forward to the third and fourth deals *on which your side will be vulnerable*. In other words, the part-score will help your side in its attempt to score a *vulnerable* game. Thus, the value of the part-score made on this particular deal is greater than usual. In this case, you should not bid game unless the odds are about 2-to-1 in your favor — for example, you need a three-two split with five cards outstanding.

Similarly, when the opponents threaten to make a part-score in a situation in which it will be of increased value, you should be prepared to pay slightly more to stop their making it than you would in the same circumstances in standard rubber bridge.

Completing the circle, we see that if the opponents are threatening to make a part-score in a situation *other* than one which gives special value to the part-score, you should not fight as hard as you would at rubber bridge to prevent them from making it. Reason? The opponents will have only a limited time in which to use the value of that part-score toward making a game.

Furthermore, you now have more reason to sacrifice against a contract which will convert a part-score into a game. Once again, the value of the part-score will expire at the end of four deals. The most obvious example occurs on the fourth deal. Usually, with both sides vulnerable, it does not pay to give up 200 or 300 to stop game if the opponents have a 60 part-score, for they retain the value of the 60 points towards game for the next deal. But in four-deal, this type of sacrifice is profitable, for you stop the opponents from collecting their 500-point game bonus, and the value of the part-score then lapses. (The 100-point bonus for a part-score is awarded only if the part-score is contracted for and made on the final deal of the chukker.)

Similarly, you should not reach for close slams when you have a part-score, for you cannot be assured that there will be enough deals remaining for you to take advantage of the fact that you have a head start on the next game. And, on the same theme, you should not be as anxious to sacrifice against an opposing game in order to protect your own part-score — it just isn't worth protecting!

SPECIAL SITUATIONS

Killing the opponents' part-score   On occasion, situations may arise on which you have the chance to conclude the chukker. Sometimes it may be to your advantage to do so. Suppose it is the fourth deal and your opponents have a part-score of 30. There are three passes to you and you hold:

♠ A K J 7 5   ♡ J 8 5   ◇ 6 5 3 2   ♣ 9

Ordinarily, you would be willing to throw the deal in. The chance of game is not great and if you open you will probably wind up paying a small penalty. Passing out the deal will, therefore, tend to show you a profit. But in the given situation at four-deal bridge you should open with one spade! The opponents will have to bid above two spades in order to complete a game, and they probably cannot do so safely or successfully since the remaining strength should be equally distributed among the other three hands. Thus, the worst that can happen to you is that partner will carry the bidding too high and you will go down a trick. But you will gladly pay out 100 points to end the chukker, because this will deprive your opponents of the value of their part-score of 30, which might prove invaluable in scoring a 500-point game bonus on the redeal. (Recall that when a hand is passed out at four-deal bridge, the same dealer deals again.)

Killing the opponents' vulnerability   When the opponents are vulnerable and you are not, your side is at a considerable disadvantage. The opponents' game and slam bonuses are all greater than yours. Thus, it is to your advantage to have these deals played in as quiet a contract as possible. A passed-out hand would be ideal if the deal moved around the table, but what happens, according to the rules of the game, is that the same dealer deals again. Thus, if a deal is passed out, the vulnerability conditions will remain the same. You should take any reasonable action to prevent this situation from occurring. For example, suppose the opponents are vulnerable and you are not and you are in fourth position holding:

♠ A 8 3   ♡ K 6 4   ◇ K 7 6   ♣ Q 9 8 2

If there are three passes to you, you should open this hand with one club! This would be a pointless opening in ordinary rubber bridge, for you have no chance of game and your partner may count on you for more strength and make a minus score for your side if you open in fourth position. But in four-deal bridge you have every reason to open: you don't want to play another deal under unfavorable vulnerability conditions. You are quite willing to pay out 50 points for down one when partner bids too high to avoid the necessity of giving your opponents another chance to score a vulnerable game (or vulnerable slam!). And since you have 12 high-card points and the other strength is scattered around, nothing serious can happen on this deal.

It is because this type of fourth-position opening is good strategy that I do not approve of the rule under which the dealer is vulnerable on the second and third deals of each chukker. Often someone will open one of these fourth-hand cheeseboxes — you can't blame him, for it is clearly his best strategy — and the result is usually a very dull contract, as the strength is sure to be evenly divided between the two partnerships.

If you adopt the variation in which the dealer is *not* vulnerable on the second and third deals, a person in position to pass the deal out on one of these deals will have vulnerability conditions favorable to himself. As we will see in the next section, he will be anxious to pass out a doubtful hand, and thus what would have been a dull deal is passed out rather than played in a boring part-score contract.

Protecting your own vulnerability The reverse of the strategy described in the previous section is *not* to open a hand not offering game prospects in third position when the vulnerability favors you. Suppose that you are vulnerable and the opponents are not, there are two passes to you and you hold:

♠ 10 4   ♡ K Q 10 9 6 5   ◇ A J 8   ♣ 7 5

In normal circumstances you would open with one heart in this position. It directs a good lead and may hamper the opponents' bidding processes. Since you have a very strong suit, there is little or no danger that you will incur a big penalty, even if partner bids aggressively.

But in four-deal bridge you should *pass!* There is virtually no hope for game when partner has passed originally. Why hope for a dull part-score result on your own vulnerable deal? Instead, pass, hoping that the player in fourth position will do the same. Of course, if the bidding is opened in fourth position, you will have a chance to enter the bidding safely (to avoid being stolen blind) because of your strong suit.

SUMMARY

In four-deal bridge, changes in scoring affect the odds on certain actions. In particular:

1] The value of a part-score varies from one hand to the next. You should be aware of the situations in which a part-score is less valuable than usual (as it often is) or more valuable than usual (as it occasionally is).

2] Because of the changing vulnerability conditions, you should act in such a way as to prevent a big score by the opponents when they are vulnerable, and avoid settling for a moderate score when your side is vulnerable.

The odds at duplicate bridge

If you want to be sure to play the odds rather than your luck, duplicate bridge is the game for you. You are never concerned with the frequency of incidence of a hand and how you should convert your knowledge into the utmost profit. The hand has occurred — not just once to you, but at every other table as well. You are concerned not with what should happen in the long run but with what is going to happen at the other tables of this game.

At duplicate bridge, the winner is not he who is dealt the best cards, but he who makes the most out of the cards he (and eventually all the other players in his position at the other tables) is dealt. It is for this reason that almost all tournament competition in this country consists of some form of *duplicate* bridge. Even in non-tournament play, duplicate gives you a chance to see just how good a player you are, as measured against others who hold the same cards; and it eliminates the chance that your good play was merely good card-holding — or vice versa.

One trouble with rubber bridge is that no one ever knows just how good a player he is. Of course, if he wins day in and day out, the other players in the club will realize he is better than they are, but the club winner is apt to get complacent that way. Who knows whether he is a good player or whether he is merely better than the others in his club? Worse yet for his self-esteem, perhaps he has just been getting an extremely good run of cards.

Almost all tournament competition in this country consists of some form of *duplicate* bridge. Money is not at stake, but Master Points. And it is quite possible to win a duplicate tournament without once having an opening bid during the entire session!

For readers not familiar with duplicate bridge, I strongly advise you to gain some experience playing this fine game, particularly since it is the best way to improve your skill. If you have never played duplicate, there are several excellent books dealing with this subject; in addition, the American Contract Bridge League, governing authority for most duplicate contests in this country, publishes a free pamphlet, *Easy Guide to Duplicate*, which you may obtain by writing to this organization.* I shall attempt here briefly to familiarize you

* *American Contract Bridge League, 125 Greenwich Ave., Greenwich,* Conn. 08630.

with a few of the main concepts which make duplicate bridge different from ordinary rubber bridge.

One notable difference is in scoring. Instead of having each hand count toward a rubber, each hand (or board) is scored as an individual unit. Thus, part-scores do not have conversion value; they are worth only their trick score. If you bid two spades and make two, you get 60 for tricks plus a special bonus of 50 for making a part-score contract. Your total is therefore 110. If you had bid two spades and made three, the result would have been 140. If you bid and make a game, you get trick score plus a bonus of 300 if you are not vulnerable and 500 if you are vulnerable. Thus, bidding four spades and making five counts as 450 not vulnerable, 650 vulnerable. Slam bonuses are the same as rubber bridge, as are penalties. You still get the 50 points for making a doubled or redoubled contract, but honors do not count. Thus, bidding and making seven spades vulnerable scores 2210 (210 for tricks, plus 500 for a vulnerable game, plus 1500 for a vulnerable grand slam).

Although this is the score on your hand, it in itself is not the determining factor as to whether you have done well or poorly. At the end of the session, each score is "match-pointed" (in a pair contest, which is the way most duplicates are played). Your "match-point score" is determined, not by how many points you actually scored, but by *how you did compared with everybody else who held your cards*.

The big difference between duplicate and rubber bridge becomes most obvious here. Suppose that, sitting East-West, on Board 5 you bid four hearts and take eleven tricks, for a score of 450. (By looking at the board or at your private score, you can tell that your opponents are vulnerable, while you are not; so you score 300 for game, plus 120 for tricks, plus 30 for the overtrick).

Is this a good score? With only this information, there is no way to tell. In rubber bridge, it would probably be a good result because you had chalked up a game; but in duplicate, your real opponents are not the North-South pair at your table, but all the other East-Wests who also hold your cards. The director works it out this way: On the traveling score slip, he awards one match point to you for each pair whose score is not as good as yours, and one-half match point for each other pair with the same score as yours. Thus, in a fairly large duplicate (13 tables), the board would be played thirteen times by thirteen different East-West pairs. Suppose your opponents made a mistake which allowed you to score the overtrick in your four-heart contract. At rubber bridge, this would be unimportant; but in duplicate, if all the other pairs scored only 420 (four hearts just making), you would receive 12 match points and your present North-South opponents would get zero! All the other East-West pairs would get slightly below average, and all the other North-South pairs would get slightly above average. (An "average score" on a given board would be half of the possible match points you could possibly acquire. Thus, on the board in question, average would be 6 match points out of a possible 12.) By scoring that apparently insignificant overtrick, you would get all the match points (in duplicate parlance, a "top"). To win the usual duplicate contest, you have to get a score of between 60% and 65%, which means that you need consistently good scores; four or five "tops" will not win for you unless your other scores are consistently average or higher.

Because a duplicate contest is scored in this way, you can never really relax; every hand is just as important as every other hand. You may bid seven spades on the first hand and make it, vulnerable, for a score of 2210. On the very next hand, your opponents, struggling all the way, may manage to make two clubs for a score of 90. That 90 may be a better score, obtaining more points, than your vulnerable grand slam! After all, if, on the first board, the twelve other East-West pairs who held your cards all were as astute as you in bidding the grand slam, you will receive only an average score; but if on the second hand, no other North-South pair did better than a score of 50 for defeating East-West in, say, one notrump, that 90 would mean a "cold top" for your opponents.

You can see upon reflection that in duplicate, you can do a number of things that would be rather strange and uncalled for in rubber bridge. For example, if your opponents bid seven hearts and you *know* they will make it, you might decide to sacrifice in seven spades if you thought you could take just *two* tricks! Their vulnerable grand slam would be worth 2210;

if you bid seven spades and went down *eleven* doubled, you would score −2100, which sounds disastrous. But if every pair were allowed to play seven hearts except at your table, you would get a cold top! In practice, of course, players rarely do this. Grand slams are frequently not bid at all tables (in fact, you can almost take it as a maxim that some pairs will not bid it). It is usually better to hope that through some miscalculation the opponents will be defeated in their grand slam; in this case, you would get a top score if no one else got to seven, or if the other players with your opponents' cards played their cards better and made seven. And even if thirteen tricks are cold, you will probably get a few match points from the other pairs who tied you. This illustration shows, however, that an action which would be completely lunatic at rubber bridge might be called for at duplicate.

Some other goings-on in duplicate might make the rubber-bridge player think he was in fantasy-land:

» Duplicate players usually scorn safety plays. They are usually right!

» Duplicate players frequently risk their contracts for an overtrick!

» Duplicate players frequently indulge in close, "hair-trigger" doubles of low-level contracts, even when the doubled contract would produce game if made!

» Duplicate players would rather play a dangerous three notrump than a cold five diamonds!

Before you turn contemptuously away from the duplicate enthusiasts, you should note the overriding principle that causes them to do all those seemingly peculiar things. In rubber bridge, the *amount* of gain is the most important thing. You will sacrifice in six spades against their six hearts if you are fairly certain it will cost only 300; even if their slam cannot be made, you haven't lost much. In duplicate, this would probably be a disaster, for the *amount* of gain is not important. How many points you stand to gain or lose is relatively immaterial; what is critical to you in duplicate is the *frequency* of gain; *how often* will your play gain or lose? In the example I just mentioned, where you were contemplating sacrificing against your opponents' seven hearts, you will do so only if you think their contract will be made. *How much* you will lose if your decision is wrong is unimportant; a zero is a zero either way.

I shall discuss briefly some of the specific differences between duplicate and rubber-bridge strategy and how you should adjust your estimate of the odds. All phases of the game are radically affected by the differences in principle. As a beginning duplicate player you should realize, first, that every hand is as important as every other hand; second, that your real opponents are the other pairs sitting in the same direction as you who will be holding your cards; and third, (this cannot be emphasized too many times) how much you stand to gain or lose by your decision does not matter; the important thing is, *how often*.

GAME BIDDING

You will recall that at rubber bridge you consistently bid game when the odds of your making the contract were about even or, particularly when vulnerable, slightly against you. You did not mind being set three times out of five, because on the other two occasions you scored enough points to offset your losses on the first three hands. At duplicate, you don't want to do this; if half the pairs playing your way are bidding the game and half are not, you will come out a loser on balance by bidding these games. On three occasions, you will get a poor score by getting a minus when half of "the field" is plus; on only two occasions will you get a good score by bidding the close game and making it when the other pairs have smaller plus scores than you.

Of course, your first question will be, "How do I know what the other pairs will be doing with my cards?" Frequently, you don't; but paradoxically, you will get the most match points by trying to estimate what the other pairs playing in your direction will do, and then doing the same thing. This is known as "going with the field" and has several built-in advantages.

First, to get a good score for the entire session, you have to avoid disasters. If you go through an evening without a single major disaster (like letting the opponents make a doubled contract, or bidding a grand slam off an ace, or giving away several tricks in defense in a normal contract), you are quite likely to win the tournament! This may be surprising to you, for you may think that experts win tournaments through their dazzling and spectacular plays and brilliant coups; but I can inform you that such is not the case. Knowledge of technique is important, of course, but much more important is simply *not making obvious mistakes*. I cannot begin to tell you how many tournaments I have won, not through any brilliant play, but just from being alert to take advantage of mistakes by my opponents. Many of your good results will come when your opponents overbid, when they misdefend, or when they miss obvious games and slams. Why should you jeopardize your results by trying for brilliancies? If you concentrate on not getting zeroes or "bottoms," you will get plenty of tops and near-tops.

Second, "playing with the field" puts you in a position where you will always get some match-points, regardless of the result. Suppose you are the dealer and pick up a balanced hand with sixteen points in high cards and a five-card suit, like this:

♠ K 10 2   ♡ A J 3   ◊ K Q 9 6 4   ♣ K 10

Your obvious opening bid is one notrump, at rubber bridge or duplicate. Your partner raises you to two notrump, and it is your decision. What do you do?

You pass, because most of the other pairs will pass. Your partner has shown about 8-9 points, and game does not seem to be a good proposition. Suppose that for a moment you were blessed with the ability to read partner's mind, and you knew that he held the following hand:

♠ J 5 4   ♡ 6 5   ◊ A 5 3   ♣ Q J 9 8 4

Would you bid the game? In rubber bridge, of course; at duplicate, no.

Why the difference? The game is an excellent one that in rubber bridge you would be unhappy not to reach. But in duplicate, the other pairs are not going to get there, and you can't afford to risk getting a zero if you are set.

Suppose you bid the game. You make it, and get a top, for (let us say) twelve match points. If you go down, however, you will get zero match points, for you remember that no other pair is bidding it (most pairs do not bid games with two balanced hands and only 24 points in high cards).

Now suppose that you stop in two notrump. Everything lies well for you, and you take ten tricks for a score of 180. You will find that you have at least an average score. First of all, most of the other pairs will be in the same contract, taking the same number of tricks as you; you will get one-half match-point from each of them. In addition, you will find that one or two pairs misbid the hand and got to the wrong contract. There are always one or two inexperienced pairs playing in a duplicate game, and they may have a result like this:

S	W	N	E
(your hand)			
1 ◊	1 ♠	Pass	Pass
2 ◊	Pass	Pass	Pass

This is not a very good bidding sequence, but it does happen. These North-South pairs will take about ten tricks, scoring 130, and you will beat them as well as tieing all the other pairs who were in the same contract as you, two notrump.

Now let us suppose that the cards lie badly and three notrump cannot be made. Again you will get better than average, and you have not risked receiving a zero.

The point here is that you can usually afford to make a decision in such a way that you "will have company" if you are wrong. Since we assume you are playing your cards accurately and not making any obvious errors, you will probably get above average by making such a decision. But you don't want to be forced into a decision in which you will get a top if you are right and a bottom if you are wrong. You would have to get three or more tops for every two bottoms, and it is pretty difficult to maintain that kind of average!

Better to wait with open jaws for your opponents and in the meantime play sound, unspectacular bridge. Remember, you will always get match points from the other pairs who are doing exactly the same thing as you.

Another aspect of game bidding is one which will really irritate the good rubber-bridge player. To him, it does not matter whether he scores eleven tricks in diamonds or nine tricks at notrump; he wants to be in the safest game contract. But in duplicate, safety is not very important. For example, three notrump, made with an overtrick, scores 430 not vulnerable. Five diamonds, just making, scores only 400. If three notrump will make with an overtrick six or seven times out of ten, it is far preferable to an absolutely laydown five clubs or five diamonds. The emphasis in duplicate is not on reaching the safest game but the highest-scoring game. Thus, a feature which will be a real red flag to the rubber-bridge bull is the paltry ten extra points that can be scored for a notrump game, as against the same number of tricks in a suit. Duplicate players will strain to play in notrump whenever they can, if a notrump contract can possibly produce the same number of tricks as the safer suit contract. You may be surprised after playing your first duplicate session to find that on a given deal you scored 620 for five diamonds, making six owing to a defensive error, and received two out of a possible twelve match points! Typically, eight of the other twelve pairs were in three notrump, scoring 630 or 660; two were in four hearts, scoring 650; and two, the pairs you beat, overreached themselves by bidding *six* diamonds. No one stopped in five diamonds. In fact the only time you will find most pairs in five diamonds is when they are sacrificing or after other competitive bidding. Minor-suit games are strictly a last resort at duplicate.

SLAM BIDDING

The most obvious characteristic of slam bidding at duplicate is that it is slightly less frequent than at rubber bridge. If you bid a slam that is not a laydown, you will almost always get an extremely poor score if you fail to make it; usually, more than half the pairs will not bid it. This is not necessarily

due to any special concepts of duplicate strategy; it is simply
that duplicate bidding in the slam zone has not reached a very
high degree of attainment. Since duplicate players have found
that conservatism pays off, they have extended that concept to
the bidding of slams. They have found that, even if the slam
is cold, many pairs will not bid it and they will get some
match points anyway. Of course, you could also argue with
just as much logic that if you bid the slam and go down, you
will have some company. But year in and year out, you will
find that, other than in a very strong field such as at a
national tournament, the majority of the field does *not* bid
close slams. So avoid bidding a slam if it is likely to depend
on a finesse. Of course, you should by all means bid a slam
if the odds of making appear to be distinctly in your favor;
conservatism should not be carried too far!

Supposing you are contemplating bidding a slam that you
feel most other pairs will bid. If your estimate is correct, the
field will try to bid six notrump and score 1440 (vulnerable),
rather than be conservative and settle for 1430 (six of a major
suit) or 1370 (six of a minor). If the slam appears to be
stone cold, you should of course prefer notrump if you think
your chances are almost as good as the suit slam.

One consideration that many duplicate players often
forget is the possibility of scoring an overtrick in a slam. Suppose the odds do not favor bidding a grand slam (and you
need really good odds at duplicate), but twelve tricks should
be cold, with a play for the thirteenth. Notrump hogs frequently find that they have got their 1440, all right, but lost
many match points to their more conservative brethren who
stopped in six hearts and made an overtrick for 1460! The play
for thirteen tricks is frequently better in a suit contract; there
are chances for ruffing tricks, suit establishment, etc., which
are not available at notrump.

In the bidding of grand slams, the safety factor finally
comes into its own. Practically no one bids a grand slam at
duplicate unless it is virtually cold. If you bid a grand slam
and are set, you will almost surely get a zero. But if you have
decided to bid a grand slam, do not worry about higher-
scoring contracts unless you can count thirteen tricks off the
top. Bidding and making seven clubs or seven diamonds, for

2140, will almost surely be a good score, even though there may be a riskier make available in a major suit, for 2210, or notrump, for 2220 (these are all vulnerable scores; not vulnerable, the numbers are 1440, 1510, and 1520).

COMPETITIVE BIDDING

Rubber bridge players will find that competitive bidding in duplicate is quite different. Sequences like this, which seldom if ever come up in rubber bridge, are common at duplicate:

W	N	E	S
1 ♡	Pass	2 ♡	Pass
Pass	Double	Pass	2 ♠
3 ♡	Pass	Pass	3 ♠
Pass	Pass	Pass	

The bidding by the North-South pair in this sequence is known as "balancing." North's double was a "balancing double," and West's three-heart bid was "balancing back in," all of which will strike rubber bridge players as unmitigated nonsense. Why should North double at the two-level when he couldn't double at the one-level? Why is South bidding at the three-level all of a sudden? In this nightmare world, it seems that all four players have gone slightly crazy. They appear to be violating every rubber-bridge concept of safety and risk — which, of course, they are.

Since every hand in a duplicate game is just as important as every other hand, a great deal of attention must be paid to the small hands, those deals in which neither side can make a game. On the vast majority of these hands, both sides can make something; paradoxically, it may be somewhat safer to contest the bidding *after* your opponents have told you that their strength is strictly limited, than to come in right away and expose your neck to the chopping-block. Let's look at a typical duplicate part-score hand.

West dealer
Both sides vulnerable

```
                    ♠ 10 9 5
                    ♡ A 9
                    ◇ Q 8 7 5 4
                    ♣ A 10 6
   ♠ A 2                          ♠ J 7 6
   ♡ K Q 5 3 2        N           ♡ J 10 6 4
   ◇ 9 6          W       E       ◇ A J 2
   ♣ K Q 9 4         S           ♣ 5 3 2
                    ♠ K Q 8 4 3
                    ♡ 8 7
                    ◇ K 10 3
                    ♣ J 8 7
```

THE BIDDING:

W	N	E	S
1 ♡	Pass	2 ♡	Pass
Pass	Double!	Pass	2 ♠
Pass	Pass	?	

No rubber-bridge player would dream of taking action with the North hand; however, any rubber-bridge player would get a poor duplicate score with the North-South cards. You can see that East-West can easily make two hearts. If allowed to play in this contract, they will score 110, and probably an excellent match-point score.

The reason North-South would get such a poor score for −110 is that their side can make two or three spades. It is a near-disaster to sell out for −110 when you could have scored 110 yourself. What makes the situation even more tricky, however, is that even if two spades could not have been made, North-South would improve their score by bidding two spades and going down one for a score of −100.

On this hand, East-West have 21 points to North-South's 19. Yet the hand "belongs" to North-South because of the good lie of the club suit, and the favorably-placed diamond jack. There is no possible way that this could have been found out during the bidding. So North-South took dangerous action in the hope of ensuring themselves a better match-point score. They had several factors in their favor: First, they knew that the East-West high-card strength was limited, because they had made no attempt to get to game; second, there was the possibility that their side could make something, too; third, East-West might bid three hearts and find themselves with a minus score.

Of course, the dangerous aspects of their action were also evident. North-South might go down in two spades and then find that neither side could make anything at this level. Also, North-South might be unable to find a good suit fit, or they might be doubled and set heavily for a near-zero. But again, on *frequency* their reopening double was the best chance of increasing their match-point score. More about these reopening bids in a moment. For the time being, you can see from this hand that both sides must take risks that rubber bridge players would consider unreasonable, just to improve their score from −110 to −100, or perhaps to +110. Competition is even more keen when neither side is vulnerable. In that case, the reopening side can even afford to get doubled as long as the set is no more than one trick. A score of −50 may be a near top when most of the other pairs your way are suffering losses of −90, −110 or −140.

Balancing

At duplicate bridge, a hand is almost never passed out in one of a suit. The same hand on which the contract might be conceded in a sociable rubber bridge game is bitterly contested at duplicate.

Reopening the bidding in fourth seat after two passes is called "balancing" or (in England) "protection." Your partner will expect, until shown otherwise, subminimum values for your call, whether or not you have previously limited your hand by passing. A takeout double, for instance, shows only about ten points in this position; of course, with a better hand, the doubler will bid again. After the auction 1♠ − Pass − Pass, double with

♠ J 2   ♡ K Q 8 3   ◇ K 7 4   ♣ Q 10 9 5

and thereafter hold your peace.

Similarly, a reopening bid of one notrump does not show a full opening bid or overcall of one notrump, or anything like it. The usual range is about 11-13 points.

♠ K 10 3   ♡ A J 2   ◇ Q J 10 3   ♣ J 10 4

is a typical reopening bid of one notrump after an opening bid of one heart by left-hand opponent is followed by two passes.

A reopening overcall at the one-level shows no more than a respectable five-card suit and scattered values:

♠ Q 7   ♡ K J 10 7 5   ◇ K 9 4   ♣ 10 9 6

would be a reopening bid of one heart after left-hand opponent has bid one club and the other two players have passed. It follows that, if one heart may indicate as weak a hand as this, the *reopening* jump bid must show more. It would make little sense to make a weak jump overcall in this position; you would rather pass and hope that somehow the opponents had missed a game. So the reopening jump overcall is a good sound hand, inviting a raise on moderate values; something like

♠ A K 10 7 6 4   ♡ J 2   ◇ A 10 9   ♣ Q 2

would be typical. Otherwise, partner might let you languish in one spade with

♠ Q 8   ♡ A 10.6   ◇ 8 7 4 3   ♣ K 10 9 7

for, for all he knows, you might have a scattered nine- or ten-count with a one-spade reopening bid. So bid two spades, and you will stand a fighting chance to reach the fine three-notrump contract.

The one time that the duplicate player will pass out a one-bid with close to an average hand or better is when he holds length in the opponents' suit. Now he faces real danger that by reopening he will allow them to find a better spot. So widespread is this practice that most good duplicate players will automatically lead a trump against a one-level contract, expecting partner to have a strong enough holding to permit the eventual drawing of trumps and prevent the opponents from scoring tricks by ruffing.

Playing against the odds

Sometimes the play of the hand in match-point duplicate seems to fly completely in the face of the odds, committing such "folly" as risking 700 points for the possibility of gaining 30. The reason is that the basis for calculating the true odds has shifted from "how much" to "how often." This is not always easy to calculate exactly, because it may involve intangibles, but in some cases the choice is clear-cut.

For example:

With both sides vulnerable, North opens the bidding with one diamond and South bids three notrump. West opens the deuce of hearts and South counts his sure tricks on this layout:

```
N:  ♠ A Q 6     ♡ 9 3     ◇ A J 10 9 8     ♣ J 7 2
S:  ♠ K J 10 3   ♡ A K 7   ◇ 6 4 3          ♣ K Q 10
```

With two heart tricks, four spade tricks and one sure trick in diamonds, South can insure his contract against any distribution of the opposing cards by establishing two winners in clubs. At rubber bridge, South takes the 100% play; he leads a club, grabs his nine tricks, chalks up 100 below the line and 500 for the rubber. Of course, if he could find one or both of the diamond honors with West he could establish three additional tricks in diamonds instead of two tricks in clubs and would make four notrump, collecting 630 instead of 600. But if East held both the diamond honors, South would be set one trick for minus 100, so he would be risking 700 points for a possible gain of 30. The chances are three to one that East will not have both diamond honors, but the one time in four that South lost his game would cost 700 points against a gain of 90 for the three times he would gain 30 points by playing diamonds instead of clubs.

Playing match points, however, let's assume that top score is 12. If you play for average on four deals, scoring 6 on each, your total score is 24. If you play for top on four deals, and make it on three, your total score is 36. The possibility that someone may reach four spades at another table means that three notrump scores even less than average and further weights the odds in favor of the diamond finesses.

Another case:

Both sides vulnerable

| N: | ♠ 7 5 2 | ♡ K J 2 | ◇ K Q J | ♣ 8 5 4 3 |
| S: | ♠ A Q 10 6 4 3 | ♡ A 7 6 | ◇ A 4 | ♣ 9 2 |

South is playing a normal four spade contract, with no adverse bidding. West leads the king of clubs, continues with the queen and leads the 10 to East's ace, which South ruffs. Presumably East also has the jack of clubs, so there is no indication from the number of points known to be held by both players as to which is more likely to hold points in spades.

At rubber bridge, declarer's correct play is clear. He insures his 620 score against the possibility of losing a finesse of the queen of spades to a blank king in West's hand by making the standard safety play of cashing the spade ace. In approximately three cases out of four — where East held K-J, K-9, or K-8 — this loses a potential 30-point overtrick. South cheerfully pays 130 points to insure against the loss of 720, and gains a further 30 (by means of a finesse against the jack of spades) in the one case where he drops the blank king.

In duplicate, however, playing a normal contract against the normal defense presumed to have taken place at all other tables, South cannot afford to give up the play for the overtrick, based roughly on the same calculation as in the preceding example. The number of points to be gained or lost yields to the number of times the gain or loss will occur. South must go to dummy with a diamond and finesse the queen of spades.

Similarly, in defense play, a defender cannot concern himself solely with a comparison of the total points to be won or lost. Assume that the opponents have sacrificed, not vulnerable, at three spades doubled against your three heart contract. If you were allowed to play and make three hearts, you would score 140 = 90, plus 50 for the part score. If you set the opponents only one trick, the most you can collect will be 100. At rubber bridge, you take the sure set. In duplicate, it may pay you to risk allowing the opponents to make their contract in order to try to set them two tricks for plus 300. At rubber bridge, you would be risking 630 points — the 100 point penalty, plus 180 in tricks and 300 for the value of the game and 50 as the bonus for making a doubled contract — to gain 200. In duplicate, you are risking what probably will be a poorer than average score — 100 against the 140 at other tables — for a shot at top score. Here, in playing for the extra trick set, you are going with the odds.

How to play card combinations

The number of different card combinations you, as declarer, can face, is virtually infinite. No one can possibly know the best possible method of maneuvering all combinations of cards. Nonetheless, the more of the "percentage plays" of different suits that you know, the more successful you will be in your quest for tricks.

As you will, I hope, remember, the "correct" method of playing a suit may be different from one hand to the next. In this section I list the best methods of play of some of the more common and more important combinations of cards you are likely to run across. In each case I give the best method of handling the combination for the different numbers of tricks you might want to take in the suit. In all situations, I have assumed that you have sufficient entries to lead the suit from either hand and reenter either hand if necessary to cash a winning trick. This last condition will not always be realistic, but there are so many different cases that it would be impossible to give even a partial list that would be meaningful.

When a restricted entry position or a new card combination arises, you must try to work out how to handle it based on general principles, or on its similarity to other combinations which are almost the same. Thus, a careful study of the listing in this section can pay big dividends, even if you do not come face to face with the actual combination given in the text.

card combination (dummy's holding on top line; declarer's holding below)	tricks wanted	best method of play
A K Q J 9 2	5	Play to drop the ten
A K Q J 9 3 2	6 5	Play to drop the ten Finesse the nine
A K Q 8 4 J 3 2	5	Cash the jack first
A K Q 10 2	4	Finesse the ten
A K Q 10 9 2	5	Play to drop the jack
A K Q 10 3 2	4 or 5	Finesse the ten
A K Q 9 3 2	4	Finesse the nine
A K Q 10 9 3 2	6	Play to drop the jack
A K Q 10 4 3 2	6 4 or 5	Play to drop the jack Finesse the ten

bridge

card combination	tricks wanted	best method of play
A K 10 4 3	5	Play to drop the jack
Q 9	4	Cash the queen, then lead the nine for a finesse
A K 4 3 2	4 or 5	Finesse the ten
Q 10		
A K Q 10	4	Play to drop the jack
4 3 2		
A K Q 9	4	Cash the ace, then the king. If an honor falls behind dummy, finesse on the third round
4 3 2		
A K 9 3 2	5	Cash the ace, then the queen
Q 8 4	4	Lead low to the eight or nine
A K 10 3 2	5	Play the ace first
Q 9 5 4		
A K 9 3 2	5	Play the queen first
Q 8 5 4		
A K J 10 (9)	4 (5)	Finesse the jack
2		
A K J 9 8	4 or 5	Finesse the jack
2		
A K J 9	3 or 4	Finesse the nine. If this loses to the ten, later finesse the jack
3 2		

card combination	tricks wanted	best method of play
A J 3 2 K 9	3	*Finesse the nine*
A K J 10 9 3 2	6	*Finesse the jack*
A K J 10 9 3 2	5	*Finesse the jack. Note that the ace should* not *be cashed first*
A K J 10 9 4 3 2	5	*Cash the ace, then finesse the jack*
A K 3 2 J 10 9	3 or 4	*Run the jack*
A K 3 2 J 5 4	3	*Play the ace, then lead toward the jack*
A K J 10 9 3 2 4	7	*Finesse the jack*
A K 9 8 7 3 J 2	5 or 6	*Run the jack*
A J 5 4 3 2 K 9	5 or 6 4	*Cash the king, then lead to the jack* *Lead small to the nine*
A K 9 4 3 J 5 2	5 4	*Cash ace, king* *Cash the ace, then lead toward the jack*

bridge

card combination	tricks wanted	best method of play
A J 5 3 2	5	Lead low to the jack
K 9 4	4	Cash the ace, then low to the nine
A 9 4 3 2	5	Finesse the jack
K J 5	4	Cash the king, then lead low to the jack
	3	Either of the above
A K 3 2	4	Cash ace and king
J 9 8 4	3	Cash the ace, run the nine
A J 4 3	4	Finesse the jack
K 9 5 2	3	Cash the ace, then lead to the nine
A K J 6 5 4 3 2	8	Cash the ace and king
7	7	Finesse the jack
A K 9 6 5 4 3	7	Cash ace and king
J 2	6	Lead low to the jack
A Q J 9	3	Finesse the nine
2		
A Q 9 8	3 or 4	Run the jack, intending to finesse the nine later unless the jack holds
J 2		
A Q 4 2	3	Lead small to the nine
J 9		

card combination	tricks wanted	best method of play
A Q J 9 3 2 4	5 or 6 3 or 4	Finesse the queen Finesse the nine
A Q 9 8 2 J 3	4 or 5	Run the jack; finesse the nine next if covered
A Q 4 3 2 J 5	4 3	Lead small to the jack Cash the ace, then small to the jack
Q J 9 8 7 A 2	5 4	Run the queen Cash the ace, then lead to the queen
A Q J 2 5 4 3	4 3	Finesse the queen, then jack Cash the ace, then lead toward the queen
Q J 5 4 3 A 9	3 or 4	Lead small to the nine
A Q 9 8 J 3 2	4 3	Run the jack. If covered, finesse the nine Finesse the queen. If it holds, run the jack
Q J 3 2 A 5 4	3	Play the ace, then lead toward the queen and jack
A Q 5 4 3 J 6 2	5 4	Finesse the queen, then play the ace Cash the ace, then lead to the jack

bridge

card combination	tricks wanted	best method of play
A 7 6 5 4 3 Q J 2	6 5	*Run the queen* *Lead low to the queen*
A Q J 4 3 2 10 9 8 7 6	6	*Play to drop the king*
A Q J 4 3 2 10 9 8 7	6	*Finesse against the king*
A Q 9 8 7 6 J 4 3 2	6	*Lead the jack, intending to finesse*
A K 10 9 4 3	3 or 4	*Finesse the ten*
A 9 3 2 K 10	3	*Lead to the ten*
A K 10 9 2 4 3	4 or 5 3	*Finesse the ten* *Play the ace, then finesse the ten*
A 10 9 4 3 2 K 5	6 5	*Cash king and ace* *Cash the king, then finesse the ten*
A K 10 9 2 5 4 3	4 or 5	*Finesse the ten*
A K 8 3 2 10 6 5	5 4 3	*Cash ace and king* *Cash the ace, then play small to the ten* *Lead small to the ten*

card combination	tricks wanted	best method of play
A 10 3 2 K 9 5 4	4 3	Cash ace and king Lead small to the ten, then cash the ace
A K 10 9 4 3 6 5 2	6	Play the ace. If an honor drops behind, finesse the ten
K Q J 9 (3) 2	3 (4)	Finesse the nine
K Q 4 3 J 6 5	3	Lead to the king, then to the queen
A Q 10 9 2	3	Finesse the ten
A Q 9 4 3 2	2	Finesse the nine, then the queen
A Q 9 8 3 4 2	4 3	Finesse the nine, then the queen Finesse the nine, then the eight
A 10 9 4 3 Q 2	4 3	Run the queen, then finesse the ten Cash the ace first
Q 6 5 4 3 A 10	3 or 4 2	Lead to the ten Play the ace and lead to the queen

bridge

card combination	tricks wanted	best method of play
A Q 10 9 4 3 2	3 or 4	Finesse the ten
A Q 10 8 4 3 2	4 3 2	Finesse the eight Finesse the queen, then the ten Lead to the ten, then cash the ace
Q 6 5 4 3 2 A 10	3 or 5 4	Finesse the ten Cash the ace, then lead to the queen
K 10 2 Q 3	2	Lead to the queen, then finesse the ten
K Q 10 9 (3) 2	3 (4)	Finesse the ten
K Q 10 9 3 4 2	3 or 4	Finesse the ten
K Q 10 3 7 6 5 4	3	Lead to the king, then to the ten
K 4 3 2 Q 7 6 5	3 2	Lead to an honor, then duck in both hands Play low from both hands first
A J 10 4 3 (2)	2	Finesse the jack, then the ten

card combination	tricks wanted	best method of play
A J 9 4 3 (2)	2	*Finesse the nine, then the jack*
A J 10 7 4 (3) 6 5 2	4 (5)	*Finesse the jack, then the ten*
K J 9 8 3 2	2 or 3	*Finesse the nine*
K J 10 9 8 7 5 4 3 2	5	*Finesse the jack*
Q J 3 6 5 4	1	*Lead to the queen, then to the jack*
Q J 9 6 5 4	1	*Lead to the queen, then to the jack*
Q 5 4 J 6 2	1	*Lead to the queen, then to the jack*
Q 9 2 J 4 3	1	*Lead to the jack, then to the nine*
K 10 9 8 6 5 4 3	2	*Finesse the ten, then the nine*

Some tables you don't need to learn

It may be interesting to know what your chances are of holding a complete suit, but about the only value of learning this astronomical figure is to teach you to look with suspicion upon the honesty of the deal (or to expect that somebody has failed to shuffle properly) if you pick up a complete suit hand. Only a mathematician gets any real satisfaction from knowing abstract percentage figures. What I want to know about the odds is how they should affect what I can expect to win or lose.

If you wish to be stubborn about odds, you can maintain that what has already appeared did not affect the original chance of any particular distribution — which is certainly true. But if you are a pragmatist, you will not insist that the chances are even that one player will hold a particular card if another player has already played it.

Perhaps the most valuable of the tables, from the standpoint of what you can learn about proper play, are those affecting suit combinations. However, the following material may also have its uses.

Tabulating the odds

THE POINT COUNT

Almost all bridge writers agree that the popular point count methods, promulgated in my books, have greatly improved the bidding accuracy of the average player and have helped make bridge the world's most popular card game. Many people, having learned the point-count rules, ask me, "What is the chance of getting each of the different point counts?" They want to know, for example, how often they will hold the 16-to-18 points required for an opening bid of one notrump, or the point ranges for various other bids.

In the following chart, I list the chance of being dealt any precise number of points (counting 4 for an ace, 3 for a king, 2 for a queen, and 1 for a jack). These values are expressed in terms of percentages; in other words, the number of times in 100 deals you can expect to hold the number of points in question.

Probability of holding a precise number of high-card points (values expressed in percentages)

number of points	% chance	number of points	% chance
0	0.3639	19	1.0361
1	0.7884	20	0.6434
2	1.3561	21	0.3778
3	2.4624	22	0.2101
4	3.8455	23	0.1118
5	5.1864	24	0.0558
6	6.5542	25	0.0264
7	8.0282	26	0.0117
8	8.8922	27	0.0050
9	9.3560	28	0.0019
10	9.4051	29	0.0007
11	8.9447	30	0.0002
12	8.0268	31	0.0001
13	6.9143	32	0.000017
14	5.6934	33	0.0000035
15	4.4237	34	0.00000071
16	3.3109	35	0.000000098
17	2.3616	36	0.00000000927
18	1.6051	37	0.00000000062991

LONG SUITS

How long is a really long suit? If you play bridge regularly, you probably have the feeling that you see a seven-card suit once in a while, but an eight-card suit (while you do get them) is a rare occurrence. This experience conforms to the expected percentages. About 3½% of all hands have a seven-card suit, but only 1 in every 200 has an eight-card suit. Longer suits are rare to the vanishing point. I estimate that my bridge career has spanned some half-million or more deals, and I don't think I have held a nine-card or longer suit more than a few dozen times. This figure is slightly below the mathematical expectancy, so perhaps I hold relatively dull cards.

For those who are interested in long suits, here are the percentages on how often you can expect to get suits of specified length.

Probability of having long suits

longest suit in your hand	% chance
4	35.0805
5	44.3396
6	16.5477
7	3.5267
8	0.4668
9	0.0370
10	0.0017
11	0.000036
12	0.00000032
13	0.00000000062991

You can see from this table that the chance of a suit of eleven cards or longer is microscopic. I can remember holding a suit of eleven cards only once (not counting the times I was the victim of a "goulash" deal). I have queried many long-time bridge addicts about big suits and only one could remember ever holding an eleven-card suit (each could remember at least one ten-card suit, however). So I guess I have no right to complain after all.

SUIT DISTRIBUTIONS

Sometimes a hand is exciting not because it contains a long suit, but because it contains skewed distributions. Voids always enliven the play because they introduce the element of the unpredictable; hands with two long suits have great playing strength and are fun to hold. If you give me a choice between:

♠ A Q 7 3   ♡ K Q 10   ◇ A Q J   ♣ Q 10 6,

20 high-card points but poor distribution, and

♠ A K 8 6 4 2   ♡ A Q J 9 5 2   ◊ 10   ♣ —

only 14 high-card points but spectacular distribution, I will take the second hand every time. As little as a doubleton spade and four hearts to the king in partner's hand will produce a virtually laydown slam in hearts. With the first hand, you will need a lot of holes filled by partner in order to make a slam, and even game is far from a certainty.

In the table that follows, I list the percentage chance of picking up each possible suit distribution.

Probability of different suit distributions

distribution	% chance	distribution	% chance
4-4-3-2	21.5512	8-2-2-1	0.1924
5-3-3-2	15.5168	8-3-1-1	0.1176
5-4-3-1	12.9307	8-3-2-0	0.1085
5-4-2-2	10.5797	7-5-1-0	0.1085
4-3-3-3	10.5361	6-6-1-0	0.0723
6-3-2-2	5.6425	8-4-1-0	0.0452
6-4-2-1	4.7921	9-2-1-1	0.0178
6-3-3-1	3.4482	9-3-1-0	0.0100
5-5-2-1	3.1739	9-2-2-0	0.0082
4-4-4-1	2.9932	7-6-0-0	0.0056
7-3-2-1	1.8808	8-5-0-0	0.0031
6-4-3-0	1.3262	10-2-1-0	0.0011
5-4-4-0	1.2433	9-4-0-0	0.0010
5-5-3-0	0.8952	10-1-1-1	0.0004
6-5-1-1	0.7053	10-3-0-0	0.0002
6-5-2-0	0.6511	11-1-1-0	0.000025
7-2-2-2	0.5130	11-2-0-0	0.000011
7-4-1-1	0.3918	12-1-0-0	0.00000032
7-4-2-0	0.3617	13-0-0-0	0.00000000062991
7-3-3-0	0.2653		

THE CHANCE OF A FIT

Very often, you are faced with a decision as to whether or not to make a risky bid of a suit at a high level. In these situations, you often wonder how likely it is that your partner

bridge

will have cards in support of your suit. The following table gives the chance of partner holding a specified number of cards in your suit. Of course, the more cards you have the fewer partner figures to have, so these numbers vary with your own length in the suit.

number of cards you hold	chance of partner holding specified number of cards	
	number	% chance
13	0	100.0000
12	0	66.6667
	1	33.3333
11	0	43.8596
	1	45.6140
	2	10.5263
10	0	28.4495
	1	46.2304
	2	22.1906
	3	3.1294
9	0	18.1760
	1	41.0937
	2	30.8203
	3	9.0406
	4	0.8693
8	0	11.4250
	1	33.7556
	2	35.2231
	3	16.1440
	4	3.2288
	5	0.2235
7	0	7.0566
	1	26.2102
	2	35.7412
	3	22.7915
	4	7.1223
	5	1.0256
	6	0.0526
6	0	4.2767
	1	19.4591
	2	33.3584

number of cards you hold	chance of partner holding specified number of cards	
	number	% chance
	3	27.7987
	4	12.0864
	5	2.7194
	6	0.2901
	7	0.0112
5	0	2.5393
	1	13.8993
	2	29.1886
	3	30.5786
	4	17.3742
	5	5.4389
	6	0.9065
	7	0.0725
	8	0.0021
4	0	1.4744
	1	9.5838
	2	24.2118
	3	31.0718
	4	22.1941
	5	9.0794
	6	2.1053
	7	0.2632
	8	0.0158
	9	0.0003
3	0	0.8355
	1	6.3892
	2	19.1676
	3	29.5922
	4	25.8931
	5	13.3165
	6	4.0353
	7	0.7018
	8	0.0658
	9	0.0029
	10	less than 0.0001
2	0	0.4610
	1	4.1199

bridge

number of cards you hold	chance of partner holding specified number of cards	
	number	% chance
	2	14.5410
	3	26.6585
	4	28.0615
	5	17.6788
	6	6.7348
	7	1.5306
	8	0.1996
	9	0.0139
	10	0.0004
	11	less than 0.0001
1	0	0.2470
	1	2.5683
	2	10.5941
	3	22.8501
	4	28.5626
	5	21.6475
	6	10.1022
	7	2.8863
	8	0.4920
	9	0.0475
	10	0.0024
	11	less than 0.0001
	12	less than 0.0001
0	0	0.1280
	1	1.5457
	2	7.4195
	3	18.7032
	4	27.5048
	5	24.7543
	6	13.8971
	7	4.8640
	8	1.0423
	9	0.1316
	10	0.0092
	11	0.0003
	12	less than 0.0001
	13	less than 0.0001

SUIT SPLITS

The table below gives the chance of finding all possible splits of the opposing cards. The number in the left-hand column is the combined total of cards held by declarer and dummy in the suit in question.

cards held	split of suit in enemy hands	% chance
12	1-0	100.0000
11	2-0	48.0000
	1-1	52.0000
10	3-0	22.0000
	2-1	78.0000
9	4-0	9.5652
	3-1	49.7391
	2-2	40.6957
8	5-0	3.9130
	4-1	28.2609
	3-2	67.8261
7	6-0	1.4907
	5-1	14.5342
	4-2	48.4472
	3-3	35.5280
6	7-0	0.5217
	6-1	.6.7826
	5-2	30.5217
	4-3	62.1739
5	8-0	0.1648
	7-1	2.8558
	6-2	17.1350
	5-3	47.1213
	4-4	32.7231
4	9-0	0.0458
	8-1	1.0709
	7-2	8.5675
	6-3	31.4142
	5-4	58.9016
3	10-0	0.0108

bridge

cards held	split of suit in enemy hands	% chance
	9-1	0.3500
	8-2	3.7798
	7-3	18.4789
	6-4	46.1973
	5-5	31.1832
2	11-0	0.0020
	10-1	0.0962
	9-2	1.4437
	8-3	9.5282
	7-4	31.7607
	6-5	57.1692
1	12-0	0.0003
	11-1	0.0210
	10-2	0.4620
	9-3	4.2348
	8-4	19.0564
	7-5	45.7354
	6-6	30.4902
0	13-0	less than 0.0001
	12-1	0.0033
	11-2	0.1170
	10-3	1.5729
	9-4	9.8307
	8-5	31.8514
	7-6	56.6247

LENGTH IN A GIVEN SUIT

The following table gives the chance that you will be dealt exactly, at most, or at least a specified number of cards in a specified suit.

number of cards	% chance of being dealt (in a specified suit)		
	exactly this number	at most this number	at least this number
0	1.279	1.279	100.000%
1	8.006	9.285	98.721
2	20.587	29.872	90.715
3	28.633	58.505	70.128
4	23.861	82.366	41.495
5	12.469	94.835	17.634
6	4.156	98.991	5.165
7	0.882	99.873	1.008
8	0.117	99.990	0.126
9	0.009	99.999	0.010
10	0.001	above 99.999	below 0.001
11, 12, 13	below 0.001	above 99.999	below 0.001

glossary

À CHEVAL In baccarat, a bet that both players will beat the bank; in roulette, covering two adjoining numbers with one chip.

ADVERTISEMENTS (ADS), ADVERTISING In gin, a discard of a card of rank equal to one desired, eg., with: ♡ 9 ♡ 8, a discard of the ♢ 7 would be an advertisement, in hopes that the opponent will discard the ♡ 7 should he hold it.

AUCTION In bridge and pinochle, the period of the game devoted to bidding; the bidding itself.

AUCTION PINOCHLE Pinochle game where players bid for the privilege of declaring the trump suit; the successful bidder gains the benefit of adding the contents of a three-card widow to his hand and discarding three other cards to replace them.

BACCARAT Casino card game in which objective is to total as near 9 as possible. (Picture cards and 10s count 0.)

BACK GAME In backgammon, the timing of the play to keep enough men in your opponent's inner table so as to prevent him from bearing off without giving you a chance to hit one of his men.

BACKGAMMON A board game played by two players, in which the object is to remove all your pieces (stones) from the playing area before your opponent removes his.

BALANCING In bridge, re-opening the auction after two passes by bidding or doubling, after it is clear that the opponents do not hold the balance of power. This action is usually restricted to duplicate bridge.

BANCO In baccarat or chemin de fer, the offer by a single player to cover the entire amount of money in the bank.

BANKER In casino games, the person against whom the bettors compete.

BAR In backgammon, the divider strip between each player's inner and outer table, on which are placed those men that have been hit and are off the board.

BAR POINT In backgammon, the first point on the outer table.

BEARING OFF In backgammon, the process of removing stones from the inner table.

glossary

BETE In pinochle, when a player fails to make his contract, he is said to go *bete*.

BIG SIX — BIG EIGHT In craps, an even money bet that a six or an eight will appear before a seven.

BINGO A variation of lotto in which the player is given the center square free.

BIRDCAGE A casino game, where three dice are spun in a cage, and the bettor wagers that one or more of the dice will show the number on which he bets.

BLACKJACK A card game in which the objective is to score as close as possible to twenty-one without going over that total.

BLACKWOOD In bridge, a convention used to determine the number of aces held by a partnership.

BLIND In pinochle, another name for the widow; in poker, and other games, a bet or raise without looking at one's hand.

BLITZ In gin, the completion of a game before one of the contestants has been able to get on score.

BLOT In backgammon, a point which is covered by only one stone, and thus capable of being hit.

BOARD In bridge, the dummy hand. In duplicate bridge, a device used to hold each thirteen card hand in a separate pocket. In backgammon, checkers, pachisi, etc., the "table" on which the game is played.

BOOSTING In auction pinochle, an attempt to force an opponent to bid too high by use of competitive bidding.

BOTTOM In duplicate bridge, a score which neither beats nor ties any other score; low score.

BOXES In gin, an award for "going gin," or for winning a hand. A box is usually valued at 25 points. Basically a "box" is one square in which the score of a deal is entered.

BUST In blackjack, having a combination which goes over 21 points. If a player goes "bust" he automatically loses.

CANASTA A variation of gin, played with a 108 card deck (two standard decks plus four jokers). In the game, a canasta is a combination of seven matching cards (up to three of which may be "wild cards" — jokers or deuces).

CASE-DOWN PLAYER In blackjack, a person who is able to remember all the cards which have been played and scale his bets and strategy accordingly.

CHECK In poker, a call to signify that the player doesn't want to bet in that turn of play.

CHECK-RAISE In poker, a raise of a bet by a person who originally chose not to bet.

CHEMIN DE FER A two-hand variation of baccarat.

CHUKKER In four-deal bridge, another name for the rubber or set of four completed deals.

CHICAGO Four-deal bridge.

COME   In craps, a method of betting that on the next roll of the dice the shooter will be successful.

COME-OUT   In craps, the first roll of the dice.

CONSECUTIVE THROWS   A variation of coin tossing in which the first person to throw a head wins.

CRAP-OUTS   In craps, a roll of 2, 3, or 12 on the come-out.

CRAPS   A casino game, in which two dice are thrown, and the objective is to wager successfully on the result of the throw of the dice.

CRIB   In cribbage, the extra hand which belongs to the dealer for scoring purposes. It is composed of four cards, two thrown by each of the players.

CRIBBAGE   A card game (usually two-hand; sometimes four-hand) in which the object is to make up different scoring combinations.

CUE-BID   In bridge, a bid of a suit first mentioned by the opponents, usually used to describe a strong hand, suited for play in any of the other suits.

DAILY DOUBLE   In horse racing, a system of betting in which the bettor must pick the winners of two specified races.

DICE   The plural of die.

DIE   A six-sided cube numbered with dots from one to six, each face of the cube having a different number. Used in craps as well as numerous board games. (Plural: dice.)

DIFFERENT STACKS   A "swindle" game in which the object is to match coins.

DON'T COME   In craps, a method of betting that on the next roll of the dice, the shooter will be unsuccessful.

DON'T PASS   In craps, betting that the shooter will either crap-out or fail to make his point.

DOUBLE DOWN   In blackjack, turning the first two cards face up, and receiving only one more card — face down — while in the process doubling the wager.

DOUBLING CUBE   In backgammon, a cube numbered in multiples of two, from 2 to 64. It is used to increase the stakes.

DRAW POKER   A card game in which each player receives five cards face down, with the option of replacing some of them later in the deal.

DUPLICATE BRIDGE   A method of playing bridge in which all players have an opportunity to play the same cards and have their results compared with one another.

ECHELONING   In bridge, a method of combining plays to afford the best opportunity to make the contract.

EVEN MONEY BET   A wager on a sports event where one contestant has been given a scoring handicap to make the odds even.

EXACTA   In pari-mutuel betting, a system of betting where the bettor must determine the first and second place finishers in proper order to win his bet.

FAR CARDS   In cribbage, those cards which are most desirable to throw into your opponent's crib, *eg.*, ♠ Q - ◇ 2, which are at opposite ends and less likely to produce a run.

FASCINATION   A variation of lotto in which small balls are rolled towards holes at the back of an electrically controlled board.

FAVORITE *vs.* UNDERDOG BETS   A bet at odds for either the favorite or the underdog of a particular event.

FIELD BETS   A bet where you must pick a winner from a long list of entries. In craps, a bet that the next roll of the dice will produce a 2, 3, 4, 9, 10, 11 or 12.

FINESSE   In bridge, the attempt to gain power for lower ranking cards by taking advantage of the favorable position of higher-ranking cards held by the opposition.

FIRST HAND   In bridge, the dealer, who is first to bid.

FIXES   In betting, an attempt to control the outcome of an event.

FLUSH   In pinochle, the A K Q J 10 of a suit, counting 150 points. In poker, a hand which contains five cards of the same suit, e.g., ♣ K - ♣ J - ♣ 9 - ♣ 5 - ♣ 2.

FOLDING   In poker, dropping out of the hand before the final outcome is decided.

FORWARD GAME   In backgammon, an attempt to get your men around the board and borne off as quickly as possible.

FOUR-DEAL BRIDGE   A variation of rubber bridge in which partners change after each four deals (hands which are played out). Vulnerability varies according to who is dealer. Also called Chicago.

FOUR-OF-A-KIND   In poker, a hand which contains four cards of equal rank. eg., ♠ 9 - ♡ 9 - ◇ 9 - ♣ 9 - ♡ 6 is four-of-a-kind.

FOURTH HAND   In bridge, the person to the right of the dealer, last to bid.

FREE SPACE, FREE SQUARE   In bingo, the center square of the five by five card, which is automatically given to the player.

FULL HOUSE   In poker, a hand which contains both three-of-a-kind and a pair. eg., ♠ A - ◇ A - ♣ A - ♡ 8 - ♣ 8 is a full house.

GAME   In bridge, the winning of 100 points below the line.

GIN   A card game for two players in which the object is to create melds of three or four cards of equal rank or touching cards of the same suit. eg., ♠ K - ◇ K - ♣ K is a meld, as is ♠ J - ♠ 10 - ♠ 9; also a complete match-up of the player's 10-card hand.

HANDLE   The amount bet on one or more races at a racetrack.

HARD COMBINATION   In blackjack, a combination using an ace as one point rather than the alternative choice of eleven.

HARD-WAY BETS   In craps, betting that an even numbered point will be made by rolling doubles. If the point is made with other than doubles, or if a seven is rolled, the bet loses.

HEARTS TRIPLE   In pinochle, a method of scoring whereby a hand played with hearts as trumps is scored for three times the normal amount.

HIGH-LOW In poker, a game in which the high hand and the low hand (in poker evaluation) split the pot.

HIGH-ROLLER A person who frequently gambles (and usually loses) at high stakes.

HIT; HIT ME In blackjack, a request to take another card in the hopes of improving one's hand.

HITTING In backgammon, the moving of a stone to a point where there is an opponent's blot, thus putting his stone "on the bar."

HOLE-CARD In stud poker, a card which is dealt face down.

HONORS In rubber bridge, the top five cards in a suit (A K Q J 10) constitute the honor cards. If all five are in the same hand, and that suit is trumps, a bonus of 150 points is awarded. Four of the top five honors count 100 points if they are in the same hand when that suit is trumps, while in notrump contracts, all four aces in the same hand are worth 150 points.

INFORMATION DOUBLE; INFORMATORY DOUBLE Other names for the take-out double.

INSURANCE In blackjack, if the dealer has an ace showing, the players are allowed to purchase insurance against the dealer holding a natural, by placing an additional bet equal to one-half the original bet.

INTERNATIONAL MATCH POINTS (IMPS) In bridge, a method of scoring used frequently in team events and occasionally in pair events. Play at IMPS is similar to rubber bridge.

JACKS OR BETTER (JACKPOTS) In poker, a variation of five-card draw, in which to make an original bet a holding of at least a pair of jacks is required.

JACKPOT In casino slot machines, the largest possible payoff, usually for three bells in a row in the three windows.

KENO A variation of lotto.

KENO GOOSE An instrument devised to allow the numbered balls used in the various lotto games to be selected one at a time at random.

KICKER In draw poker, an extra card held for the draw in an attempt to get a second pair or to fool an opponent.

KNOCK In gin, an attempt to score points when the unmelded cards in a hand add up to a low number. The knock ends play at that point. It succeeds when your opponent's unmelded cards total more than do yours.

LABOUCHÈRE A system of money management in betting.

LAYOFF In gin, a method of reducing one's total by adding matching cards to the melds of the opponent.
In betting, placing an additional bet so as to minimize one's risk of loss.

LEAD DIRECTING DOUBLE In bridge, a double of a contract asking partner to lead a specified suit — usually one bid by you, your partner, or dummy's first bid suit.

LIGHTNER DOUBLE In bridge, a double of a voluntarily bid slam, requesting an unusual lead. It bars the lead of a trump or a suit bid by the defenders.

LIMIT POKER   In poker, a system of betting whereby the stakes are predetermined.

LINE   In gin, a credit given for winning a hand — usually the equivalent of one box.

In rubber bridge, the dividing strip above which penalties, bonuses, overtricks and honors are scored, and below which are scored the points for making contracts leading towards game.

LINE BET   In roulette, a bet placed on five numbers at once. A chip is placed on the line separating, for example, the numbers 1, 2, 3, 0 and 00.

LOTTERY   A drawing of lots to determine winners among those who bought chances.

LOTTO   A game of chance played with cards having numbered squares corresponding with numbered balls drawn at random, and won by covering five squares in a row.

MAIN POT   In table-stake poker, the pot into which all players bet equally.

MAJOR SUITS   In bridge, spades (♠) and hearts (♡) constitute the major suits. Their value is 30 points per trick.

MATCHPOINT SCORE   In duplicate bridge, the score achieved when awarded one point for each team beaten and one-half point for each team tied on a particular deal.

MELD   In gin, a sequence of three or more cards of the same suit or three or four cards of the same rank.

In canasta, three or more cards of the same rank which have been placed face up on the table. (A wild card may be used to form a meld.)

In pinochle, any combination which has point scoring value.

MINOR SUITS   In bridge, diamonds (◇) and clubs (♣) constitute the minor suits. Their value is 20 points per trick.

MORNING LINE   In horse racing, the odds set by a professional odds-maker. These are used by bettors to assist them in making their betting selections.

MUGGINS RULE   In cribbage, if a player fails to count his points correctly, his opponent may invoke the Muggins rule, and thus collect the discrepancy between the amount claimed and the actual tally.

NATURAL   In blackjack, a two-card combination of an ace with a picture card or ten, thus adding up to the "perfect" total of twenty-one.

In craps, a seven or eleven on the come-out.

In canasta, a canasta consisting of no wild cards.

NEEDLE-IN-A-HAYSTACK   A swindle game in which a matchstick is dropped onto a checkered tablecloth, with the wager being whether or not the matchstick will land on one of the lines.

NONVULNERABLE   In bridge, playing without having scored a game in the rubber.

NOTRUMP   In bridge, where no suit is played as trumps. The first trick scored at notrump is valued at 40 points, while the rest are 30 each.

NUMBERS GAME   An illegal lottery.

ODDS   The ratio of probability that one thing will happen rather than another.

ONE-ARMED BANDIT   Slang name for a slot machine, so named because of its one handle, and the small returns which it gives.

ONE-CARD DRAWS   In draw poker, where a player exchanges only one card in his hand.

ONE PAIR   In poker, a combination of cards in one hand which includes two cards of equal rank.

eg., ♠ A - ♢ K - ♣ K - ♡ 6 - ♣ 3 is a hand containing a pair of kings.

ONE ROLL BETS   In craps, the bettor wagers as to the exact roll of the dice on the next roll.

ONE UNIT BET   In a favorite vs. underdog bet, a wager consists of one unit. The odds quoted mean that if you wager one unit, you will win the stated amount.

OVERCALL   In bridge, any action other than pass taken by an opponent of the preceding bidder.

OVERLAY   In horse racing, a quotation of higher odds at the track than in the morning line.

PACK   In canasta, the discard pile.

PARLAYS   In horse racing, placing the entire winnings from one race into the next, hoping to pyramid winnings.

In roulette, a bet on a combination of numbers.

PARTIAL   In bridge, a contract p .yed below the level of game.

PART SCORE   In bridge, a score below the line not enough for game.

PASS   In bridge, refusal to make any bid.

In craps, a successful roll of the dice.

PAT HAND   In draw poker, those hands which will not generally improve by exchanging any cards.

PICTURE CARD   In card games, the king, queen and jack.

PINOCHLE   A card game played with a 48-card deck of four suits, each having two cards each of 9's, 10's, Jacks, Queens, Kings, and aces.

In the game pinochle, the meld of the ♠ Q and ♢ J, valued at 40 points.

PIPS   The spots on the cards; in backgammon, an expression to describe the various points on the board.

PIVOT BRIDGE GAME   In rubber bridge a game in which a partnership plays one rubber together, then the players change partners.

PLACE   In horse racing, coming in second.

PLACE NUMBERS   In craps, the numbers 4, 5, SIX, 8, NINE, and 10 are place numbers. You wager that the number which you choose will appear before a seven does.

POINT   In backgammon, one of the twenty-four places to which the stones may be moved.

In craps, the number which the player must throw before he throws a seven in order to win his bet.

POINT SPREAD   In betting on sports, a handicap given one team to theoretically equalize the two competitors.

POKER   A card game in which the player bets that he holds a better hand than any of his opponents.

POKERINO   A version of lotto, similar to fascination, in which the objective is to form poker hands.

POT   In poker, the place where all bets are put; the total of those bets.

POT LIMIT   A method of betting in poker in which a player may bet as much as is in the pot at his turn to bet.

PREEMPT   In bridge, an opening bid at a high level, made with a long suit and few high cards, in an attempt to shut out the opponents.

PREEMPTIVE JUMP OVERCALL   In bridge, a use of a jump overcall as preemptive, in an attempt to cram the opponents' bidding space.

PRIME   In backgammon, a holding of six consecutive points so that your opponent cannot get past.

PROBABILITY   The chance of an event happening.

PROBABILITY ONE   The probability of an event occurring that must happen.

PROBABILITY ZERO   The probability of an event occurring that can never happen.

PROTECTION   Synonym for balancing.

PUNTER   In baccarat and chemin de fer, the person who plays against the banker.

QUINELLA   In pari-mutuel betting, predicting the first two finishers in a particular event.

RED-BLACK   In roulette, a system of betting that the ball will land on the color you pick.

ROULETTE WHEEL   In roulette, the revolving wheel with 38 small pockets numbered one through thirty-six plus 0 and 00, into which a small ball is thrown. Bets are placed to guess which pocket the ball will land in.

ROYAL FLUSH   In poker, the highest ranking hand, being the highest five cards in a suit. ♠ A - ♠ K - ♠ Q - ♠ J - ♠ 10 is a royal flush.

RUBBER   In bridge, the continuous playing of hands until one side scores two games.

RUFF   In bridge, the playing of a trump to a trick to which another suit had been led.

SACRIFICE   In bridge, to bid higher than the opponents' game or slam, in the hopes that the penalty will be less than if the opponents were to fulfill their contract.

SAFETY PLAY In bridge, the sacrificing of a potential trick in order to guarantee making the contract.

SCHNEID OR SCHNEIDER In gin, a shutout, in which the scores become doubled.

SECOND HAND In bridge, the player to the left of the dealer.

SHOE In casino card games, a device which holds up to six decks of playing cards in such a way as to prevent illegal dealing of the cards.

SHOOTER In craps, the player who is rolling the dice.

SHORT SLIP In numbers, a slip on which there have been more bets placed than money received.

SHOW In horse racing, the third place finisher.

SIDE POT In table stakes poker, a pot created when one or more players no longer have enough currency to meet the last bet, so that the others can continue.

SLAM In bridge, a contract in which the objective is to lose either one or no tricks.

SLOT MACHINE A casino machine with three wheels, each with pictures on it. The objective is to match three pictures and thus win.

SOFT COMBINATION In blackjack, a combination of cards in which an ace is counted as eleven points as opposed to one point.

SPADES DOUBLE In pinochle, a method of scoring whereby a hand played with spades as trumps is scored for twice the normal amount.

SPLITTING In blackjack, the option to take the first two cards, if equal in rank, and play them as two different hands, meanwhile doubling the original investment.

STAND PAT In draw poker, not to draw any cards, an action usually reserved for when a pat hand is held.
In blackjack, not to draw additional cards.

STARTER In cribbage, the card which is cut after the players have discarded into the crib. The starter card then becomes part of all hands for scoring purposes.

STAYMAN CONVENTION In bridge, a convention used over notrump bids to help locate a four-four major suit fit.

STONES In backgammon, the markers used by the players.

STRAIGHT In poker, a hand consisting of five cards in sequence. ♠ 10 - ♡ 9 - ♡ 8 - ♣ 7 - ◇ 6 is a straight.

STRAIGHT FLUSH In poker, five cards of the same suit in sequence. ♡ 6 - ♡ 5 - ♡ 4 - ♡ 3 - ♡ 2 is a straight flush.

STRANGERS In gin, cards in your hand which will not help to make a meld. (Also applies to cards discarded by the opponent which do not help to make a meld.)

STUD POKER A poker game in which four cards are dealt face up, and the remainder face down.

glossary

TABLE STAKES   In poker, a method of betting so that each player may bet up to the amount of money he has on the table at the beginning of the hand.

TAKE-OUT DOUBLE   In bridge, a double of an opponent's bid which requests partner to bid his best suit.

THREE-OF-A-KIND   In poker, a holding of three cards of equal rank. ♠ 8 - ♡ 6 - ♡ 3 - ◇ 3 - ♣ 3 is three-of-a-kind (three 3's).

THIRD HAND   In bridge, the player directly opposite the dealer.

TILE   A backgammon stone; a mahjong piece.

TOP   In duplicate bridge, a score which beats the results of all other pairs playing the hand.

TOTE MACHINE   In horse racing, a machine which keeps track of all bets which have been placed, and determines the proper pay-offs.

TWENTY-ONE   Another name for blackjack.

TWIN DOUBLE   In horse racing, a method of betting which requires selecting the winners of four pre-selected races.

TWO-PAIRS   In poker, two different pairs of two cards of equal rank. ♡ 10 - ◇ 10 - ♠ 5 - ◇ 5 - ♣ 2 is a hand containing two-pairs.

UNDER CUT   In gin, to produce a hand of lower count than the total on which an opponent has knocked. Sometimes this lower total is achieved by laying off on opponent's melds.

VULNERABLE   In bridge, having scored one game towards rubber.

WHEEL OF FORTUNE   A gambling device with numbers on it; more or less a vertical roulette wheel.

WIDOW   In auction pinochle, the three cards left over after the three players have been dealt fifteen cards each. The player bids for the right to replace any or all of the cards in the widow for a similar number of cards in his hand.

WIN   In horse racing, to finish first.

878

65